FICTION   Leskov, Nikolai Semenovich, 1831-1895
          The Amazon, and other stories / Nikolai
       S. Leskov ; translated with introduction
       by David Magarshack.   Westport, Conn. :
       Hyperion Press, 1977.
          282p.   (Classics of Russian literature)
       (The Hyperion library of world literature)
          Reprint of the 1949 ed. pub. by Allen &
       Unwin, London.
          Contents: The Amazon.-A little mistake.-
       The March hara.
          1. Short stories   I. Title
       BAL 11/79   76-23884

ndexed:
hort Story Index

LESKOV

THE AMAZON
AND OTHER STORIES

CLASSICS OF RUSSIAN LITERATURE

HYPERION PRESS, INC.
Westport, Connecticut

Nikolai S. Leskov

THE AMAZON

AND OTHER STORIES

TRANSLATED WITH INTRODUCTION BY
DAVID MAGARSHACK

LONDON
———
GEORGE ALLEN & UNWIN LTD

Published in 1949 by George Allen & Unwin, Ltd., London
Hyperion reprint edition 1977
Library of Congress Catalogue Number 76-23884
ISBN 0-88355-495-X (cloth ed.)
ISBN 0-88355-496-8 (paper ed.)
Printed in the United States of America

Library of Congress Cataloging in Publication Data

Leskov, Nikolai Semenovich, 1831-1895.
  The Amazon, and other stories.

  (Classics of Russian literature) (The Hyperion
library of world literature)
  Reprint of the 1949 ed. published by Allen & Unwin,
London.
  CONTENTS: The Amazon. — A little mistake. — The
March hare.
  I. Title.
PZ3.L5647Am7 [PG3337.L5]   891.7'3'3   76-23884
ISBN 0-88355-495-X
ISBN 0-88355-496-8 pbk.

INTRODUCTION

THERE WERE THREE FACTORS in Leskov's life which left an indelible mark on his writings.

To begin with, Leskov came in close contact with the common people as a child and it was then that he, to use his own phrase, "learnt to love the people." He was born in a small village in the province of Orel, the son of a poor civil servant, in 1831. His grandmother, Alexandra Vassilyevna Alferyeva, and his nurse, Anna Stepanovna Kalandina, both of whom he immortalised in many of his stories, were women of the people, and they instilled in him a deep regard for the illiterate and often inarticulate peasant. Later he acknowledged it himself by declaring that he did not learn to know the Russian people, as other prominent Russian writers did, "from conversations with Petersburg cabbies," but that he grew up among the people. "The people regarded me as one of them," he wrote, "and I still have many personal friends among them. I have therefore no need either to raise them on stilts or trample them under my feet."

The second factor in Leskov's life which helped to shape his art was that, on leaving the Civil Service in 1857, he joined the English firm of Scott and Wilkins, one of the directors of which, "the Russified Englishman," Alexander Yakovlevich Scott, was his uncle by marriage. As a member of this firm, Leskov had to travel all over Russia, and it was during these travels that he obtained his material for his amazingly kaleidoscopic view of human life.

Finally, there is the fact that Leskov was practically a self-taught man. He was sent to the Orel grammar school at the age of ten and left it five years later without finishing the eight-year course. Instead of attending to the dry school curriculum, he preferred to spend most of his free time rummaging among the books of the large library of Prince Mossalsky to which he had access. In his own words, he read "almost every book in this library." He then joined the Civil Service and became a junior clerk in the Orel criminal court. Three years later he got himself transferred to Kiev, where his uncle was Professor of Medicine at the university and where he had many opportunities of filling up the gaps in his education. It was also during the years he spent in the capital of the Ukraine that he obtained his masterly knowledge of the Ukrainian language which he used with great effect in many of his stories, including *The March Hare*. But the "stigma" of lacking a university education clung to Leskov all his life, and the question, "Aren't you a graduate of Kiev University?" was always sure to rouse his anger. It is, however, true to say that because he was a self-taught man, Leskov, as a writer, is entirely free from any "literary" taint, with the result that his writings are invariably life-like and his language rich and idiomatic.

Leskov's first efforts as a writer were in the field of journalism. His articles dealing with different aspects of Russian social and economic life began to appear in 1860. His first stories came out in 1862, and for the next thirty-three years he devoted himself wholly to literature.

In a letter to a friend, Leskov defines his attitude towards literature in these words :

"I love literature as a means which enables me to express what I regard as truth and what I esteem to be good for humanity at large. If it no longer expresses that, I do not regard it as of any further use and I do not value it any more. To look upon literature as an art is not my point of view . . . The term 'art for art's sake' is entirely incomprehensible to me. No! Art must be of some benefit to man, for it is only then that it acquires a definite meaning . . . The same thing applies to literature : if a writer cannot serve truth and goodness by it, there is no reason why he should go on writing and he might as well give up his profession and do something else . . ."

As regards his method of work, Leskov's ideas were influenced by the same reasoning. "I cannot even imagine, as I cannot imagine myself a tall man," he declared during the last years of his life, "how any writer can sit down to write a novel or a short story if he does not know why he is writing it. I can never tell beforehand, of course, whether my story will turn out as well as I should like, but I do know *why* I am writing this story or novel and what I want to say by it."

Leskov's writings are richly colloquial. He acquired his great mastery of the Russian language at first hand by association with all manner of people whose individualities of speech he treasured and reproduced in his writings. What characterises his art most, however, is his profound knowledge of the human heart and his great wisdom and humanity, and it is those qualities chiefly that assured him a large reading public in his lifetime and secured him his unique position among the Russian writers of the first rank.

The three stories in this volume present a new facet of Leskov's art to the English reader. *The Amazon* is one of his famous studies of women. The heroine of the story is a procuress, and the fact that emerges from it is that prostitution is not only a social, but also a human problem, a problem of character as well as economics. It was first published in 1883. *A Little Mistake* is a humorous story of particular charm. Ivan Yakovlevich, the "saint" in this story, is Ivan Yakovlevich Koreysha, the "seer" who spent half his life in a Moscow lunatic asylum and who enjoyed a tremendous popularity among certain classes of the population of the ancient Russian capital in the fifties and sixties of the last century. It was also published in 1883 and was later adapted for the stage.

Introduction

The March Hare is the last long short story which Leskov wrote. It was finished in 1895, one year before his death, but was first published only in 1917. Leskov himself summarised the idea of the story in the words : "In the story *The March Hare* I am trying to show that ideas can be fought only with ideas and that violent measures for the suppression of ideas are likely to produce the most unexpected results."

To the translator, Leskov presents many insuperable problems and any attempt to reproduce Leskov's own mannerisms and extravagances of style is bound to fail since their effect depends to a large extent on the peculiar characteristics of spoken Russian as contrasted with the "literary" language. Leskov's style is often brilliant and sometimes bizarre, but it is hardly ever *racy* in the sense of lively and piquant. His writings abound in words and expressions which a literary purist might condemn as "slang." There is, besides, the further point that Leskov uses many words and expressions which are incomprehensible to the modern educated Russian reader, either because they are "local slang" or because they are obsolete, and to look for similarly obscure expressions in English would be to sacrifice the effect of immediacy which Leskov always strove to convey. On the whole, therefore, I considered it best to base my translation on the living language of today.

D.M.

CONTENTS

THE AMAZON

My life has been a school of morals,
And death itself is but a lesson new.

A. Maykov

CHAPTER ONE

"NOW, NOW, DON'T START AN ARGUMENT with me, there's a dear !"

"Come, come, my dear Domna Platonovna, why shouldn't I have an argument with you ? Why indeed should you think that nobody ought to breathe a word against you ?"

"It isn't me, dear, it's you, all of you, who think yourselves so clever that you're ready to start an argument about everything under the sun ! You'd better wait a bit longer, dear. When you're as old as I am, then it'll be time for you to argue. People who haven't had any experience don't appreciate the way things are done in Petersburg, and my advice to them is to sit still and listen to what older people, who know all the circumstances here, have to say."

It was thus that Domna Platonovna, a great friend of mine who sold lace for a living, used to stop me every time I happened to disagree with her about the world and people in general. It was thus that she used to stop any of her friends who were so bold as to express an opinion which was contrary to Domna Platonovna's own convictions. The circle of Domna Platonovna's friends was very large ; indeed, as she used to say herself, it was "vast" and very varied, including as it did shop-assistants, counts, princes, liveried flunkeys, inn-keepers, actors and rich merchants. In a word, Domna Platonovna's friends belonged to every class and breed. As for her women friends, she had thousands of them, but having rather a low opinion of the fair sex, she was not particularly proud of them.

"Women," she used to remark whenever the occasion arose, "why, I know them inside out ! It's as if I had them all here !" Domna Platonovna would clench her fist and show it to me. "That's where I've got them," she'd repeat, "right in there !"

13

So great and heterogeneous was the circle of Domna Platonovna's friends in so populous a city as St. Petersburg that to
many people it was a matter of real wonder, and some of them
could not help asking her with a gasp of unconcealed admiration, "My dear Domna Platonovna, how do you do it ?"

"Do what ?"

"I mean how do you manage to know them all ?"

"Know them all ? Of course, I know them all, dear. I know
almost everybody who's anybody here."

"But how did you get to know them ? There must, surely,
be some explanation of it."

"It's all because I'm so simple-hearted, dear."

"Oh ? Are you quite sure it's only because of that ?"

"Why, yes, dear. You see, they all love me because I'm such
a simple soul, and it's just because of my simplicity and the
goodness of my heart that I've had to put up with so much
sorrow in the world, swallow so many insults, have so many
people slander and traduce me and, I don't mind telling you,
dear, even beat me, yes, beat me many a time ! But for all that,
people can't help loving me."

"I suppose that's why you know the world and its ways so
well, isn't it ?"

"Yes, dear, I know this rotten world well enough, that I do.
Know every rogue in it, just as if I had him here in the palm
of my hand. And there's something else I'd like to tell you, but
on second thoughts perhaps I'd better not . . . ." Domna Platonovna would add, looking a little embarrassed and falling into
a muse.

"Why, what is it ?"

"Well, dear," she'd reply with a sigh, "if you want to know,
it's like this : today, you see, they're always thinking out some
new trick and everyone seems to be getting more and more
clever."

"How do you mean they're getting more clever, Domna Platonovna ?"

"I mean, dear, that nowadays while you think you're getting to know a man by looking at his face, he, as like as not, will trip you up with his foot. Why, it's a real wonder to me, it is, that there should be so many people about whose only business in the world is to cheat you and tell you lies : one man thinks he's got a clever idea into his head, but another one gets one that is even cleverer."

"But really, Domna Platonovna, isn't there anything else but cheating in the world ?"

"Now, don't you start arguing with me, dear ! Better tell me what's your opinion of the world today ? Can you find anything else in it but deceit and cunning ?"

"But surely, Domna Platonovna, there are good men in the world, too ?"

"Yes, dear, I daresay you'll find them in the cemeteries among our parents, but they're not much good to us, are they ? As for them who're still alive, they're all villains, black-hearted villains, all of 'em : it's just one abomination of desolation, it is, dear."

"So according to you, Domna Platonovna, everybody you meet is either a rogue or a liar and you can't trust any of them, is that it ?"

"I didn't say anything about not trusting them, dear. Trust them by all means, if you must. Look at me : I trusted a general's wife, that Shemelfenig woman, trusted her with twenty-seven yards of lace, I did, but when I went to see her the other day and said to her, 'Would you mind settling that old account of mine, madam ?' she, if you please, said to me, 'But I've paid you already !' I says to her, I says, 'You have not paid me, madam ! I've never got a penny from you !' but she screamed at me, 'How dare you speak to me like that, you low creature? Get out!' and her footman, of course, at once seized me by the arms and put me out into the street. I left my piece of lace there, but, thank goodness, it wasn't an expensive one. That's how much you can trust them!"

"But," said I, "there's only one here and there like that."

"One? No, dear, not one. Their name's legion. Mind you, in the old days when our gentry still owned their peasants, it may have been true to say that it was only among the lower orders that you were likely to come across a thief, but nowadays when they have no more peasants, they don't mind doing a bit of thieving of their own. Why, doesn't everybody know who stole the diamond necklace at that ball the other evening? Yes, dear, nowadays nobody minds getting something that doesn't belong to him. Take, for instance, that Mrs. Karaulova, Avdotya Petrovna. To look at her you'd say she was a real lady, but she pinched a lace collar under my very nose at that country house of hers!"

"How do you mean she pinched it? Just think what you're saying, my dear Domna Platonovna! Would a lady steal a lace collar?"

"To be sure, she stole it, dear, just like anybody else. I wonder what you'd say if I told you that directly I noticed that one of my lace collars was missing, I said to her, speaking very politely and diplomatically, of course, 'Pardon me, madam,' I said, 'I think I've dropped a lace collar here. You didn't see it by any chance, did you? For,' I said, 'I'm sure one of my lace collars is missing.' What do you think she did? She slapped my face, that's what she did, dear, and said to her footman, 'Show her out!' So, of course, I was turned out immediately. I says to the footman, I says, 'My dear sir, you're in service here and you ought to know that I can't afford to lose my property.' And he says to me, 'Of course, you can't afford it,' he says, 'but that's the way she always acts.' That's all there is to it, dear. She can afford to act as she likes, seeing what her position in the world is, but I, being poor, have to hold my tongue."

"So what do you think that shows, Domna Platonovna?"

"What does that show, dear? Well, it's hardly my business to think what that shows since it's they who do the showing out. But that everybody's a rogue nowadays, that, dear, is something you'd better not try arguing with me about, because, thank God, I've only to look at a man's face to tell what he's like inside."

So how is one to argue with Domna Platonovna after that? No. However clever a dialectician you may be, Domna Platonovna is quite certain to get the better of you in an argument, for you won't be able to convince her whatever you say. The only thing you can do is show her the door, but that, of course, is a different matter. Otherwise you may be sure that she will always have the last word.

CHAPTER TWO

I FEEL I MUST DESCRIBE Domna Platonovna to my readers at greater length.

Domna Platonovna is not a tall woman; in fact, she is rather short, but she looks big. This optical illusion is caused by the fact that Domna Platonovna is, as they say, broad in the beam, and what she lacks in height, she makes up for in breadth. Her health is not particularly good, although no one seems to remember her ever being ill, and to look at her you would never suspect that there was anything the matter with her. Her bosom alone is so immense that you cannot but be overcome at the sight of it. But she herself, Domna Platonovna, I mean, is always complaining about her poor health.

"To look at me," she'd say, "you would think I was robust, but there isn't any real strength in me as in other women of my size, and as for my sleep, it is just dreadful! Heavy is not the word for it. The minute my head touches the pillow, off I go and for all I care you can put me in the garden to scare away the birds. Until I've had my fill of sleep, I'm as good as dead. Yes, that's what I am, as good as dead!"

Domna Platonovna regarded her mighty sleep, too, as one of the ailments of her corpulent body and, as we shall see later, it had, in fact, given her a lot of trouble and caused her much unhappiness.

Domna Platonovna enjoyed nothing better than to pester people about the state of her health and ask them for medical advice. She would describe her ailments to them at great length, but she refused to take any medicines and believed only in "Haarlem" drops, which she called "Harem" drops, and a phial of which she always carried in the right-hand pocket of her capacious silk *capote*. According to her own account, she was always somewhere about forty-five years of age, but to judge by her fresh complexion and her cheerful mien, no one would give her more than forty. At the time of my first acquaintance with her, Domna Platonovna's hair was of a dark brown colour, and there was not a single grey hair to be seen on her head. Her skin was quite unusually white and her red cheeks glowed with health, which, however, never satisfied her, for she used to buy some French *papier poudré* in the upper gallery of the Arcade, which greatly deepened the natural colour of her cheeks, a colour which steadfastly refused to be affected by any of her troubles or by the Finnish winds and fogs. Domna Platonovna's eyebrows looked as if they had been made of black satin : they were as black as jet and they shone with an unnatural glitter, for Domna Platonovna used to smear them thickly with a kind of black preparation and draw them into a thin line with her fingers. Her eyes were just like two black plums besprinkled with fresh morning dew. A mutual friend of ours, a Turkish prisoner of war by the name of Ispulat, who had been brought to St. Petersburg during the Crimean war, could never gaze calmly at Domna Platonovna's eyes. So potent was their influence on him that the poor fellow would completely lose his head and begin to give voice to his admiration in loud, ecstatic tones.

"Oh, what beautiful eyes ! What lovely Greek eyes !"

Any other woman would, of course, be flattered by so sincere a compliment, but Domna Platonovna was never taken in by these Turkish blandishments and she always insisted on her pure Russian origin.

"Don't talk such rubbish, you damned infidel !" she'd reply with a merry twinkle in those "Greek" eyes of hers. "Don't you dare tell me such a thing again, you big-bellied toad ! I come of a well-known and respectable family, I do, and there aren't any Greeks in the factory in our town and never have been !"

Domna Platonovna's nose was hardly what you might call a nose, so small, slender and straight was it. A nose like that you never come across on the Oka or the Zusha and, if you do, it is by mere accident. Her mouth, though, was rather big : you could tell at once that she'd been fed with a large spoon as a baby, but it was a pleasant mouth none the less and it looked so fresh, of a regular shape, with scarlet lips and teeth that might have been cut out of a young turnip. In a word, not only on an uninhabited island, but even in so big and populous a city as St. Petersburg any man who regarded the kissing of a pretty girl as a kind of duty would not by any means consider it a hardship to kiss Domna Platonovna. But there could be no doubt that the greatest attractions of Domna Platonovna's face were her chin, a chin that was a real peach, and the general expression of her features, which was so soft and child-like that if the thought ever crossed your mind how a woman whose face bespoke such bottomless good-nature could talk of nothing else but human treachery and malice, you could not help saying to yourself, "Oh, curse you a hundred times, Domna Platonovna, for, damn it ! one look at your face is enough to conjure up such a multitude of the most dreadful problems in my head !"

Domna Platonovna was of a very sociable disposition ; she was a really cheerful soul, good-hearted, not given to taking offence easily, rather simple-minded, perhaps, and a bit superstitious, too, but, on the whole, honest and straightforward, although, to be sure, as in every Russian, there was a streak of cunning in her. Work and worry were Domna Platonovna's usual lot and she did not seem to be able to live without either. She was always busy, always rushing about, always worrying about something, devising some new scheme or other, or carrying it out.

"I live a lonely life," she used to say, "have no one except myself to look after in the whole world and yet to earn my bare living I have to lead a most aggravating sort of existence, running about the market like a scalded cat, and if it isn't one, then it is another who's always trying to catch me by the tail."

"But," you'd sometimes say to her, "you can't possibly do everything at once, can you?"

"Well, perhaps not everything," she'd reply, "but all the same let me tell you that it's very trying. Well, so long at present, good-bye, dear : there are people waiting for me in a dozen different places!" and she'd actually rush off in a devil of a hurry.

Domna Platonovna quite often realised herself that she did not labour for her bread alone and that her hard work and aggravating existence could be made considerably less hard and aggravating without any harm to her own personal interests ; but she just could not restrain herself from bustling about.

"I can't bear the thought of losing any business," she used to say. "I'm jealous, you see, of anyone else getting it. To see something coming my way is enough to make my heart leap with joy."

But, as a matter of fact, what Domna Platonovna was jealous of was not that anybody should derive any profit from some business she might lose. No. That side often left her strangely cold. What did matter to her was that she might miss the worry and bustle involved in bringing the business to a successful issue.

"He's deceived me, the villain !" or "She's deceived me, the beast !" she'd go on complaining all day long, but next time you met her, she was again rushing about and worrying herself to death for the same villain or beast and telling herself beforehand that they would quite certainly deceive her again.

Domna Platonovna's business which gave her so much trouble was of a most diverse character. Officially, to be sure, she was just a seller of lace, that is to say, women of the artisan class and wives of poor merchants and priests used to send her from "their own parts" all kinds of lace collars, strips of lace material and cuffs which she hawked around Petersburg, or, in summer, around the different holiday resorts in the vicinity of the capital, sending back to "their own parts" the money she received after the deduction of her commission and expenses. But, besides her lace business, Domna Platonovna engaged in a most complicated business of a private character, in the carrying out of which the lace and the collars merely played the part of a pass to places where she would not otherwise have been admitted. Thus she found husbands and wives for all sorts of people, found purchasers for furniture and second-hand ladies' garments, raised loans for people with and without security, ran a kind of domestic agency of her own, finding jobs for governesses, caretakers and footmen, took confidential messages to the most famous *salons* and *boudoirs* in town of the sort that could not possibly be entrusted to the post and brought replies from the ladies in question, ladies surrounded by an atmosphere of frigid piety and devotion to good works.

But in spite of all her enthusiasm and connections, Domna Platonovna never got rich or even made a comfortable living. She had enough for her own needs, dressed, in her own words, "decently" and never begrudged herself anything; but she never had any spare money, either because she was too preoccupied with her different business worries or because her customers often deceived her, and, besides, all sorts of curious accidents always happened to her with her money.

Her chief trouble was that she was an artist : she got too much carried away by her own handiwork. Although she would invariably tell you that she had to work so hard for the sake of her daily bread, that claim of hers was scarcely just. Domna Platonovna loved her work as an artist loves his art : to contrive something, to collect something, to concoct something and then to admire her own handiwork—that was the main thing, that was what she really cared about, that was what she spent her money on and sacrificed any profit she might have obtained from the business in question which a more practical business woman would never have sacrificed.

Domna Platonovna found her vocation by sheer chance. At first she was quite satisfied with hawking her lace and it never entered her head to combine her trade with any other occupation ; but the magic of our capital transformed this rather absurd Mtsensk woman into the accomplished factotum whom I knew as the inimitable Domna Platonovna, a woman who applied her native wit to any kind of business and who secured an entrée everywhere. Soon she had established herself so firmly that it was quite impossible for her not to get in wherever she wanted. She always carried a large embroidered bag on her arm, she was always dressed in a brand-new silk *capote*, round her neck she always wore a lace collar with large, tapering points, and round her shoulders a blue French shawl with a white border, in her free hand a snow-white linen handkerchief, and on her head either a violet or a mauve gros-de-Naples band, in a word, a perfect lady ! And her face ? Why, it was meekness and piety itself ! Indeed, Domna Platonovna possessed the invaluable gift of being able to control the expression of her face at will.

"Without it," she used to say, "I shouldn't be able to do anything in my line of business : you must never show whether you're an Ananias or just a common or garden rascal."

In addition, Domna Platonovna had a very polite form of address. For instance, she'd never say in a drawing room, as others would in her place, that she'd been to "the public baths," but she would say, "I had the great pleasure, sir, of visiting a bathing establishment yesterday," and she'd never say, as others would, of a pregnant woman that she was pregnant, but

she'd always say "she's in the family way," or something of
the kind.

She was, generally speaking, a lady of the most impeccable
manners and, if necessary, she was quite able to impress people
by her education. But in spite of all that, Domna Platonovna
was never known to show off, and she was what one might call
a highly patriotic woman besides. Since her political horizon,
however, was rather narrow, her patriotism, too, was of the
narrowest kind, that is to say, she thought it her duty to speak
highly of her own Orel province and to do her utmost for any
man or woman who hailed from "her own parts."

"I'd like to know what you make of it," she used to say to
me. "I know quite well that our Orel people are the worst
scoundrels and the biggest thieves in the world and yet even if
you were the blackest villain in your own town, even if you
were worse than that cross-eyed Turk, Ispulat, I should never
let you down and I wouldn't change you for the most honest
and upright man from another province."

I'm afraid I could offer her no explanation of it. Both of us,
in fact, were greatly puzzled, and all we could do was to ask
each other :

"Now, why's that really ?"

CHAPTER THREE

I GOT ACQUAINTED WITH Domna Platonovna by sheer chance. At the time when I first met her I had a room in the flat of a Polish lady, the wife of a colonel, who spoke six European languages, not counting Polish, and who invariably ended up her conversation in any of those languages in her native tongue. Domna Platonovna knew hundreds of such colonels' wives in St. Petersburg and she carried out different commissions for almost every one of them : affairs of the heart or affairs of business or, again, both business and heart affairs. My own landlady was, as a matter of fact, a highly educated lady who knew the world, carried herself with the utmost decorum, used to pretend with some success that what she liked most about people was their sincerity and humanity, read a lot, was thrown into unfeigned raptures by the poets and liked to recite the lines from the Polish poet Maczewski's "Maria" :

Everything in this world will death destroy,
There's a canker in the loveliest of roses.

It was in my landlady's flat that I met Domna Platonovna for the first time. I was sitting at the table and drinking tea while the colonel's wife recited to me :

Everything in this world will death destroy,
There's a canker in the loveliest of roses.

Domna Platonovna came in, uttered a prayer, stopped at the door and bowed in every direction, although there was no one else in the room except my landlady and myself, placed her voluminous bag on the table and said :

"Well, here I am !"

At that time Domna Platonovna wore a brown silk *capote*, a blue French shawl, a lace collar with tapering points and a mauve gros-de-Naples head-band, in short, she was dressed in her uniform, in which I would beg my readers to picture her to themselves in their imaginations..

My landlady was very glad to see her, although she seemed perhaps to have blushed slightly at her entrance. She welcomed her in a friendly way, though with a certain reserve.

"Why haven't you been to see me for such a long time, my dear Domna Platonovna?" the colonel's wife asked her.

"I was very busy, ma'am," answered Domna Platonovna, sitting down and observing me closely.

"What were you so busy with?"

"Well, there's you, ma'am, and there's somebody else and somebody else again and I'm always trying to do my best for all of you and that's why I'm so busy," replied Domna Platonovna, and, after sipping her tea in silence for a while, she said, "That business you asked me about, ma'am . . . You remember, don't you? Well, I went there the other day and I spoke to . . ."

Here I got up and took my leave.

That was absolutely all that happened at my first meeting with Domna Platonovna, and it looked as if our acquaintance would hardly thrive, but thrive it did.

A few days after that meeting I was sitting in my room when there was a knock at my door.

"Come in," I said without looking round.

I could hear that something very large had crept into the room and was moving about in it. I looked round and saw Domna Platonovna.

"Where, my dear sir," she asked, "is your icon?"

"There," I said, "over the curtain in the corner."

"Is it a Polish icon or one of ours, a Christian one?" she asked again, raising her hand slowly to cross herself.

"I believe it's a Russian one," I replied.

Domna Platonovna shielded her eyes with her hand, gazed at the icon for some time and then just dismissed it with a wave of the hand, "Makes no difference," so to speak, and uttered a prayer.

"Where can I put my bag?" she asked, looking round the room.

"Put it where you like," I said.

"If you don't mind," she said, "I shall put it on the divan for the time being," and, putting down her bag, she sat down herself.

"What a nice visitor!" I said to myself. "Doesn't stand on ceremony, does she?"

"Fancy, how small icons are nowadays, you can hardly see them," Domna Platonovna began. "It's a new fashion, I suppose. All the aristocratic families in town have these small icons, but I must say I don't like it."

"Why don't you like it?"

"Why should I? It means that they're anxious to hide God away so that you can't find Him, doesn't it?"

I said nothing.

"But really," Domna Platonovna went on, "an icon ought it be of a proper size, oughtn't it?"

"What size would you suggest?" I asked. "Is there a proper size for an icon, Domna Platonovna?" and having said that, I somehow, you know, began to look on her as an old friend.

"Of course there is!" Domna Platonovna said with conviction. "Just look at our merchants, my dear friend! They always have an icon of the right size: you couldn't miss it even if you wanted to, and with a lamp that sheds its radiance all round, everything as it should be. But these tiny icons, why, what else do they signify but that our gentry are trying to run away from God and that God Himself is far from them. The other day, it was during Holy Week, I went to see a general's wife and while I was there a footman came in and announced the arrival of the clergy. 'Tell them I'm busy,' she said. 'Why should you tell them that, ma'am?' I asked. 'Isn't it a great sin not to admit them?' But she said, 'I hate priests!' Well, of course, it's her business," continued Domna Platonovna. "If she doesn't want to have 'em in her house, she needn't have 'em, but what I say is, if you don't like the men sent to your house, He who sent them won't like you."

"Oh," I said, "what a shrewd woman you are, Domna Platonovna!"

"Well, my friend," replied Domna Platonovna, "you must have your wits about you nowadays, you know. How much do you pay for your room?"

"Twenty-five roubles."

"That's a lot of money, dear."

"Well, as a matter of fact, I, too, think it's rather a lot to pay."

"Why don't you move?"

"Oh," I said, "it's too much bother."

"Your landlady is pretty, isn't she?"

"Now, please," I said, "leave my landlady out of it."

"Tut-tut," she said, "tell that to someone else, not to me. I know the kind of scoundrels you men are!"

"Well," I said to myself, "you certainly put a nice construction on everything, my dear lady."

"They're clever, though, the Polish women, I mean," said Domna Platonovna, yawning and crossing her mouth. "They don't do anything for nothing."

"You shouldn't say such things about my landlady, Domna Platonovna," I said. "She's an honest woman."

"Who said she wasn't an honest woman, dear? There's no question here of her being honest or not : she's still a young woman."

"I'm sure you know what you're talking about," I said, "but whatever it is I assure you I have nothing to do with it."

"Well," said Domna Platonovna, "I daresay you haven't,

dear, but you may have, you know, you may. I know the Petersburg circumstances all right and I needn't waste any words on them."

"I can see, my dear lady," I said to myself, "that I shan't be able to convince you."

"But remember," said Domna Platonovna, bending over me and giving me a soft tap on the shoulder, "never take any advantage of the poor soul : pay her for your room !"

"But I do pay her for my room !" I protested.

"That's right, dear, because the first thing a man who makes an impression on a poor woman does, is to live at her expense."

"Now, really, Domna Platonovna," I tried to stop her, "what are you talking about?"

"Ah, my friend, a woman, and especially a Russian woman, is so very stupid about love. 'Take it, darling, take everything I have!' Poor creature, she's ready to cut off her right arm for him and he, the low cad, is only too pleased to make use of her."

"That is very reprehensible, I'm sure," I said, "but you're not by any chance suggesting that I'm her lover, are you?"

"No, but you should take pity on her all the same, dear. For, say what you will, a woman is a poor helpless creature, ever such a helpless creature she is! They all ought to be thrashed within an inch of their lives to keep them away as far as possible from you, villains that you all are. And really, dear, why is it that the world seems to be so full of wicked men? What are they good for? And then again, look at it another way and the world would be a dull place without them, for sometimes you do seem to miss them. Oh, the devil take 'em!" Domna Platonovna exclaimed angrily, spat, and went on, "The other day I went to see Mrs. Domukhovskaya, another colonel's wife . . . Do you know her?"

"No," I said, "I don't know her."

"A real beauty !"

"Is she?"

"Yes, a Polish lady."

"Well, what about it?" I asked. "You don't expect me to know every Polish woman in town, do you?"

"But she isn't a real Polish lady, she's a convert, one of our faith."

"I'm afraid," I said, "that doesn't help me much. Even if Mrs. Domukhovskaya isn't really a Polish lady, but one of our faith, I still don't know who she is. I don't know her, I tell you!"

"Her husband's a doctor."

"I thought you said she was the wife of a colonel."

"Well, and so she is. What's that got to do with it?"

"Oh, never mind," I said. "What about her?"

"Well, you see, dear, she fell out with her husband."

"Oh?"

"Yes, dear, they seem to have disagreed about something and they decided to go their own ways. Anyway, that's what that Lekanida woman did. 'Can't stand his high moral tone, Domna Platonovna,' she says to me."

I just nodded.

"'Can't stand his antics,' she says to me. 'My nerves,' she says, 'can't put up with his tantrums any more'."

I again nodded silently.

"Nerves, indeed, I thought to myself," Domna Platonovna went on, "why don't I suffer from nerves? A month passes and her ladyship, I see, has rented a flat. 'Am going to get lodgers,' she said. Well, I thought to myself, got sick of your husband, have you? Let's see the sort of trouble you're letting yourself in for now! Couldn't live decently while your husband was looking after you, so now, my dear girl, try to live by your own wits and may the Lord help you. For pride goes before a fall, it does, and when you have had enough of it, you'll be glad to go back to him, but he, my pretty one, may not be so glad to have you back! After another month I went to see her again and, as I expected, she had a lodger all right, a fine-looking fellow, except that he was maybe a bit on the thin side and a bit pockmarked, too, poor soul. 'Oh, my dear Domna Platonovna,' she says to me, 'I've such a nice lodger,' she says, 'such perfect manners, so well educated and so kind-hearted. Does everything for me, the dear man does, looks after all my affairs, he does!'"

So I said to her, "They've all got perfect manners nowadays, my dear," I said, "but since he looks after all your affairs for you, I suppose nothing could be more legal than that, could it now?"

I was just joking, you understand, but I could see that she'd taken offence, in fact, she got red in the face and looked daggers at me and we didn't part on the best of terms, I can tell you. Well, as I look at it, dear, everybody knows best what's good for him and, I thought, if that lodger of·hers is really a good man, no one in his right mind would condemn her and God Himself would probably forgive her. I saw her twice afterwards and every time I found her in her little room crying her eyes out.

"What's the matter, my dear?" I asked her. "A bit too early for tears, isn't it?"

"Oh, my dear Domna Platonovna," she said, "I'm so unhappy!" and not another word would she say.

"What are you so unhappy about?" I asked. "Not in trouble, are you?"

"Oh, no," she said, "thank God it's not that."

"Well," I said, "if it isn't that then there's nothing to worry about."

"I haven't got a penny, Domna Platonovna," she said.

"So that's it," I thought to myself. "That certainly is bad." But I know, of course, that when people find themselves penniless it is only right to cheer them up a bit. "What does money matter, my dear?" I said to her. "If you haven't got any money today, you'll get some tomorrow. What about your lodgers?"

"One has paid me," she said, "but I'm afraid two of my rooms are empty."

"I'm sorry to hear that, my dear," I said, "for in your business there can be nothing worse than empty rooms. But what about that sweetheart of yours?"

I asked her right out, without ceremony. However, she did not reply, but went on crying. Poor thing, I felt so sorry for her, for I could see that she was just a weak, silly woman.

"Well," I said, "if he really is such a rotter, then why not get rid of him?"

That made her burst out sobbing bitterly and biting the ends of her wet handkerchief.

"They're none of them worth crying over or breaking your heart for, the dirty rotters," I said. "And if you don't want to have anything to do with him any more, then it's good riddance to bad rubbish! I shall find you another one who'll not only cherish you, but will be a real help to you and never give you any occasion to cry, let alone break your heart."

But she began to wave her hands at me frantically.

"Don't, don't, don't!" she cried, flinging herself on her bed and burying her face in the pillows, her body shaking so violently that it was a wonder her dress did not split at the back.

As it happened I knew a merchant (his father owned a shop in Surovskaya Lane) who was very anxious that I should introduce him to a young lady. "Please, Domna Platonovna," he said to me, "introduce me to a nice girl or even to a married woman, I don't mind which, so long as she's highly educated. I'm fed up with uneducated women!" I could well believe it, for his father and the other menfolk in his family were all married to fools, and he himself was also married to a real nitwit of a woman. Every time I went there, she was sitting about sucking boiled sweets.

Now, I thought to myself, what could be nicer than to bring him and Lekanida together? But I could see that she hadn't learnt her lesson yet, so I left her : let her, I said to myself, ripen in the sun a little longer!

For about two months I didn't go near her. Mind you, I was very sorry for her, but I thought if the fool had no sense and did not appreciate what was good for her, then nobody could do anything for her. Anyway, about Lent I happened to be in the same house where she had her flat, sold some lace there, and I suddenly took a fancy for some coffee, simply dying for a cup of coffee I was. So I said to myself, 'Why not go and see Mrs. Domukhovskaya? Surely, Lekanida Petrovna won't mind treating me to a cup of coffee!' I went up the back stairs and opened the kitchen door, but there was nobody there. "Keeping open house, it seems," I said to myself. "Take anything you like!" for there was the *samovar* and the pots and pans and everything on the shelves.

No sooner did the thought cross my mind (I was walking along the passage just then) than I heard something going bang, bang, bang. Good gracious, I thought, what could that be? I opened the door of her room and there was that sweetheart of hers—he was an actor, and not what you might call a good actor, either, although he liked to call himself an artist—well, there he was, standing over Lekanida with a riding whip in his hand.

"Oh, you brute! You brute!" I shouted at him. "What are you doing to this poor, helpless woman, you brute?" and I rushed between them, shielded myself with my bag and just rushed between them!

Domna Platonovna paused and addressed herself to me.

"So you see," she said, "what bullies like you do to a poor woman !"

I held my peace.

Well (Domna Platonovna went on with her story), so I separated them. He stopped horsewhipping her in my presence and she—why, she began to apologise for him !

"Don't take it so seriously," she said to me. "He was only joking !"

"Well, my dear," I said to her, "if he was only joking, then of course it's all right, but all the same you'd better make sure you haven't split your dress open from laughing at his jokes !"

However, they seemed to make it up : he went on living at her flat, but he didn't pay her a penny, the villain didn't.

"Is that all ?" I asked.

"Certainly not !" replied Domna Platonovna.

After a little time the rows started again. He began knocking her about almost every day, and just at the time she took in a woman lodger, one of those young provincial ladies, a merchant's wife. Well, everybody knows what our merchants' wives are like : the minute they leave their homes, they're ready for any mischief. So, as I said, that artist fellow carried on as before and, in addition, he began making up to the woman lodger. Well, there were such goings on there that I even stopped visiting Lekanida Petrovna.   •

"This is no business of mine," I thought to myself. "You've made your bed, so now lie on it."

Only on the thirteenth of September, on the eve of the raising of the Holy and Life-Giving Cross, I went to the Znamenye Cathedral for evening mass. Walking out of the church after the service, I saw Lekanida Petrovna kneeling on the top of the steps by the entrance. Poor soul, she looked so miserable, kneeling there in an old, threadbare coat and crying as if her heart was about to burst. Well, I couldn't help feeling sorry for her again.

"How are you, Lekanida Petrovna?" I said, going up to her.

"Oh, my dear Domna Platonovna," she said with tears streaming down her cheeks, "I'm so glad to see you! I'm sure it must have been God Himself Who sent you here!"

"Well, my dear," I said to her, "I shouldn't think it was God who sent me, for God only sends disembodied angels as His messengers and I'm as great a sinner as anybody else. There, there," I said to her, "stop crying, my dear, and let's go somewhere where we can sit down under a roof and where you can tell me what your trouble is. Perhaps I could think of something to help you."

So we went.

"Has that brute been knocking you about again?" I asked.

"I haven't got anyone any more," she said, "brute or no brute."

"But where are you going?" I asked her, for her flat was in Seshtilavochnaya Street and she was turning into Gryaznaya Street.

It seemed that she had no flat any more, either. Little by little everything came out: the little furniture she had, had been taken away by her landlord for arrears of rent, her sweetheart had disappeared, and a good thing, too, if you ask me! and she was living in a little room which she rented from Avdotya Ivanovna Dislen. Now Avdotya Ivanovna is one of the meanest women in town, proud though she is of her gentility and of being a major's daughter. As mean as they make 'em, that's her! I was nearly dragged off to a police station on account of that mean cat, silly old fool that I am!

"I know that Dislen woman very well," I said to Lekanida. "My dear," I said, "she's a real harpy, she is !"

"But what can I do ?" she wailed. "Dear Domna Platonovna, what can I do ?"

And she wrung her hands, poor soul, so that my heart bled to look at her.

"Won't you come to my place ?" she asked.

"No, my dear," I said. "My heart bleeds for you, poor thing, but I shall not go to that Dislen woman's flat. I nearly got locked up by the police once on account of that worthless creature, I did. Why not come to my place instead, my dear, if you want to talk to me ?"

So she went with me to my place. I gave her tea, did my best to make her warm and comfortable, shared whatever the good Lord had sent me for supper and even put her to bed with me.

"Does that satisfy you ?" Domna Platonovna interrupted her story and turned to me.

I nodded silently.

That night, I can tell you, she scared me good and proper. She'd lie quietly for a while, then she'd give a start, sit down on the bed and begin to wail.

"Dear Domna Platonovna," she'd say, "what am I going to do with myself ?"

I could see that it was getting very late, so I said, "Stop worrying, my dear, and go to sleep. We'll think of something tomorrow."

I could hardly keep awake, for I'm such a sound sleeper. At last I managed to fall asleep and I slept like a log until it was time for me to get up. When I woke up I saw that Lekanida was sitting on a chair in her chemise with her legs crossed under her and smoking a cigarette. She looked such a picture, so lovely, so white—just like soft down in white satin !

"Would you mind putting on the *samovar*, my dear?" I asked.

"I'll try," she said.

She slipped on her cheap cotton skirt and went into my little kitchen. I stayed in bed, feeling a little lazy that morning. She brought in the *samovar* and we had tea.

"Do you know what I've been thinking of, Domna Platonovna ?" she asked.

"I'm afraid I don't, my dear," I replied. "No use trying to guess somebody else's thoughts, is it ?"

"I was thinking of going back to my husband," she said.

"Well," I said, "what could be better than being an honest woman again ! But are you sure, my dear, that he will take you back ?"

"Oh, he's such a good man !" she said. "I realise now that he's a much better man than any of them."

"I'm very glad he's such a good man, my dear," I said, "but how long is it since you left him ?"

"I left him almost a year ago."

"Oh, so it's almost a year since you left him, is it ? That," I said, "is quite a long time, my dear lady."

"What do you mean by that, Domna Platonovna ?" she said.

"Oh, nothing, my dear," I said, "except that I'm just wondering if he hasn't got somebody in your place, some pretty miss who can cook a nice meal for him or bake some fine pastries."

"I hadn't even thought of it," she said.

"That's the trouble, my dear, that you hadn't even thought of it," I said. "None of you ever do, none of you ever think of it ! But you should have thought of it, my dear, for if you had, you wouldn't have been in such a mess now !"

That fairly floored her, that did. I could see that she was

eating her heart out, the poor creature. She bit her lips and said so softly that I could only just catch her words, "I'm sure he isn't like that at all!"

"Oh, you little fools!" I thought to myself. "You think nothing of jumping like goats into a row of peas, but when it comes to your husband, then it's a different matter! 'My husband may be an awful bore, but he mustn't even glance at a whore!'" It fair makes my blood boil every time I hear some silly woman talk like that!

"I hope you don't mind my saying so," I told her, "but, as I see it, you have no right to talk like that. What kind of a man is your husband, what special kind of a man, I mean, is he that you should say he's not 'like that?' I shall never believe it. I can't help thinking that he's just like the rest of them : flesh and blood! And as for you, my dear," I said, "you'd better consider that as a woman you didn't observe your marriage vows very strictly, so why should he be blamed if he did the same as you, particularly, my dear angel, as a man is just like a hawk : he swoops down, ruffles up his feathers, shakes himself and off he flies where his fancy takes him, while all a poor woman knows is the way from the door to the kitchen stove!"

And addressing herself to me, Domna Platonovna said, "To one of you fellows a poor woman is just what a bagpipe is to a fool : he plays a few tunes on it and throws it away. Isn't it so?"

I made no reply and Domna Platonovna, I'm glad to say, did not wait for my reply, but went on :

Well, so this grand lady of mine, this Lekanida Petrovna, said to me after I had finished talking to her, "I shan't hide anything from my husband," she said, "I shall tell him everything. I shall confess and let him do what he likes with me."

"If you don't mind my saying so, my dear," I said, "that

doesn't sound good sense to me, either, for however much you've sinned, what is the good of telling your husband about it? What's done, is done. He won't thank you for telling him about it, will he? So take my advice, my dear, and don't say a word to him about it."

"No, no," she said, "I don't want to lie to him."

"It doesn't matter whether you want to or not," I said. "People say it's a sin to steal, but you must have your meal!"

"No, no, no!" she went on. "I shan't tell him a lie, I shan't! Deceit is such an awful thing!"

She went on like that and I could do nothing to change her mind.

"First of all," she said, "I shall write and tell him everything, and if he forgives me, I'll go back to him immediately I receive his letter."

"All right, my dear," I said, "do as you think best. I can see that you won't listen to sense. One thing about you women, though," I said, "does seem funny to me. For you seem to be acting according to quite new rules : when you make up your minds to be unfaithful to your husbands, you don't tell them anything about it, but when it comes to going back to them, you consider it a point of honour to tell them all about your iniquities. Be warned in time, my sweet," I said, "or you'll be sorry for the rest of your life!"

Well, I was right, of course. She wrote her letter and goodness only knows what she did say to her husband in it, probably explained everything. However, there was no reply. She'd come to see me and cry and cry, but ... there was no reply!

"I shall go back to him whether he replies or not," she said. "I don't mind slaving for him for the rest of my life."

I thought it over and ... well, I couldn't help thinking that there might be something in what she said. After all, she was very pretty and even if her husband should get nasty, things might turn out right in the end if he saw her every day and at night . . . well, flesh is weak! The cuckoo that calls at night, they say, always sings longer than the one who only calls in the daytime.

"Very well," I said, "go back to him, for after all a husband isn't a lover : a man's more likely to take pity on a poor erring woman if she's his wife."

"But, my dear Domna Platonovna," she said, "where am I to get the money for my fares?"

"Why," said I, "haven't you got any money of your own at all?"

"Not a penny," she said, "I even owe my landlady for my rent."

"Well, my dear," I said, "money is not so easily come by these days and least of all here."

"But aren't you sorry for me?" she cried. "Can't you see my tears?"

"What about your tears, my dear?" I said. "Tears are one thing and money's another. I'm very sorry for you, as you know, but Moscow doesn't believe in tears, the proverb says. Nobody will give you any money for your tears, my dear."

She just went on crying and I sat beside her and, as we were talking to each other, there was a knock at the front door and in walked that colonel . . . now, what's his name?

Domna Platonovna paused and looked at me.

"What are you asking me for?" I said. "I'm sure I don't know his name."

"A Uhlan . . . now what do they call 'em? . . . engineer?"

"What does it matter, Domna Platonovna?" I asked.

"Larkin I think his name was, or was it? Anyway, it was a bird–like name and it began either with an L or a K . . ."

"Never mind his name!"

"You see, dear, I know so many people and I can always tell you where they live, but blest if I can remember their names!"

However (Domna Platonovna continued with her tale), in walks that colonel and, catching sight of Lekanida through the half-open door, starts teasing me about her and whispers in my ear:

"Who is the young lady?"

She's quite a grown-up woman, you know, but he called her a young lady: looked much younger than her age, she did.

I told him who she was.

"Does she come from the provinces?"

"You guessed it the first time," I said. "She does come from the provinces."

Not being a young scamp to whom every pretty face is fair game, but a man of some position and rank, he liked a woman, for a short time, at any rate, to be modest and to observe certain rules, not like our Petersburg ladies who have neither modesty, nor shame and, as for principles, a girl with a shaven head has more hair than *they* have principles! That was why he was so glad to hear that Lekanida was from the provinces.

"Do me a favour, Domna Pantaloonovna," he said (all army men, it seems have such a habit: they won't call me Domna Platonovna, but Domna Pantaloonovna!) "I don't mind what it costs me, Domna Pantaloonovna," he said, "but arrange this matter for me, will you?"

I said nothing at all to him, but just raised my eyebrows and motioned in the direction of Lekanida, giving him to understand that it was, so to speak, "difficult."

"It isn't out of the question, is it?" he asked.

"That, my dear general," I said, "I can't possibly say, because everything depends entirely on what she decides to do and

41

although," I said, "I'm not very hopeful, I shall do my best for you."

He immediately said to me, "Don't let's waste any words, Domna Pantaloonovna. Here's fifty roubles—let her have them at once!"

"Did you give her the money?" I asked Domna Platonovna. "Don't be in such a hurry, dear," Domna Platonovna replied. "If you want to hear my story, you mustn't interrupt me."

I accepted the money, for, I thought to myself, although, to be sure, I had never discussed a matter of the sort with her and hardly knew under what pretext to give her the money, yet knowing the Petersburg circumstances as well as I do, I could not help concluding that the poor thing would probably be too glad to take the money. So, leaving the colonel in the other room, I went back to Lekanida and said, "I can see, Lekanida Petrovna, that you've been born with a silver spoon in your mouth, for we've just been talking about money and here it is!"

She began asking me excitedly, "Who gave you the money? How did it happen? Where did you get it from?"

I said in a loud voice, "God has sent it to you," and, bending over, I whispered in her ear, "The gentleman in the other room has asked me to give it to you because he wants you to be friends with him . . . Go on," I said, "take it!"

I looked at her, and there were big tears in her eyes and they began rolling down her cheeks on to the table just like large peas. I couldn't tell whether she was pleased or not, but what was there to cry about?

"Come on," I said, "don't be silly, take the money and just go to the other room for a minute, while I stay here and pretend to be busy! . . ."

"Well," Domna Platonovna addressed me, "what do you say? Done her a good turn, hadn't I? And so quickly, too!"

I looked at Domna Platonovna : there was not a glimmer of subterfuge in her eyes, not a trace of cunning about her lips, her speech was sincere and frank, her whole face expressed her keen desire to do the poor, penniless girl a really good turn and her fear lest something should happen to destroy the unexpected piece of good fortune which seemed to have dropped out of the blue, fear not for what she, but the luckless Lekanida, might lose.

"Well, what do you say?" Domna Platonovna exclaimed, jumping up from her seat and striking the table a resounding blow with her hand, her face flushing angrily. "Did I or did I not do all I could for her? But she, the mean creature, what did she do? Why, she rushed out of the room without saying a word to me and ran down the back stairs, howling at the top of her voice! Disgraced me, she did! I went quickly back to my little room and he, too, snatched up his hat and made off. I looked round and there was her old, worn out merino-wool coat. She must have forgotten it. You wait, my pet, I thought to myself, I shan't let you off so easily when you come back, that I shan't, you hussy, you!"

In a day or two (Domna Platonovna resumed her story after having calmed down), I came back home and lo and behold! her ladyship had honoured me with a visit! Although I was not particularly angry with her, being very quick-tempered but never nursing a grudge against people, I pretended to be furious with her.

"Good evening, Domna Platonovna," she said.

"Good evening, my dear," I said. "Have you come for your coat? Here it is."

"I'm sorry, Domna Platonovna," she said, "but I got so frightened the other day."

"Well," I said, "thank you very much, my dear. I must say you repaid me for my kindness, that you did. If I'd been your worst enemy, you could hardly have done it better."

"I was so frightened, Domna Platonovna," she said. "Please, forgive me."

"I've nothing to forgive you for," I said, "but I don't like people to kick up a row in the house where I live, run down the stairs and scream the place down. You must remember," I said, "that the tenants here are respectable people and the landlord, too, is a moneylender, people come to him at all hours of the day and he does not want to hear any screams in his house."

"I'm sorry, Domna Platonovna, but—don't you see?—I never expected such a proposal."

"Are you so different from anybody else," I said, "that such a proposal should have offended you? Why, there's no law against anybody making you any offer he likes, for you're a woman who's in need of money. Besides, no one was trying to force you to do anything, so there was no reason at all why you should have made such a row, was there?"

Well, she kept on imploring me to forgive her, and, of course, I forgave her, began talking to her as if nothing had happened, and even offered her a cup of tea.

"I've come to ask you to help me, Domna Platonovna," she said. "Can you tell me how I can earn enough money to pay for my fares to my husband?"

"How do you expect to earn it, madam?" I asked. "You've had your chance, and you missed it, now you'd better think of something yourself. I'm sure I don't know how you can earn any money."

"I can sew," she said, "and I can make hats."

"Well, my dear," I said, "I know all about that. I know the Petersburg circumstances better than you. Such work, even if you were lucky enough to get it, is done by professional seamstresses and even they would walk about in rags, if they did not get their clothes by selling their favours."

"So what shall I do?" she asked, and started wringing her hands again.

"What you should have done," I said, "was not to have been so particular, for then you could have gone back to your husband the next day."

Oh, how she flared up at that! Her cheeks flamed and her eyes blazed. "What are you saying, Domna Platonovna?" she cried. "Do you really think I'd do a thing like that?"

"Didn't you do it, my dear, without asking me?"

She reddened even more. "That," she said, "was different. It was my fault, no doubt, but I couldn't help myself because I was in love, but to do such a vile thing now that I have repented and made up my mind to go back to my husband—no, never!"

"I don't know what you're talking about, my dear," I said. "I can't see anything vile about it. If you ask me, a woman who's made up her mind to turn over a new leaf should not snap her fingers at such an opportunity."

"Well," she said, "I do snap my fingers at that proposal of yours!"

"A great lady, aren't you? You didn't mind living in sin for months with that ruffian of yours, but when it's a question of business, when your own peace of mind depends on it, when your only chance of living a decent life in the future is at stake, you won't take the one step necessary to give you all you want, you can't spare a minute, can you?"

I looked again at Domna Platonovna. No, there was nothing at all about her that distinguishes those who specialise in the training of victims of the "social malady"; on the contrary, there sat before me a very good-natured woman and she talked her abominations with an air of imperturbable conviction in her own goodness and the inexcusable stupidity of Mrs. Lekanida Domukhovskaya.

"You're in the capital now," I said (Domna Platonovna continued), "and here nobody will give you anything for nothing, nobody will lift a finger to help you, let alone give you money."

So we had our talk and she went away. Off she went and I don't think I saw her again for the next fortnight. At last the poor thing showed up again, and again she was in tears, moaning and groaning.

"Sigh as much as you like, my dear," I said to her, "you may sigh until there's no more breath left in your body, but knowing the Petersburg circumstances as well as I do, I can tell you that your tears won't improve your position a bit."

"Oh dear," she moaned, "I've cried my eyes out, my head aches, and I've got such an awful pain in my chest. I've even applied for help to charitable institutions, been everywhere, but got nothing."

"Well," I said, "it's your own fault, isn't it? You should have asked me first about those charitable institutions and you'd have saved yourself a lot of unnecessary trouble. People go there only to wear out their last pair of boots."

"Just look at me," she said. "What an awful sight I am!"

"I can see, my dear, I can see," I replied, "and I'm not in the least surprised, either, for sorrow, they say, only improves a crab's complexion. I'm sorry, my dear, but I can't do anything for you."

She spent about an hour in my place, crying all the time and, to tell the truth, I was beginning to get a bit fed up with her.

"What's the use of crying?" I said to her at last. "Crying

won't help you, will it ? Wouldn't it be much better to swallow your pride and give in ?"

I could see that though she never stopped crying, she listened to me and was no longer angry with me.

"I'm afraid, my dear," I said, "there's nothing else you can do. Remember," I said, "you're not the first and you won't be the last."

"Oh, if only I could borrow fifty roubles from somewhere, Domna Platonovna," she said.

"Nobody will lend you fifty copecks, let alone fifty roubles," I said. "This isn't just any town, it's a capital city. You had fifty roubles in your hands, but you weren't clever enough to keep them, so what can *I* do for you ?"

So she cried and cried and went away. A little later, on the eve of St. John of Rhyl I think it was, two days before the holy day of the Icons of the Kazan Virgin, I felt a little indisposed. The night before I'd been to see a merchant's wife in Okhta and I suppose I must have caught a cold coming back on that terrible ferry. I stayed at home and didn't even go to morning mass. Put some grease on my nose and stayed in bed. It was on that day that Lekanida Petrovna did me the honour of paying me another visit. She came in without her cloak, just covered with a kerchief.

"Good afternoon, Domna Platonovna," she said.

"Good afternoon, my dear," I replied. "Why aren't you dressed properly ?"

"Oh," she said, "I've only come out for a minute," but I could see that she was greatly upset, for her face kept on changing colour, red one minute and white as a sheet another. She didn't cry any more, though. I must say that gave me a nasty shock, that did, for I could not help thinking that the Dislen creature must have thrown her out into the street.

47

The Amazon

"You haven't had any unpleasantness with that Dislen woman, have you?" I asked.

Her lips twitched and I could see that she wanted to tell me something, but couldn't bring herself to.

"What's the matter, my dear? Do tell me, please."

"I've come to you, Domna Platonovna," she said.

I was silent.

"How are you, Domna Platonovna?" she said.

"Nothing to grumble about," I said. "One day's just like another with me."

"Well," she said, "I . . . I'm dead beat."

"I expect," I said, "there's been no change in your position, either."

"I'm afraid not," she said. "I've been everywhere, I really don't think I know the meaning of shame any more : been to all sorts of rich people for help. I was told there was a rich man in Kuznechy Lane who helps poor people. I went to see him and I went to see another in Znamensky Square."

"And how much, my dear, did they give you?"

"Three roubles each."

"You're lucky," I said. "I know a merchant at Five Corners who changes a rouble into copecks and distributes a copeck each to the poor on Sundays. 'In the eyes of God,' he says, 'it's like doing a hundred good deeds.' But as for getting your fifty roubles," I said, "I don't think you'll find a rich man in the whole of Petersburg who'd give them to you for nothing."

"I think you're wrong," she said. "I'm told there is one man who'd give me the money."

"Is there now? Who told you that? Whoever met a man like that?"

"A woman told me about it. We waited together to see that rich merchant in Kuznechy Lane. There's a Greek on the Nevsky, she told me, and he helps people a lot."

48

"Why does he help people?" I asked. "Just because he likes the look of them?"

"He just helps people, Domna Platonovna, that's all."

"Fiddlesticks!" I said. "Don't make me laugh!"

"But why shouldn't you believe it? That lady told me he had helped her. She's been separated from her husband for six years, and every time she goes there, she gets fifty roubles."

"She was pulling your leg, that lady of yours," I said.

"She was not," she said. "I'm sure she wasn't."

"She's lying, my dear," I said. "I shall never believe it. Who ever heard of a man giving a woman fifty roubles for nothing?"

"But I'm telling you it's true!"

"Why?" I asked, "Have you been there yourself?"

She flushed crimson, poor thing, didn't know where to hide her face.

"Really, Domna Platonovna, what are you trying to suggest? You don't think there's anything wrong, do you? Why, he's eighty years old! Many well-educated women go to him and he demands nothing from them."

"Is it only your beauty he likes to admire?" I said.

"*My* beauty? Why do you insist that I've been there?" she asked, reddening to the roots of her hair.

"Why shouldn't I? Can't I see that you've been there?"

"Well, what if I have? All right, I have been there."

"Well," I said, "I'm glad you were so fortunate as to visit such a fine house."

"I didn't notice anything particularly fine about it," she said. "I just went to see the lady who knows him and I told her about my circumstances. At first, she, too, suggested that I should do what the others had been telling me to do, but as I wouldn't hear of it, she said to me, 'Wouldn't you like to go and see a rich Greek who doesn't ask anything and helps many pretty women?' She gave me his address and she told me that he had a daughter who was studying to play the piano. She advised me to go there and say that I was a music teacher, but insist on seeing him personally. She assured me that he'd do nothing to annoy me and that he'd give me the money. You see, Domna Platonovna, he's such a very old man!"

"I don't see anything," I said.

I noticed that she was getting angry with me for being so dense, not that I was so stupid, either, for I could see very well what she was driving at, but I wanted to make her properly ashamed of herself so that her conscience should prick her just a little.

"But why don't you see it?" she asked.

"Because," I said, "I just can't make out what it is all about, and, what's more, I don't want to know what it's all about, either."

"Why don't you?"

"Because," I said, "it's an abomination! It's disgusting!" I said. "Fie, for shame!" I said.

I made her feel ashamed all right that time. She blinked at me a few times, then she flung herself into my arms and burst out crying, asking me again and again where she could get the money for her fares.

"But haven't you got your fares?" I asked. "Didn't he give you the money for your fares?"

"No," she said, "he only gave me ten roubles."

"Why only ten? He gives fifty to everybody, doesn't he? Why did he give you only ten?"

"Goodness knows," she exclaimed angrily, and even stopped crying for sheer vexation.

"So that's it! It seems you didn't quite please him, did you? Oh," I said, "you fine ladies! Didn't I, an ordinary woman, give you much more sensible advice than that fine lady of yours?"

"Yes," she said, "I realise it myself now."

"You should have realised it before," I said.

"Well, Domna Platonovna," she said, "I've now . . . I've made up my mind," and she looked down on the ground.

"What have you made up your mind about?" I asked.

"What else can I do?" she said. "I'm afraid, Domna Platonovna, I just must do as you said. I can see there's nothing else left for me to do. If only he were a decent man . . ."

"Very well," I said, trying not to embarrass her by my words, "I'll do my best for you. I'll look round. Only remember, my dear, be sensible and don't go changing your mind!"

"Of course not," she said, "I understand . . ."

I could see that the words were almost choking her, but she said in a firm voice, "See what you can do, Domna Platonovna, I'll try to be sensible."

I found out from her that the Dislen woman had given her notice to clear out of her room, and not only that, but she'd taken the ten roubles the poor thing had brought from that Greek and had, in fact, already thrown her out, taking her things, the few rags she still had, in payment of the rent she owed her.

"Well," I said, "I'd expect that from that cat."

"I think," she said, "she just wanted to sell me."

"You could hardly have expected anything else from her," I replied.

"I helped her out many a time when I had money," she said, "but now she treats me just as if I were a street walker."

"Well, my dear," I said, "you needn't look for gratitude from people today. The more you help them, the more eager they are to do you a bad turn. When they're drowning, they'll promise you the keys of heaven, but when they're safe again, they won't offer you even an ordinary doorkey."

I talked to her like that and it never occurred to me that she herself, the hussy, would show her gratitude to me in just the same way.

Domna Platonovna fetched a deep sigh.

I saw that she wanted to ask me something (Domna Platonovna went on), so I said to her, "What is it, my dear? Do you want to ask me something? Speak up, there's a dear, I shan't bite you."

"When will it be?" she asked.

"Well, my dear," I said, "you must have patience. You can't do such things just like that."

"But I have nowhere to go to, Domna Platonovna."

I have a little room (if you come up to see me one day, dear, I'll show it to you), where I keep my things, the few things I have, and if a young lady should be looking for a job or just waiting for something to turn up, I usually rent it to her. Just then the little room was free, so I told Lekanida to move in and stay there for the time being.

Her moving in just meant that she stayed there in what she came : that mean Dislen creature had taken all she had for the money Lekanida owed her.

Seeing how poor she was, I gave her a dress a merchant had given me as a present, a lovely dress it was, too, crêpe-de-chine or whatever the material is called. I couldn't wear it myself because it was too narrow in the waist. The dressmaker, the silly woman, had made a proper mess of it and, as a matter of fact, I am not very fond myself of fashionable dresses, too tight round the bosom they are, if you ask me, and that's why I always walk about in a *capote*.

Anyway, I gave her that dress and some lace, too. She altered the dress, sewed on a bit of lace here and there and made herself a lovely garment. I myself went and got her a pair of shoes with little tassels and high heels, and I gave her a few lace collars and cuffs, in short, got her up like a princess, so that not only was she pleased, but she need not have been ashamed to show herself in it to anybody. I couldn't help saying to her, "You're a really smart woman now, my dear! You certainly know how to dress!"

So one week went by and then another and we seemed to be getting on very nicely together : I was out all day on business and she stayed at home. Then suddenly I was asked by a woman, and not just an ordinary woman, either, but a real lady, though not in her first bloom—an ugly-looking Jezebel she was, as a matter of fact—if I could get her a young student as a tutor for her son. I knew, of course, the kind of student she wanted.

"He must be clean," she said to me, "not one of those what-d'you-call-'ems—Socialists, for they, I expect, don't even know where to buy soap !"

"No, of course not, ma'am," I said, "we certainly don't want any of them. They are no good for anything."

"And," she said, "he must be a grown-up man. I don't want anyone looking like a baby or the children won't pay any attention to him."

"I see what you mean, ma'am," I said.

So I found her a student : a youngish fellow, but well grown and very clean, too, understands everything without having to be told. I went to see the lady about that business, gave her the student's address, told her when to expect a call from him and the rest of it and explained to her that if she didn't fancy him, I could find her another. So that was settled and I left. As I was walking down the stairs, I saw in the hall a general I knew who had just come in. This general (he wasn't a real general, but a high civil servant) was a highly-educated man, lived in a sumptuously furnished house with large mirrors, chandeliers, gold everywhere, carpets, footmen in white gloves, a smell of expensive scent in every room. In short, the house belonged to him and he lived on two floors, like a real lord. As you entered the house, his own suite was on the ground floor on the left, eight rooms occupied by himself, and on the right there was another suite in which his son, who was married, had lived for the past two years. The son, too, had married a very rich woman, and everybody in the house could not praise her enough, everybody agreeing that she was a very kind-hearted young lady. The only trouble was that she was suspected to be suffering from consumption, looked very thin, she did. On the first floor, just on top of that fine staircase—such a wide staircase it was with flowerpots on either side—the old lady herself lived—the general's wife, just like a blackgrouse on her feeding ground, with her children and their tutors. Lived in great state, they did!

The general saw me and said, "How are you, Domna Platonovna?" A very civil gentleman!

"How are you, sir?" I replied.

"Been to see my wife?" he asked.

"Yes, sir," I said. "I've been to see her ladyship your wife, brought her some lace, I have."

"Got anything else besides your lace? Something pretty?"

"Yes, indeed, sir," I said. "I've always got something nice for nice people."

"Well, let's go for a stroll," he said. "The weather's so lovely," he said.

"Yes, sir," I said, "the weather's certainly very lovely, we seldom get such a fine day."

He walked out of the house and I followed him and his carriage followed behind us. So we walked along Mokhovaya Street together, the general and I, such a nice gentleman he was and so unaffected, ever so simple and kind.

"Well," he said, "what nice thing have you got for me today, Domna Platonovna?"

"I've got something for you, sir," I replied, "which I know you will appreciate."

"Are you quite sure you're telling me the truth?" he asked.

He did not believe me because he was a man of great experience, always went to all the circuses and ballets, knew his way about everywhere, especially where pretty girls were concerned.

"Well, sir," I said, "I don't want to boast, for I believe you know me well enough, sir, to realise that I never talk at random; but if you feel like it, you can come up to my place any time you please. It's always better," I said, "to see a thing for yourself than to hear it praised."

"So you're telling me the truth, are you? Something worth while, eh?"

"I don't want to waste any more words, sir," I replied. "It isn't the sort of merchandise that needs advertising."

"All right," he said, "we shall see."

"You're welcome, sir," I said. "When are we to expect you, sir?"

"I shall probably come up one day this week," he said.

"I'm afraid that won't suit me, sir," I said. "You'd better tell me on what day to expect you for certain and we shall be waiting for you, for, you see, sir," I said, "I'm not always in myself. A wolf is fed by his feet, as the saying is."

"All right," he said, "in that case I'll come straight from the office the day after tomorrow, on Friday."

"Very good, sir," I said. "I'll tell her to expect you."

"And," he asked me, "haven't you got something nice in this bag of yours?"

"Yes, sir," I said, "I have a piece of lovely black lace here. Your wife took half of it," I lied to him, "and the other half I've still got. Worth twenty roubles, it is, sir."

"Give her that from me," he said. "Tell her *her good genius* is sending it to her," he said it as a joke, but he gave me twenty-five roubles and, "Keep the change," he said, "and buy yourself something with it!"

Well, you could have knocked me down with a feather! Without as much as having cast an eye on her, he was already giving me such a present!

He got into his carriage at Semyonovsky Bridge and I walked home along the Fontanka embankment.

"Well, Lekanida Petrovna," I said, "you're a very lucky woman!"

"Why? What happened?"

So I told her everything just as it happened. I praised him without, however, concealing the truth. He was not very young, I told her, but he was a very important-looking gentleman, stoutish, wore fine linen, a pair of gold spectacles . . .

But she just sat there all of a tremble.

"There's nothing to be afraid of, my dear," I said. "He may look terrifying to some of the officials of his department, but your business with him is of quite a different kind. You see if he won't be kissing your hands and feet one day. One Polish lady I introduced him to," I said, "did anything she liked with him, and she even managed to have her own lovers besides and he got them excellent jobs. She used to tell him they were her brothers. You can take my word for it, my dear, and have no fear of him, for I know him very well. That Polish lady, for instance, used to beat him! She'd make a scene and knock his spectacles off so that the glass would go tinkling all over the place, and you're as well educated as she. In the meantime," I said, "here's a present for you from him," and I took out the lace and put it in front of her.

When I came back home again in the evening, I found her sitting at the table darning a stocking, her eyes red with weeping. The lace, I noticed, was still lying where I had left it.

"Why don't you put the lace away?" I asked her. "You should have put it in the chest of drawers. It cost a lot of money, you know."

"What do I want it for?" she said.

"Well, if you don't want it, my dear," I said, "I'll give you back the ten roubles I got for it."

"Just as you like," she said.

I picked up the lace, made sure that it was all there, rolled it up and, without measuring it, put it back in my bag.

"You owe me for my dress," I said, "but I shan't charge you too much for it. What do you say if I sell it to you for seven roubles? Your shoes cost me another three roubles, so that we are quits now. As for the rest, we'll settle it later."

"All right," she said and burst into tears again.

"I can't for the life of me see what you're crying about now," I said.

"Don't begrudge me my last tears," she said. "You needn't worry about my looks. He'll like me all right."

"Well," I said, "I've done all I could for you, my dear, so you needn't be so high and mighty with me. Look at her! The airs she's giving herself!"

So I just stopped talking to her. Thursday came and went and I still did not talk to her. On Friday I had my tea and, before leaving, I said to her, "You'd better get yourself ready, my lady. He'll be coming today."

"Today?" she exclaimed, jumping up from her chair. "Are you sure it is today?"

"Didn't I tell you that he promised to call on Friday? And it was Thursday yesterday, wasn't it?"

"Oh, my dear Domna Platonovna," she said, biting her fingers, "please, please . . ." and down she flopped at my feet.

"What's the matter?" I said. "Have you lost your senses?"

"Save me!"

"What shall I save you from?"

"Have pity on me! Protect me!"

"What are you talking about?" I said. "Didn't you ask me to arrange it for you yourself?"

She just buried her face in her hands and sobbed and sobbed, "Please, Domna Platonovna, tell him to come tomorrow, tell him to come the day after tomorrow!"

Well, I could see that it was a waste of time listening to her, so I slammed the door and went away. Let him come, I said to myself, and they'll soon reach some understanding. It wasn't the first time I'd seen women act like that: they're all a bit silly at first.

And turning to me, Domna Platonovna said, "What are you looking at me like that for? I'm telling you the truth: all of them act as if their hearts would break."

"Go on, Domna Platonovna," I said.

"Well, what do you think that hussy did?"

"How should I know what the devil made her do?" I could not help exclaiming in a sudden fit of fury.

"Aye, dear, it was the devil all right who made her do a thing like that!" Domna Platonovna said, as if complimenting me on my insight.

Such a man (she went on), such an important gentleman and she didn't even let him into the house! He knocked and knocked, rang the bell, but she just sat there without answering the door. The cunning she-devil! I never thought she'd have the sauce to do a thing like that. Sitting there behind a locked door, as if she wasn't in at all!

I went to see him the same evening without knowing what had happened. They let me in at once and I asked him, "Well, sir, did I deceive you?" But he looked daggers at me. Told me everything that had happened and how he went away with nothing.

"That's not the way to treat decent people, Domna Platon-ovna," he said.

"I've never heard of such a thing, sir," I said. "I suppose, she must have gone out a minute for something and she didn't hear you," but to myself I thought, "Oh, you little beast, you rattlesnake, you shameless hussy!"

"Come again tomorrow, sir," I said to him. "I give you my word that everything will be all right."

I left him and ran all the way home and when I came in I shouted at her, "Oh, you little beast, what have you done to me now? You've probably ruined me with such a man. Why, not only you, but all your relations and the whole of your province aren't worth his little finger! A word from him and all of you, aye, and the officials of your province, too, will vanish from the face of the earth! What are you playing the grand lady for, you good for nothing idler? What do you think I'm feeding you for? A poor woman like me, you can see yourself how I'm running about day and night trying to earn a few pence here and a few pence there! Can't you see for yourself what an aggravating life I live? And now I've got to feed you, too, have I?"

What names did I not call her! Oh, I was so mad at her that I called her every name under the sun. I felt like scratching her eyes out, I did.

Domna Platonovna brushed away a tear from one of her eyes and added in parenthesis: "I can't help feeling sorry for her even now when I remember how I abused her then!"

"You pauper, you! Call yourself a gentlewoman, do you?" I said to her. "Get out of my house! I don't want to see you again! I hate to breathe the same air as you!" and I even pulled her by the sleeve towards the door.

I was so furious that I didn't know what I was doing. And, really, I seemed to have completely forgotten that I had invited such an important gentleman to come to see her next morning!

No sooner did I tell her to clear out than she got up and made for the door. I was beginning to feel sorry for her, but when she turned away without speaking a word and made for the door, I got furious with her again.

"Where are you off to, you so and so?" I shouted at her.

I can't even remember the names I called her.

"Don't you dare to leave!" I said. "You're to stay here!"

"No," she said, "I'm not going to stay here another minute. I'm going," she said.

"You'll do nothing of the kind!" I said. "Don't you dare to go!"

"But if you're so angry with me, Domna Platonovna," she said, "I'd better go."

"Angry?" I said. "Why, I'm not only angry with you, but I shall beat you black and blue in a minute."

She uttered a little scream and rushed straight to the door, but I caught her by the hand and pulled her back and, furious as I was, I slapped her face six times as hard as I could.

"You're a thief!" I shouted at her. "A thief and not a lady!"

She remained standing in the corner where I had struck her, trembling like a jelly, but even then, mind you, she did not forget she was a lady.

"What have I stolen from you?" she asked.

"You'd better tidy your hair," I said, for I had made a proper mess of her coiffure. "So you want to know what you have stolen from me, do you?" I went on. "Why, you slut, haven't I fed you for two weeks? Haven't I dressed and shod you? I'm running about all day long," I said, "trying to earn an honest living, leading such an aggravating life and now must I be robbed of my last crust of bread because you've got me into trouble with such an important man?"

While I was talking, she quietly did up her plaits into a coil, filled a jug with cold water and washed her face. Then she brushed her hair and sat down at the window without saying a word, only from time to time putting the back of the metal hand-mirror to her burning cheeks. I pretended not to look at her, put out my lace on the table and tried to busy myself, but I could see that her cheeks were burning.

"Oh," I thought to myself, "I shouldn't have insulted her like that, brute that I am!"

The longer I stood at the table, the sorrier I felt for her, and the more I thought of what I had done, the more I pitied her.

"It's that kind-hearted I am!" Domna Platonovna addressed me. "Can't get the better of that good nature of mine. I felt angry with myself for having struck her. Although I knew that it was all her own doing and that she deserved what she got, I was still sorry for her."

So (Domna Platonovna went on with her story) I rushed out for a moment to the pastrycook's in the basement of our house and bought a few pastries for her. As soon as I came back, I put the *samovar* on the table, poured her out a cup of tea and offered it to her with the pastries. She took the tea and a pastry from my hands, bit off a piece of the pastry and just kept it there between her teeth and . . . smiled, yes, smiled a gay kind of smile, while tears were rolling down her cheeks. The tears didn't just flow out of her eyes, they gushed out in a flood, just as if you took a cut lemon and squeezed the juice out of it.

"Now, now," I said, "don't take it to heart so, there's a dear!"

"Never mind," she said, "never mind, never mind . . ." and she went on repeating that "never mind" of hers without stopping.

"Good Lord," I thought, "she hasn't gone out of her mind, has she?"

I splashed some cold water on her face and after a while she calmed down and seemed to have completely recovered. She sat down on the edge of the bed and there she remained sitting for a long time. My conscience was still pricking me for the way I had treated her, so I said a prayer a priest had taught me while I was still in Mtsensk, a special prayer against madness, beginning with the words, "O merciful Mother of the most merciful God, holy and pure Virgin," and afterwards I took off my gown and, going up to her in my petticoat only, I said, "Listen to me, Lekanida Petrovna, it is written in the Scriptures, 'Let not the sun go down upon your wrath' so please forgive me for forgetting myself. Come, my dear, let's be friends!" Then I bowed to the ground before her and I took her hand and kissed it. Yes, I kissed her hand, and she bent over me and touched my shoulder with her lips and, then, she also kissed my hand, and we embraced and kissed each other.

"My dear friend," I said, "believe me, I didn't do it out of spite or out of greed, but for your own good!"

I went on talking to her like that, stroking her head, and she said breathlessly:

"I know, I know . . . Thank you, Domna Platonovna, thank you."

"You realise, my dear," I said, "that he'll be here tomorrow, don't you?"

"Yes," she said, "I realise that. Let him come. Yes, let him come."

I went on stroking her head and smoothing her hair round her ears, and she sat there without taking her eyes off the icon.

The lamp burnt so gently before the icon and its radiance fell upon her face and I could see that she was moving her lips, but no sound came from them.

"What are you doing, my dear?" I asked. "Are you praying?"

"No, Domna Platonovna," she said, "I just can't help it."

"I thought you were saying your prayers, my dear," I said, "but you mustn't go on talking to yourself like that. It's only lunatics who talk to themselves."

"Oh, Domna Platonovna," she said, "I think I must be mad. What am I doing? What am I doing?" she went on repeating, smiting her breast with all her strength.

"It can't be helped, my dear," I said. "I suppose this is the hard heritage that has been appointed to you."

"How do you mean this heritage has been appointed to me? I was an honest woman! O God, O God, where are you? Where are you, O God?"

"It is written," I said, "that no man has ever seen God and that He is nowhere to be seen."

"But where are the good, merciful Christians? Where are they? Where?"

"The Christians, my dear, are here."

"Where?"

"What do you mean where? They are here, the whole of Russia is Christian, we're all Christians, you and I are Christians."

"Yes, yes, of course," she said, "I know that we're Christians . . ."

I glanced at her and I saw a strange look come into her face as she said those words, just as if she was talking to someone who was invisible.

"Good gracious, my dear," I said, "you haven't really lost your reason, have you? What are you trying to frighten me for? What are you murmuring against your Creator for?"

The Amazon

She calmed down again, but soon she burst into tears once more and started talking softly to herself.

"Why have I done it?" she said. "Why have I been my own worst enemy? Why did I listen to those people? It is they who made me quarrel with my husband, it is they who told me over and over again that he was a tyrant and a brute, but it wasn't true! It was I, stupid and pampered fool that I was, who poisoned his life instead of making him happy. Oh, you wicked people, you've misled me, you promised me untold riches, but forgot to mention the rivers of burning brimstone. My husband doesn't want to know me any more, he doesn't want to look at me again, he doesn't even read my letters, and tomorrow, to-morrow . . ." she shuddered violently. "Mother," she cried, "oh, mother, if you could only see me now, my darling! If you, my pure angel, could only look at me now from your grave! Oh, Domna Platonovna, you can't imagine the care she lavished on us! What a fine life we had, always dressed in spotlessly clean clothes . . . Oh, everything was so lovely in our house, mother adored flowers . . . She'd sometimes take me by the hand and we'd go for long walks in the country together . . . . across fields and meadows . . ."

That night I had a most extraordinary dream. I fell asleep on her bed listening to the story of her childhood, just as I was in my petticoat, so I fell into a heavy sleep. Now, I usually sleep like a log and I never have any dreams, except perhaps sometimes I dream about somebody trying to burgle my flat, but that night I kept on dreaming of woods and meadows and gardens and about her, too, about Lekanida Petrovna, I mean. I saw her in my dream as a little girl, such a pretty little girl, too, with fair, curly hair, carrying a bunch of flowers in one hand and followed by a little dog, a little white dog, which was barking all the time, bow-wow, bow-wow, bow-wow! as if he was angry and wanted to bite me. I bent down to pick up a stick to drive the dog away and just at that moment a dead hand was suddenly thrust out of the ground and it caught me here by the wrist. I woke up and I found that I had been asleep there the whole night and that it was time for me to get up. I must have lain on my hand with all my weight, for it had gone dead.

I got up, said my prayers and had my tea, but she was still asleep.

"Get up, Lekanida Petrovna," I said, "it's late. Your tea is on the table. I'm going out now, my dear."

I kissed her on the forehead as she lay on the bed. I was sorry for her just as if she was my own daughter, but as I went out of the front door, I took out the key quietly, locked the door on the outside and put it in my pocket.

"That," I thought to myself, "should make things a lot easier all round!"

Then I went straight to the general and said, "Well, sir, now everything depends on you. I did my best for you, but you'd better hurry!" and I gave him the key.

"Surely, my dear Domna Platonovna," I said, "that's not the end of your story, is it?"

Domna Platonovna laughed and shook her head, as if wishing to say, "Oh, how funny people are!"

I came home late on purpose that day (Domna Platonovna went on) and I was surprised to see that no lamp was lit in any of the rooms.

"Lekanida Petrovna!" I called.

I heard her moving about on my bed.

"Are you asleep?" I asked, hardly able to restrain my laughter.

"No, I'm not asleep," she replied.

"Why don't you light a candle?" I asked.

"What do I want a light for?" she replied.

I lit a candle, blew on the charcoal in the *samovar* and then called to her to get up and join me in a cup of tea.

"Don't want to," she said, turning her face to the wall.

"Well, why don't you get up and go to your own bed? I have to make my bed."

She got up, glowering like a wolf, looked frowningly at the lighted candle and shielded her eyes from the light.

"What are you covering your eyes for?" I asked.

"It hurts me to look at the light," she replied.

So she went off to her cubby-hole and I could hear her fling herself on her bed without undressing.

I undressed and said my prayers as usual, but all the time I was dying to know how they had fared, the two of them, while I was out. I was afraid to pay the general another visit, for, I thought to myself, I might get into hot water again. I ought, of course, to have asked Lekanida about it, but she did not seem in the mood for exchanging intimacies with me. Let's try a bit of cunning, I thought, and going into her room, I said, "Has anyone called while I was out?"

She was silent.

"Why don't you answer my question, my dear?" I asked.

She turned on me furiously and said, "What do you want to ask me questions for?"

"What do you mean?" I said. "I'm the landlady here, aren't I?"

"You know everything perfectly well without asking me about it," she said, and, mind, she was speaking in quite a different tone to me now.

But, of course, I knew all I wanted to now. I went back to my room and I heard her sighing all the time, and while I was undressing and until I fell asleep, she was still sighing.

"So that's the end of your story, Domna Platonovna?" I asked.

"No, dear," she replied, "that is only the end of the first act."

"And what happened in the second act?"

"In the second act that hussy declared war to the death on me, that's what happened in the second act, dear."

"How did that happen?" I asked. "That seems to be interesting, Domna Platonovna!"

"Well, dear, it happened just as things usually happen in life. As soon as a man feels his power, he begins to behave like a swine!"

"How long did it take for her attitude towards you to change?"

"How long? Why, the very next day she showed herself in her true colours!" Domna Platonovna replied and resumed her tale :

I got up early as usual and got the *samovar* going. Having made tea, I went to her little room and sat down beside her bed with my cup of tea.

"Get up, Lekanida Petrovna," I said, "have a wash and say your prayers, it's time for a cup of tea."

Without saying a word, she jumped out of her bed all dressed as she was, and I noticed that a piece of paper fell out of her pocket. I bent down to pick it up, but she swooped down on it like a hawk.

"Don't touch it," she said, grasping it in her hand.

I saw that it was a hundred rouble note. "What are you growling at me like that for, my dear?" I said.

"I shall growl at you if I like," she said.

"Calm yourself, my dear," I said, "I'm not that Dislen landlady of yours! Nobody will take away what belongs to you in my house."

Not a word did she say in reply. Drinking my tea, she was, but too proud even to look at me! Who would not feel hurt at being treated like that? However, I let that pass too, thinking that she was still feeling upset and, indeed, I could see how every now and then a shiver would pass across her bare chest (her chemise was cut very low). She had, as I mentioned before, a lovely body, pink and white, just like soft down in satin, but that morning her skin seemed to have gone dark and her bare shoulders, poor thing! were covered with goose-pimples, as if from cold. "A pampered miss finds the first cold blast a bit disconcerting," I thought, and I even pitied her in my heart, little dreaming that she could be so spiteful!

When I came home in the evening, I found her sitting before a candle sewing herself a new chemise, and on the table in front of her lay three or four more already cut out for sewing.

"How much did you pay for the linen?" I asked.

"I'd thank you not to bother me in future with any of your conversation, Domna Platonovna," she replied in an unnaturally quiet voice.

I shot a glance at her: she looked entirely self-composed, as if she wasn't a bit angry with me. All right, my dear, I thought to myself, if you're so high and mighty, then I too will be quite different with you!

"In my own house, Lekanida Petrovna," I said to her, "I am the mistress and I can say whatever I like, and if," I said, "you don't like my conversation, then you can go where you like."

"Don't worry," she said, "I'm going."

"But before you go," I said, "you'd better settle your account. Honest people don't leave without paying what they owe."

"You needn't worry about that, either," she said.

"I'm not worrying," I said, and I went on to tell her what she owed me for board and lodging for the six weeks she had been at my place : ten roubles for her room, fifteen roubles for her food and, I said, "Let's say another three roubles for tea and three more roubles for your laundry, making altogether," I said, "thirty-one roubles." I forgot to charge her for the candles, and it quite slipped my mind that I had also taken her with me twice to the baths.

"Very well," she said, "you'll be paid all that."

When I returned home in the evening of the following day, I found her again sitting at the table and sewing herself a chemise and on the wall, just opposite her, there hung on a nail a lovely new cloak of black satin with a gros-de-Naples lining and padded with down. It made my blood boil to think that it was through me, through my zeal for her, that she had got it all and that she should be buying everything now without me and even in an underhand way.

"If I was you, my dear," I said, "I should not have been in such a hurry to buy myself cloaks, but would first have paid my debts."

She at once put that dainty hand of hers into her pocket and, taking out a wrapped-up piece of paper, handed it to me. I unwrapped the paper and found exactly thirty-one roubles there. I took the money and "Thank you very much, madam," I said, calling her "madam" on purpose.

"Don't mention it," she said without even deigning to look up at me from her work.

She kept on sewing and sewing, the needle simply flying between her fingers. "You just wait, you green serpent, you!" I thought to myself. "Don't you give yourself such airs, my girl, just because you paid what you owed me!" And I said aloud, "You've paid me for my expenses, Lekanida Petrovna, but what do you propose to give me for the services I've rendered you?"

"What sort of services?" she asked.

69

"Do you want me to explain it to you?" I asked. "Can't you understand yourself?"

She went on sewing, pressing the hem down with her thimble. "Let him who wanted your services," she said without looking up, "pay you for them."

"Wasn't it you who wanted them most?" I said.

"No," she replied, "I didn't want them at all, and," she added, "I'd be greatly obliged if you left me alone!"

How do you like that? The impudence of the woman! However, I ignored it, left her alone and didn't talk to her again.

The following morning, it was just about breakfast time, she put on the chemise she'd been sewing, wrapped up the others which weren't ready yet in a kerchief, dressed and, bending down and taking out a cardboard box from under her bed, got a new hat out of it . . . It was a lovely hat! and it suited her perfectly . . . She put it on and said, "Good-bye, Domna Platonovna!"

Again I felt sorry for her as if she was my own child. "Won't you wait and have a cup of tea with me, my dear?"

"No, thank you," she said, "I shall have tea at my own place."

At her own place, if you please! Well, heaven forgive her, I ignored that, too. "Where are you going to live?" I asked.

"In Vladimirskaya Street," she said, "in Tarkhov's house."

"Oh, I know it very well," I said. "It's a nice house except that the house-porters there like to run after girls."

"I assure you," she said, "I'm not interested in house-porters."

"Of course not, my dear, of course not!" I said. "Have you rented a room there?"

"No," she replied, "I've taken a flat. I'm going to live there with my cook."

"So that's the way things are with you now!" I thought to myself and said aloud, "You're a real one, aren't you?" and I shook a finger at her, joking like. "Why did you deceive me then? Why did you tell me you wanted to go back to your husband?"

"So you think I deceived you, do you?" she said.

"What did you expect me to think?" I said. "If you really wanted to go back to your husband, you wouldn't have rented a flat, would you?"

"I'm sorry for you, Domna Platonovna," she said, "you don't seem to understand anything."

"Don't try to be too clever with me, my dear," I said. "I can see that you've managed everything beautifully!"

"What are you talking about?" she exclaimed. "Do you think sluts like me go back to their husbands?"

"Oh, my dear," I said, "what are *you* talking about? Slut, indeed! I know women who're ten times worse than you and who still live with their husbands!"

She was standing at the door just then and was about to open it and go out, when she suddenly smiled and, turning to me, said, "Forgive me, Domna Platonovna, for having been angry with you. I can see now that one ought never to be angry with you, for you are such a stupid woman!"

That was her way of saying good-bye to me! Nice, wasn't it? "Well," I thought, after she had gone, "stupid or not, I seem to be cleverer than you, anyway, for I did exactly what I liked with you, clever and educated lady that you are!"

So that was how we parted. We had not exactly quarrelled, but we had not been particularly nice to each other, either. I did not see her after that day for I should think almost a year. I happened to have been particularly busy at the time, married off four merchants, found a husband for a colonel's daughter, got a wife for a State Councillor, the widow of a merchant, and in between there were lots of other things to be seen to and, of course, there was also my lace to sell—I was sent yards and yards of it at the time from the provinces, so what with one thing and another the time passed. Well, one fine day it so happened that I had to visit the house of the general to whom I had introduced my Lekanida, to see his daughter-in-law. His son I had known a long time : a chip of the old˙block he was, like father, like son ! Anyway, so I went to see the general's daughter-in-law, who wanted to sell me a white silk cloak, but she wasn't at home : gone to Voronezh, I was told, to pray at the tomb of St. Mitrofany. Well, I said to myself, why not go and see her husband for old times' sake ?

I went in through the back door, but found no one there. I peeped into one room, then into another and suddenly I heard Lekanida's voice. "Darling," she was saying, "I love you. You're the only treasure I have in the whole world !"

"Well, well," I said to myself, "so my dear Lekanida Petrovna is having a fine time, it seems, making love to father and son !" and off I went, without making a sound, the same way I came in. I started making enquiries, for I was curious to find out how she had got to know the son. Well, it seemed that it was the son's wife who took pity on her and began visiting her surreptitiously, all because, you see, she was so sorry for her, because of her being such a nice, educated young lady, Lekanida, that is. Well, so my dear Lekanida had paid her back in the same coin as she had me. All right, it was none of my business, so I said nothing about it and, in a manner of speaking, I even became an accomplice in her treachery, for even where I ought to have spoken out, I never showed by a look that I knew what was going on.

Nearly another year passed. At the time, Lekanida lived in Kirpichny Lane. It was the fourth week of Lent and I was getting ready to go to confession when, walking through Kirpichny

Lane one day, I looked up at the house where she lived and I said to myself, "What an awful shame I haven't made it up with Lekanida Petrovna! I'm now getting ready to partake of the holy Eucharist and what could be more seemly than being friends with her again?" So I went in. She lived in such style that you couldn't ask for anything better, even the parlour maid looked a real lady.

"Tell your mistress, my pretty one," I said to her, "that Domna Platonovna, the lace woman, would like to see her."

She went in, and returning almost at once, said, "Please come in."

I went into the drawing room where everything was in very fine style, too, and there on a divan sat Lekanida Petrovna and the general's daughter-in-law : they were both of them having coffee. Lekanida met me just as if nothing had happened between us, just as if we had seen each other only the night before.

I, simple-hearted that I am, began to congratulate her on her nice flat, saying, "What a lovely flat you have, my dear ! I hope the Lord will shower even greater blessings upon you !"

She began talking quickly in French to the other one, and I couldn't understand a word they were saying to each other. I just sat there like a fool, staring at the walls until I began to yawn.

"Oh, I'm so sorry, Domna Platonovna," Lekanida suddenly said to me, "would you like some coffee ?"

"Thank you, my dear," I said, "I shouldn't mind a cup."

She at once rang a silver hand-bell and said to her maid, "Dasha," she said, "see that Domna Platonovna has some coffee, will you ?"

Fool that I am, I did not at the time realise what she meant by her "see that she has some coffee !" But in a minute or two the same Dasha came in and announced, "The coffee's ready, ma'am."

"Thank you," said Lekanida to her and, turning to me, she said, "Won't you go with her to the kitchen, Domna Platonovna? She'll see that you have some coffee!"

Well, that was the last straw! I was ready to burst with anger. "I shall expose her!" I thought to myself, still controlling myself, though.

I got up and said, "Thank you very much, Lekanida Petrovna, you're very kind I'm sure, but poor as I am," I said, "I can afford my own coffee."

"Why are you so angry with me?" she asked.

"Why?" I said, looking straight into her eyes. "Because, my dear, you did not mind eating my food at my table with me and now you want me to have coffee with your maid. No wonder I'm feeling hurt."

"But Dasha's an honest girl," she said, "and her company cannot possibly be an affront to you," and it seemed to me that, as she said it, she was smiling to herself.

"Oh, you viper," I thought to myself, "I've nourished you in my bosom and now you're turning on me, are you?" and I said aloud, "I haven't said a word against the young lady's morals, but I didn't expect you, Lekanida Petrovna, to put me at a table with your servants!"

"And why shouldn't I, Domna Platonovna?" she asked.

"Because, my dear," I said, "you ought to remember what you were and you should take a look at yourself now and consider to whom you owe it all."

"I remember very well," she said, "that I was an honest woman and that now I'm trash and that I owe it all to your kindness, Domna Platonovna."

"Quite right, my dear," I said, "you are nothing but trash! I'm telling you that straight to your face and I don't care who hears me: you're trash! You were trash and trash you are and it was certainly not I who made you trash!" And picking up

74

my bag, I said, "Good-bye, your ladyship!" and was about to
leave them, when the general's daughter-in-law, the sickly one,
jumped up from her seat looking all flustered and shouted at me:

"How dare you speak like that to Lekanida Petrovna?"

"Why shouldn't I, pray, speak to her like that?" I asked.

"Lekanida Petrovna," she said, "has been very kind to you,
but I shan't allow her to be insulted in my presence : she's my
friend!"

"Some friend!" I said.

But here Lekanida, too, jumped to her feet and screamed at
me, "Get out of here, you abominable creature!"

"Oh," said I, "so I'm an abominable creature, am I? Well, I
may be abominable, but I've never made love to other women's
husbands. However bad I may be, I never tried to seduce a
father and his son by flaunting my charms before them. That's
what your friend has done, madam," I said, addressing the
general's daughter-in-law, "this dear friend of yours?"

"You lie," she said. "I shall never believe you. You're saying
that about Lekanida Petrovna out of spite!"

"Well," I said, "if it is out of spite I'm saying that, then
you'll have to excuse me, Lekanida Petrovna, if I expose you
now!" And I laid it all on the table before them, told them
everything I had heard Lekanida saying to the other woman's
husband, and went away.

"Well, and what happened then, Domna Platonovna?" I
asked.

"The old gentleman would have nothing to do with her
after that scandal."

"And the young one?"

"The young one did not keep her, did he? With the young
one everything was, as they say, *pour amour*, he was in love with
her and she with him! A worthless baggage like that, but she,

75

if you please, could not live without love. Yes, she had to have a real love affair same's a police officer has to have a pair of trousers. But now she makes do without love, she does!"

"How do you know that?" I asked.

"How do I know it, dear? Why, the poor thing has to make do without love living the life she does now. One day it's a prince, another—a count, then an Englishman, and the day after an Italian, and the day after that some Spaniard. That is no longer love, dear, but filthy lucre. Goes out shopping like a countess and you should have seen the carriage in which she goes driving on Nevsky Avenue, the horses alone must have cost her thousands . . ."

"So since then you haven't been meeting her, have you?"

"No, dear. Not that I bear her any grudge, but I've never been to see her again. To tell you the truth, I don't care what happens to her now! The other day I went to see a lady in Morskaya Street and, as I came out, I met her coming up the front steps of the house. I let her pass and said to her, 'Good morning, Lekanida Petrovna!' She went green in the face, bent over to me from the top step and, smiling sweetly, said, "Good morning, you beast!"

Here I could no longer contain myself and burst out laughing.

"Yes dear," Domna Platovna assured me, "that's what she said to me : 'Good morning, you beast!' I wanted to say to her, 'Don't you beast me, my dear, you're a proper beast yourself now,' but her servant was coming up the steps, carrying a large umbrella, so I thought to myself, 'Go in peace, my French marquise'!"

CHAPTER FOUR

FIVE YEARS HAVE PASSED since the day when Domna Platonovna told me the story of Lekanida Petrovna. During those years I left St. Petersburg several times, coming back again to hear the city's ceaseless din, to look at the pale, worried, crushed faces of its inhabitants, to breathe the stench of its exhalations and to give way to fits of the blackest melancholy during its consumptive "white nights." Domna Platonovna was still the same. She used to come across me accidentally in whatever part of the city I happened to live, welcomed me always with open arms and friendly kisses, and never tired of complaining about the treacherous machinations of man who seemed to have picked her out as his favourite victim and perpetual plaything.

Innumerable were the stories Domna Platonovna told me during those five years and in all of them she was always trampled upon, insulted and humiliated, a sacrifice to her own virtues and a martyr to her own eternal solicitude for the happiness of other people.

These diverting and ingenuous tales of my dear, simple-hearted Domna Platonovna abounded in all sorts of strange and wonderful adventures. It was from her that I learnt about different kinds of weddings, deaths and inheritances ; it was she who told me of the latest thefts, burglaries and confidence tricks ; it was entirely due to her that my eyes were opened to every instance of open and covert immorality in the capital ; it was she who initiated me into the various Petersburg mysteries, and it was she, finally, who gave me the latest news about you, my friends, who hail from the same parts as Lekanida Petrovna, and about your edifying adventures—yes, about you who bring to us from the wide Volga, the limitless Saratov steppes, the gentle Oka and the golden, thrice-blessed Ukraine, your fresh, healthy bodies, your ardent, but far from wicked hearts, your quite insanely audacious faith in fate or chance or in your own strength and your dreams which are of no use whatever to anybody here.

But let us return to our friend Domna Platonovna. You must not be offended, dear reader, whoever you may be, if I speak of Domna Platonovna as our mutual friend. Since I am assuming that every reader of mine possesses at least a nodding acquaintance with Shakespeare, I should like him to remember Hamlet's words : "Use every man after his desert, and who should 'scape whipping." It is indeed difficult to penetrate into the secret places of a man's heart !

So Domna Platonovna and I kept up our meetings and friendship ; she went on looking me up and, although she was always hurrying off somewhere on some important business errand, she used to stay with me hours at a time. I, too, visited Domna Platonovna at her flat, not far from the cathedral, and I saw the cubby-hole where Lekanida Petrovna took refuge until her act of renunciation, and the pastrycook's shop where Domna Platonovna had bought the pastries with which to please and comfort her and, finally, I had the good fortune to see two freshly arrived "young ladies" who had come to St. Petersburg in search of happiness and found themselves in Domna Platonovna's flat "in Lekanida's place." But what I could never discover from Domna Platonovna was how she had reached her present position, or how she came to hold her highly original views about her own absolute uprightness and the insatiable craving for every kind of evil-doing on the part of the rest of mankind. I wanted very much to know what happened to Domna Platonovna before she got into the habit of meeting all objections with, "Now, now, don't you start an argument with me, there's a dear, for I know everything much better than you." I wanted to know what that blessed

merchant's family on the Zusha was like in which this plump
Domna Platonovna had grown up, this woman in whom
prayers and fasts and her own chastity, of which she was inordi-
nately proud, and her pity for the unfortunate were combined
with barefaced lying in her professional capacity as match-
maker and an artistic flair for bringing about short-lived
marriages, not for love, but for money, etc., etc. How, I
wondered, could all that be accommodated in one fat little
heart where such an amazing harmony reigned that one
moment Domna Platonovna was driven by her feelings to slap
the weeping Lekanida Petrovna's face time after time and the
next moment to rush downstairs to buy her some pastries; the
same heart which contracted painfully when she dreamt about
Lekanida Petrovna as a little girl in her Sunday clothes going
for a walk with her mother, but which beat calmly when she
invited some fat hog to defile the same Lekanida Petrovna who
could not even protect her body any more by locking the door!

I realised very well that Domna Platonovna did not engage
in that kind of business as a profession, but looked upon it
in the St. Petersburg way, and accepted it as a kind of law that no
woman could possibly extricate herself from any trouble except
through her own moral downfall. But all the same, what
exactly are you, Domna Platonovna? Who first gave you the
idea of following this path? But Domna Platonovna, for all her
talkativeness, could not be induced to talk about her past.

One day, however, it so happened that Domna Platonovna,
quite accidentally and of her own accord, told me how *simple*
she had been and how "they" had *taught* her so that at last she
no longer believed anybody or took anything on trust. Do not
expect, dear reader, to find anything coherent in this story of
Domna Platonovna, which will hardly help anyone to understand the mental process of this Petersburg business woman.
I am telling you what happened to her later just to entertain

you a little and, perhaps, to give you a chance to reflect upon that blind, but terrible force of "the Petersburg circumstances," which not only produce a Domna Platonovna, but also deliver into her hands those who rush across a river without troubling to look for a ford, the numberless Lekanidas over whom Domna tyrranised here, while everywhere else she would have realised herself that in their company she was nothing but a pariah or, at best, a clown.

CHAPTER FIVE

I WAS ILL AT THE TIME. I lived in Kolomna in a flat which was, to quote Domna Platonovna's description of it, "a bit peculiar." It consisted of two spacious rooms in an ancient wooden house owned by a little, wooden-faced old woman. Her husband, a merchant of great piety, having only recently died, my landlady, as behoved her widowed state, engaged in money-lending and let out her former bedroom with its huge double-bed and the adjacent sitting room with its enormous icon-case before which her late husband used to offer up his daily prayers.

In my so-called "parlour" I had a divan upholstered in real Russian hide, a round table covered with a cloth of faded violet plush with an entirely colourless silk border, a table-clock with a copper negro, a stove with a figure in high relief in a cavity where home-made liqueurs were usually placed to mature, a long mirror of excellent quality with a bronze harp on the top ledge of its tall frame. On the walls hung an oil-painting of the late Emperor Alexander I, and beside it, behind the glass of a heavy, gilt frame, a huge lithograph depicting four scenes from the life of Queen Guinevere, a portrait of the Emperor Napoleon in infantry uniform and another in cavalry uniform, a mountain landscape, a dog swimming in its own kennel, and a portrait of a Russian merchant with a medal on an Anne ribbon. In a far corner stood a tall, three-tiered icon-shrine with three large icons with dark visages which gazed sternly out of their shining, gilt garments ; in front of the shrine was a lamp which was always carefully lit by my pious landlady and below, under the icons, was a little cupboard with semi-circular doors with a bronze ridge instead of a handle. All this gave me the feeling that I was not living in St. Petersburg, but in

Zamoskvoryechye, the old merchants' quarter of Moscow, or even in the provincial town of Mtsensk itself.

My bedroom was even more Mtsensk-like : it sometimes seemed to me that the enormous double bed in whose feather-beds I sank as in a sea, was not a bed at all, but the town of Mtsensk itself, which was carrying on an incognito existence in St. Petersburg. No sooner did I sink in those featherbed waves than a kind of narcotic, poppy-like substance descended like a veil on my eyes and hid from them the whole of St. Petersburg with its cheerful boredom and its boring cheerfulness. It was there, in that becalming Mtsensk atmosphere, that I was again destined to have long heart-to-heart talks with Domna Platonovna.

I caught a cold and the doctor ordered me to stay in bed for a few days.

On one of those days, about twelve o'clock on a greyish March morning, I was lying in bed, already convalescing from my illness, and, having read as much as I fancied, I was thinking that it would not be a bad idea if someone came to see me. No sooner did that thought cross my mind than the door of my parlour opened with a creaking noise and I heard Domna Platonovna's cheerful voice exclaiming, "Oh, how lovely everything is here, dear. What fine icons and how gloriously they shine ! Yes, dear, you have got a lovely place !"

"Is it you, my dear Domna Platonovna?" I asked.

"Of course, it's me," she replied. "Who else would it be but me?"

We exchanged greetings.

"Sit down, please," I urged Domna Platonovna.

She sat down in an armchair opposite my bed and put her little hands, in one of which she grasped her snow-white linen handkerchief, on her knees.

"What's wrong with you?" she asked.

"Caught a cold," I replied.

"Lots of people are suffering from stomach complaints at present," she said.

"There's nothing wrong with my stomach," I said.

"Well," she said, "if there's nothing wrong with your stomach, you'll soon be better. You've got a lovely flat, dear."

"Not bad, Domna Platonovna," I said.

"An excellent flat. I've known your landlady, Lyubov Petrovna, a long time. She's a fine woman. She was a bit touched in the head one time and she used to scream in different voices, but I expect that must have passed off now."

"I don't know," I said. "I've never heard anything. She doesn't appear to be screaming any more."

"Oh, dear, I'm in proper trouble just now," said Domna Platonovna in a most pitiful voice.

"Why, what's the matter, Domna Platonovna?"

"Oh, such awful trouble, dear, such awful trouble that . . . it's something terrible, really, trouble and bad luck all together. Can't you see what I'm carrying my lace in now?"

Leaning over I had a look and I saw that Domna Platonovna's lace was lying on the little table, tied in a black silk kerchief with a white border.

"Are you in mourning?" I asked.

"Yes, in mourning indeed and *what* mourning!"

"I'm sorry to hear that," I said, "but where's your bag?"

"Why, dear, it's my bag I'm in mourning for. It's gone, yes . . . my bag's gone!"

"How do you mean it's gone?"

"Well, dear, it's just gone, and for the last two days every time I think of it I cannot help saying, 'O Lord, am I really such a miserable sinner that Thou shouldst try me like that?' You see, it all happened in such a funny way: it all began with a dream. I dreamt that an unknown priest came to see me and he brought me a loaf, the kind of loaf they bake in our town out of wheat porridge. 'Here,' he said, ' take this loaf, woman.' 'Father,' I said, 'whatever do I want this loaf for ?' But you can see now what he brought me that loaf for, can't you ?—to warn me that I was going to lose something !"

"How did it all happen, Domna Platonovna ?"

"Oh, it happened in the queerest way, dear. You know the merchant's wife, Mrs. Kosheverova, don't you ?"

"No," I said, "I don't know her."

"Oh, well, if you don't know her, then it doesn't matter. I'm an old friend of hers, or, perhaps, I shouldn't say, dear, that I'm a friend of hers, for she's a most spiteful woman and as mean as they make 'em ! I just happen to know her, just as I do you, dear. The other evening I went to see her and, to my misfortune, I stayed a bit late. She kept on saying to me, 'What's your hurry, Domna Platonovna ? Please, stay a little longer !' Drat the woman, has nothing to do, so she's worrying herself to death because her husband isn't jealous, although heaven knows why he should be jealous, seeing that she's as ugly as sin and that her tongue is as long as a parrot's. She told me she had toothache once and the doctor told her to apply a medicinal leech to her tooth, but the district nurse's boy applied it to her tongue instead and ever since her tongue has been swollen. I had some other business to see to that evening, had to visit a house at Five Corners to see a merchant who wants me to find him a wife, but that Kosheverova woman wouldn't let me. 'Wait,' she said, 'let's have a glass of Kiev brandy and, besides,' she said, 'Fadey Semyonovich will be coming from evening mass soon and then we'll have a cup of tea. What are you in such a hurry for ?' 'But I *am* in a hurry, dear !' I said, but to my misfortune I did stay and drank so much of that vodka, or brandy, or whatever it was, that my head began to spin. 'You'll have to excuse me, Varvara Petrovna,' I said, 'it's very kind of you, I'm sure, but I can't drink another drop.' But she wouldn't leave me alone, kept on begging me to have a little more, but I said, 'No, dear, you'd better not ask me to have a drop more. I know how much is good for me and I can't possibly have another drop, dear, not another drop!' She says to me, 'But you'll wait for my husband, won't you?' I said, 'No, my dear, I shan't wait for your husband, either.' So I put my foot down and insisted on going, for, you see, my head was going round and round. So, my dear sir, out of the gates I went, then turned into Razyezhaya Street, thinking, I'd better take a cab, and there was the cab, just waiting for me at the corner of the street. I says to the cabby, 'What will you charge me, my fine fellow, to the Znamenye Cathedral of the Holy Virgin?' and he says, 'Fifteen copecks, lady!' 'Oh, no,' I said, 'five copecks!' Well, he wouldn't agree, so I walked along Razyezhaya Street. It was very light, the street lamps were burning. gaslight in the shop-windows . . . I said to myself, 'I'll get home on foot rather than pay fifteen copecks to that hooligan for taking me a few yards in his cab.' Then all of a sudden, dear, there sprang out of the ground a funny kind of man—goodness only knows where he'd come from—in an overcoat, a hat and goloshes, in a word, a real gentleman! I tell you, dear, I couldn't for the life of me make out where he had sprung from so sudden like. 'Excuse me, madam,' he said (called me 'madam,' the rascal did), 'could you tell me where Vladimirskaya Street is?' 'Yes, sir,' I said, 'go straight ahead till you come to the first turning on the right . . .' But no sooner did I say that, raised my hand, you know, to show him, than he gave a pull at my bag, 'Thanks very much, lady,' he said, 'greatly obliged I'm sure!' and off he ran in the opposite direction. 'Oh, you hooligan,' I said, 'you rogue!' thinking that he'd just been playing a silly trick on me, but then, looking for my bag, I saw that it was gone! 'Help, help!' I shouted. 'Stop

thief, stop thief!' and I started running after him, knocking
against people, catching hold of people's hands, dragging them
after me, shouting, 'Help! A man's run off with my bag!' So
I ran and ran until I was tired out, but there was no trace of the
thief. And indeed how could a person of my size hope to catch
a fast-running rogue like him? I turned to the people in the
street : 'Oh, you rogues,' I shouted, 'what are you staring at me
for? Are you Christians at all? Can't you help a poor woman
that's been robbed?' Anyway, I ran and ran and then I stopped
and began to howl at the top of my voice like a fool. Sat down
on a kerbstone and howled. A whole crowd gathered round
me and I could hear them saying to each other, 'Must be drunk!'
But I said to them, 'You're drunk yourselves, you rogues. I've
had my bag snatched from my hand just this minute.' Here a
policeman came up. 'You'd better come to the police-station
with me, lady,' he said. So we went to the police-station and
there I started another row. Then an inspector came out of a
door and said, 'What are you making such an infernal noise for,
woman?' 'Oh, sir,' I said, 'I've just had my bag snatched
out of my hands in the street!' So he said, 'We'll have to have
a written report about it.' So they wrote the report and then
he said to me, 'You can go now.' So I went. Next day I came
back. 'What about my bag?' I asked. 'You can go home now,'
they said. 'Your report has been sent off. You'll have to wait.'
So I waited and waited until I got a summons to call at the
police-station. When I came there, they took me to a big room
where there were hundreds of bags. A police captain, a very
civil gentleman, good-looking, too, said to me, 'Can you
identify your bag?' I looked and looked, but mine was not
among them. 'No, sir,' I said, 'my bag isn't here.' So he said,
'Give her a paper!' 'What's this paper for, sir?' I asked. 'It is
an official notice that you've been robbed,' he said.' 'But how
will that paper help me, sir?' I asked. 'Well, madam,' he said,

'what else do you want me to do for you?' So they gave me the paper which said that I had been robbed and said, 'Go to the lost property office now.' So off I went to the lost property office and showed them the paper and out came an official in a colonel's uniform and he took me to a room where there were thousands of bags and he told me to look for mine among them. I looked, but mine was not there. 'Wait,' he said, 'the general must sign your paper first.' So I waited hours till the general arrived and he was given my paper and signed it. 'What has the general signed on my paper?' I asked an official. 'He signed that you've been robbed,' he replied. So now I always carry this paper about with me," Domna Platonovna finished the story about the loss of her bag.

"Yes, by all means, carry it about, Domna Platonovna," I said.

"Who knows, dear, it may turn up one day."

"Well," I said, "the most unlikely things do happen sometimes."

"Yes, indeed," she said. "If I had known I'd have stayed the night at Mrs. Kosheverova's."

"If only," I said, "you'd agreed to pay the cabby what he had asked you!"

"Oh, don't speak to me of the cabby, dear," she said. "He, too, was a rogue. They're all birds of a feather, the blackguards."

"Now, really, Domna Platonovna," I said, "how can you say such a thing? Why, there are so many of them for one thing!"

"Don't you start arguing with me, dear! I know how little the rogues can be trusted, believe me. I know all their rogueries like that!" Here Domna Platonovna clenched her fist, and, raising it, regarded it with a certain pride. "When I was still new here, one cabby did something to me which, I can tell you,

was much worse than bag-snatching," she said, putting dow
her hand. "Gave me a nasty fall, he did, and picked me clea
into the bargain."

"A fall?" I said. "How on earth did he do that?"

"Just pitched me out, that's how. It happened in winter.
had to go to the other end of the town to deliver a cloak to
lady in the cadet corps barracks. A little woman she was and s
delicate-looking you'd think she couldn't hurt a fly, but whe
she started bargaining, she'd scream the place down, the prima
donna! When I came out of there, it was already getting dark
It gets dark very early in winter, you know. I was hurryin,
along, for I was anxious to get back to Nevsky Avenue as soo
as possible, when suddenly a cabby appeared from behind
street corner, one of those hairy little peasants, you know. '
don't charge much, lady,' he said. I offered him fifteen copeck
to the Znamenye Cathedral . . ."

"But, my dear Domna Platonovna," I interrupted her
"How could you have the heart to offer him so little?"

"Well, dear, as you see, I could. 'Take you the quick way,
he said. 'Oh, all right,' I said, sitting down in the sledge. I hac
no bag at the time and I used to carry everything abou
wrapped up in a kerchief, just as I'm doing now. So that devi
of a cabman took me the quick way, somewhere behind th
fortress and across the Neva and as he came to the bank of the
frozen river, opposite the Liteynaya embankment, he tumblec
me out into a hole in the ice, just as if, you know, somebody
gave the bottom of the sledge a big blow and I . . . well, I just
tumbled out. I was pitched out one way and my bundle flew
out goodness knows where. I got up, soaked to the skin, for the
holes in the ice were full of water. 'Oh, you rogue,' I shouted
at my cabby, 'what have you done to me, you rogue, you!'
But he said, "This is the quickest way, lady. Sorry I pitched you
out, but it ain't my fault.' 'How do you mean, it isn't your fault,

you brute? Is that the way to treat your fare?' But he, the
blackguard, went on saying, 'This way, ma'am, people always
get chucked out. That's why I only took fifteen copecks from
you because you didn't mind coming the quick way!' Well,
what was one to say to such a ruffian? I wiped my clothes and
started looking round for the bundle, for as I told you, I was
pitched out one way and my bundle another. All of a sudden
an officer appeared at my side, or perhaps he wasn't an officer,
but a civil servant, he wore some kind of uniform, anyway,
and he had a moustache, that's about all I can remember of him,
and he began abusing my driver, calling him all sorts of names.

"'Why weren't you more careful, you rogue,' he said, 'and
with so fat a lady as your fare, too?' Oh, he was so angry with
the cabby that he nearly knocked his teeth out. 'Sit down,
madam,' he said, 'please, sit down in the sledge and let me put
the cover over you.' 'But I've dropped my bundle, sir,' I said.
'It fell out of the sledge when that monster tipped me out.'
'Here's your bundle, madam,' he said, handing it to me. 'Go
on, you rogue,' he shouted to the driver, 'and look sharp! And
you, madam,' he said to me, 'don't hesitate for a moment to
box his ears, if he tips you out again!' 'Thank you very much,
sir,' I said, 'but I'm afraid we women are quite helpless against
such villains!' So off we drove. When we came to my house,
I got out and said, 'I have half a mind to punish you, you
villain, and take at least five copecks off your fare, but I don't
want any more trouble with you, so,' I said, 'here's your fifteen
copeck bit!' But he said, 'It wasn't my fault, ma'am. You can't
help tipping your fare out if you takes the quick way. It didn't
do you no harm, ma'am,' he said. 'It'll make you grow,' he
said. 'Oh, you scoundrel,' I said, 'what a pity your former
master didn't thrash you enough.' But he cried to me, 'Look
out, madam, don't drop what he put in your bundle!' and
'Gee-up!' he shouted at his horse and off he drove. I came home

put the *samovar* on the table and picked up my bundle to make sure that it hadn't got wet. I undid it and nearly dropped dead, I tell you. Wanted to scream, but no sound would come from my throat, wanted to rush out of the house, but my feet wouldn't move! . . ."

"What was in that parcel?"

"What was in it? Why, I'm ashamed to tell you. Just some rubbish."

"What kind of rubbish?"

"Well, you know what kind of rubbish—a pair of torn, dirty pants, that's what was in it."

"But how did they get there?"

"That I don't know myself, dear. You see, I couldn't see how he managed to take 'em off on the Neva and put 'em in my bundle. It seemed uncanny to me. I looked and looked and couldn't believe my eyes. I rushed off to the police station, 'This isn't my bundle!' I shouted. 'All right,' the policeman said, 'it isn't your bundle. What about it?' So I told him and he took me straight to the criminal department, where I told them my story again, but the detective just laughed. 'Must have been coming from the public baths, the scoundrel,' he said. Well, I don't know where he was coming from, but how could he have palmed off such a bundle on me?"

"In the dark," I said, "that wouldn't be so difficult, Domna Platonovna."

"But what about the cabby? You remember I told you he said to me, 'Don't drop what's been put into it!' What did he mean by that?"

"You should have examined your bundle when you sat down in the sledge," I said.

"However sharp you look, dear," she said, "if they want to cheat you, they'll cheat you."

"Well," I said, "there you're a bit . . . er . . ."

"Now, now," she interrupted me, "please don't talk about things you don't know anything about, dear. They'll cheat you under your very nose, make out you are something you aren't. I can tell you of a case where I myself was cheated under my very nose. I was walking along the street one day—it was shortly after my arrival here—and I had to cross over Apraxin bridge. It used to be very crowded there, not like now since the fires, now it's a pleasure to walk there, but then it was just too awful. All right, so I was walking along when suddenly, out of nowhere it seemed, a young fellow accosted me, a handsome-looking chap : 'Want to buy a chemise, madam ? A lovely chemise !' I had a look at it and it was a brand-new chemise of excellent quality, a cotton one it was, but, as I said, of first-class quality, you could not have got such cotton material anywhere for less than sixty copecks a yard. 'How much do you want for it ?' I asked. 'Two and a half roubles,' he said. 'What about letting me have it for a little less than half the price ?' I asked. 'Which half ?' he asked. 'Any you like,' I said, for I'd been long enough here to have learnt that if you are offered anything for sale, you must always give half the price they ask you. 'No, madam,' he said, 'I can see it's no use offering you anything decent,' and he was about to pull the thing out of my hand, but I said, 'Give it to me,' for I could see that it was worth at least three roubles even to someone who didn't need it. 'Will you take a rouble for it ?' I asked. 'Let's have it back,' he said and, pulling it out of my hand, he wrapped it under his coat, looking round to make sure that nobody had seen him. Well, I thought, it must have been stolen, and I was walking away when he jumped suddenly out of the line of hawkers and said to me, 'All right, madam,' he said, 'here you are and let's have the money quick,' he said, 'you ain't half lucky today, madam !' he said. I gave him a rouble note and he gave me the same crumpled up chemise. I put my purse back into my pocket and as I unwrapped my purchase, something fell out of it at my feet. What was it? Why, some old shavings you find inside furniture. Not knowing all the Petersburg circumstances at the time, I looked and looked at it wondering what it could mean, but when I glanced at my other hand in which I thought I was holding the chemise, I saw that it was not a chemise at all, but just a worthless rag. A rag, just a rag, dear, half a yard long. And the hawkers and shop-assistants in the street raised an awful clamour, 'Come on, ma'am, look at our stuff: lovely linen for silly women!' And one of 'em rushed up to me and said, 'We've a lovely second-hand winding sheet for you, ma'am, beautiful material!' But I took no notice. Get away with you, I thought to myself. The fact is, dear, I was flabbergasted, aye, and scared, too, for I couldn't for the life of me think where that rag had come from. I tell you I saw the chemise with my own eyes and suddenly it turned into a rag! Aye, dear, they're capable of any villainy. Do whatever they ike with you, they do. Do you know colonel Yegoopov?"

l "No, I don't know him."

"How do you mean you don't know him? A fine figure of a man with a big paunch: a very handsome man. Nine horses killed under him during the war and he escaped untouched: they wrote about it in the papers."

"Afraid I still don't know him," I said.

"Well, what do you think one villain did to him and me? It's something they ought to put into a novel and not just any novel, either, but one of the best, or, better still, they ought to put it on the stage . . ."

"Don't keep me in suspense, Domna Platonovna," I said. "Do go on with your story."

"Yes, dear, it's a story worth telling all right. What's his name now? . . . There's a surveyor here . . . Kumoveyev or

Makaveyev, served in the seventh company of the Izmaylovsky regiment . . ."

"Never mind!"

"Never mind? Why, he's the real villain of the piece, he is!"

"I mean, never mind his name!"

"Oh, his name? Well, yes, there's nothing wrong with his name, just an ordinary name, but the man himself's a villain, one of the worst villains in town. Kept pestering me, he did, 'Find me a wife, Domna Platonovna.' I said to him, 'With pleasure,' I said, 'I'd be delighted to find you a wife! Give me a little time and I will find you a wife.' Looked quite handsome, the creature did, good complexion and nice moustache, well waxed and pointed upwards. So I began looking for a wife for him, rushed about here, there, everywhere, and found one at last, a girl from a merchant's family, her father owns a house on the Sands, good-looking, too, she was, red cheeks, plump . . . There was something wrong with her nose, it's true, a sort of blemish on the bridge, but it wasn't much, really, a mark left by scrofula, poor dear! So I brought the two of them together, her and that villain, I mean, and everything seemed to be getting on as well as could be! I kept an eye on him, of course, for I had heard a rumour that he had got himself engaged to a girl, a merchant's daughter she was, too, and wormed two hundred roubles out of her to get himself clothes, giving them a kind of receipt, but, as it turned out, the receipt wasn't worth the paper it was written on and they couldn't do anything to him, either. Now, of course, knowing the sort of man he was, I kept an eye on him and went to see him from time to time to make sure he hadn't run off. Well, so one day, my dear sir, I went to see him and, perhaps, I should have told you before that he lived in two rooms : one was his bedroom and the other a kind of sitting room. I went in and I found that his bedroom door was locked and in his sitting room an important-looking gentleman was sitting in an armchair and smoking a pipe, a gentleman of some importance he was because he wore a kind of sash over his shoulder. That was the colonel Yegoopov I mentioned, dear.

"Well," Domna Platonovna went on, "I turned to him and asked him, 'Is Stepan Matveyevich at home, sir?' He just shook his head sternly, but said nothing, so that I couldn't really be sure whether the surveyor was at home or not. Perhaps, I thought, he had a young lady with him in the bedroom, for although he was about to get married, *that* doesn't make much difference, does it? So I sat down and waited. But you can hardly sit in a room with a person without speaking, for if you don't say anything, people may think that you're too silly to open your mouth. So I said to him, 'What lovely weather we're having just now, sir.' He glared at me and boomed out as though speaking from the bottom of an empty barrel, 'What did you say?' So I said again, 'We're having such nice weather, sir,' but he boomed back, 'Fiddlesticks, ma'am, nothing but damned dust!' Now, of course, it was quite true that there was rather a lot of dust about, but all the same I couldn't help thinking, 'And who might you be, my dear sir, to growl at me so angrily?' So I said to him, 'Are you by any chance a relative of Stepan Matveyevich or just a friend of his?' 'A friend,' he said. 'What an excellent man Stepan Matveyevich is, sir!' I said. 'A rotter,' he said, 'a first-class rotter!' So I said to myself, 'That means that Stepan Matveyevich isn't at home,' and aloud I said, 'Have you known him for some time, sir?' 'Yes,' he said, 'I've known him when the woman was still a maid.' 'Why, sir,' I said, 'I, too, have known him as long as that, for many a maid has grown into a woman since, but I haven't noticed anything wrong about that.' Well, he says very scornfully, 'What have you got in your attic—straw?' 'Excuse me, sir,' I said, 'thank God I haven't an attic but a head on my shoulders and there isn't any straw in it, but what the Lord has appointed to be there for every man.' 'Talking through your hat,' he said. 'A country yokel,' I thought to myself, 'that's what you are—a country yokel!' Suddenly he began questioning me. 'Do you know his brother Maxim Matveyevich?' 'No, sir,' I replied, 'I don't know him, and if I don't know a man I never pretend to know him.' 'This one here,' he said, 'is a rogue, but the other one is an even bigger rogue. Deaf!' 'Beg your pardon, sir,' I said, 'did you say he was deaf?' 'Yes,' he said, 'when I say deaf, I mean deaf. Born deaf in one ear and grown deaf in the other. Can't hear a thing with either.' 'Dear, dear,' I said, 'how extraordinary!' 'Nothing extraordinary about it,' he said. 'What I mean, sir,' I said 'is that it is very extraordinary that one brother should be such a handsome man and the other should be deaf.' 'Exactly,' he said, 'that's what I mean, too : there's nothing extraordinary about it. I have two sisters and each of them has a huge red birthmark on her cheek, just like a big toad, not that it makes any difference to me!' 'I expect,' I said, 'your mother must have got frightened when she was in the family way.' 'A maid,' he said, 'upset the *samovar* on her belly.' I said very politely that I was sorry to hear that. 'Maids are the limit, sir,' I said, 'never look what they're doing.' He said to me then, 'I take it, madam,' he said, 'that you're not altogether a born fool and I'd therefore like to ask you your opinion about a certain matter. That deaf brother of his, you see, is very keen on exchanging horses.' 'Yes, sir,' I said. 'So wishing to get him out of that bad habit of his,' he said, 'I gave him a blind horse in exchange for one which wasn't blind, one, you know, which always rushes into a fence with its head.' 'Yes, sir,' I said. 'Well,' he said, 'the other day I wanted to get a bull from his farm. I paid him for a bull, but when the animal arrived I found that it wasn't a bull at all, but a steer.' 'Goodness gracious,' I said, 'what a shame! I don't suppose a steer's any good to you, is it?' 'Well, of course,' he said, 'if it's a steer, then it's no damn good to me. Well, so now I'm going to play a trick on him, the deaf one, I mean. I've got an I.O.U. from his brother Stepan Matveyevich for one hundred roubles and I know that neither of them has any money, so I'm going to show them the sort of fellow I am.' 'That's right, sir,' I said, 'I don't suppose there's anything to stop you from showing them that.' 'Well, so I just want to warn you, madam,' he said, 'that Maxim Matveyevich is a scoundrel, and as for his brother, I'm just waiting for him to come home before I put him in the debtors' jail.' 'I don't know either of them very well, sir,' I said, 'but seeing that I'm getting a wife for Stepan Matveyevich, I oughtn't to say anything against him.' 'Getting a wife for him?' he roared at me. 'Yes, sir.' 'Oh, you fool!' he said, 'Don't you know he's married?' 'You must be mistaken, sir,' I said. 'Mistaken?' he roared. 'Why, he's got three children.' 'Dear me,' I said and I thought to myself, 'Well, Stepan Matveyevich, what a joke you've played on me to be sure!' And I said aloud, 'I can see, sir, he's a swindler all right.' But the colonel said to me that if I wanted to find a husband for some likely girl, he'd be only too glad to oblige, for, as a matter of fact, he was himself looking for a girl to marry. 'With pleasure, sir,' I said. 'I'm not joking, madam,' he said, 'I mean it.' 'Very well, sir,' I said, 'I'll do it with pleasure.' 'Don't you believe me?' he asked. 'Why, of course, I believe you, sir,' I said, 'for if a man feels an inclination to settle down and give up his state of bachelorhood, he can't do anything better than marry a nice girl.' 'I don't mind if she's a widow,' he said, 'so long as she has capital.' 'Of course,' I said, 'there's nothing wrong about a widow.'

"So we discussed the whole matter then and there and he gave me his address and I began to visit him. You can't imagine the trouble that wretch caused me! A big man he was and quite mad, talked to people just as the spirit moved him. Of course, people have different dispositions, but I pity any woman who married a man like Yegoopov! He'd suddenly get up, for instance, glare at you with bulging eyes, his face purple like a bed-bug that's had a good feed on you, and roar at you, 'I'll turn you inside out, I'll flay you alive!' To look at him in one of his mad fits, you'd think somebody must have hurt his feelings badly, but usually it was some trifle or other. Well, I found him a wife, a merchant's widow, just a match for him, as if made to order, a carcase as big as his. Well, my dear sir, I introduced them to each other and everything went off well and an engagement party was arranged.

"I arrived at the party with him, the colonel, I mean. There were crowds of people there, relatives and friends of the fiancée, all of them well-to-do people, but among the guests I also noticed that surveyor, Stepan Matveyevich. I said nothing, although to tell the truth, I didn't like his being there a bit. 'I suppose,' I said to myself, 'he must have been released from the debtors' jail and he's here by invitation from the colonel.'

"However, everything seemed to be going on all right. The engagement had been officially announced, the betrothed had been blessed with the icon, and nothing untoward had happened. The fiancée's uncle, the merchant Semyon Ivanych Kolobov, to be sure, arrived at the party drunk and began telling everybody that Yepootov wasn't a colonel at all, but the son of Fyodorovna, the bath-house attendant. 'Let someone lick him behind the ear,' he said, 'and he'll immediately start a fight : he always does. I know him very well,' he went on shouting, 'he's just put on his epaulettes to show off. I'll tear his epaulettes off, I will!' But the people wouldn't let him do that and, to prevent any mischief, Semyon Ivanych was locked up in an empty room. But all of a sudden, just as the father of the fiancée raised the icon to bless the betrothed couple, an awful, blood-curdling howl was heard in the room and then a voice said very clearly, 'Do not sing of Isaiah when Emmanuel is in the womb.' Dear me, how everybody in the room got scared! The poor fiancée was terribly embarrassed and Yegoopov glared angrily at me with his bulging eyes. 'What are you glaring at me for?' I thought. 'Eyeing me like the devil a priest!' In the meantime, somebody in the room again began to moan and again a voice said very clearly, 'Dust covereth the face of heaven when a bride to a married man is given. Pray to God, poor, deceived woman, cry your eyes out.' They tried to discover the owner of that terrifying voice, but all in vain, and, my goodness, what a to do there was! The father of the fiancée put down the icon and rushed at me, vowing to thrash me within an inch of my life, and I, seeing how black things looked for me, lifted up my skirt as high as I could and just ran as fast as my feet would carry me. Yegoopov swore that he had never been married, asked them to make enquiries, if they wished, but the mysterious voice went on proclaiming so loudly that all in the room could hear it, 'Do not be deceived, brethren, do not heap dust and ashes upon the head of the maid!' The party broke up in terrible confusion and who do you think was to blame for it all? Well, after a week, Yegoopov came to see me and said, 'It was that blackguard of a surveyor,' he said, 'it was he who was speaking through his navel!' "

"Through his navel, Domna Platonovna?" I asked.

"Yes, dear, his navel or his belly, or the devil knows through what he proclaimed those slanderous lies of his," Domna Platonovna said. "As I told you before, dear," she went on, looking at me gravely, "they're all trying to outwit each other, everybody is trying to trick and deceive everybody else and, take my word for it, in the end they'll embroil the whole State in their knaveries and throw it to the dogs!"

I must confess that Domna Platonovna's sombre view of the future of the Russian State rather confounded me, for I myself

hardly expected such an awful fate to be in store for us all.
Domna Platonovna, naturally, noticed the confusion into
which her prophecy had thrown me and she wished to enjoy
to the full the political sensation she had created.

"I mean every word of it, dear," she said, raising her voice
one note higher. "Just think, dear, of all the new tricks they're
now inventing. One starts flying, which only birds have been
given to do, another starts swimming like a fish and thinks
nothing of going down to the bottom of the sea, a third, like
the man on Admiralty Square, is swallowing sulphurous fire,
a fourth talks through his belly, a fifth does something else no
human being should do ... Why, I should not be at all surprised
if Satan himself was not today at their beck and call, for whatever they do, is certainly not to man's advantage, but to his
eternal undoing. I don't mind telling you, dear, that I was once
thrown to the devil myself and suffered ignominiously at his
hands!"

"Dear me," I said, "did that really happen to you?"

"It did!"

"Please don't keep me in suspense, dear Domna Platonovna!
Tell me about it."

It happened a long time ago (Domna Platonovna said), about
twelve years ago. I was young then and inexperienced and,
having just lost my husband, I decided to engage in some
business. But what kind of business? I made up my mind that
the best thing I could do in the ladies' line of business was to
sell cloth, for a woman understands more about that kind of
trade than any other. So I decided to buy some cloth in the
market and then sit down on a bench by some gates in our
town and try to sell it. I went to the market, bought the cloth
and was about to return home with it, but the question arose
how I was to take it home with me? While I was thinking

about it, a cart driven by a team of three horses rode into the yard of the inn where I was stranded.

"We were bringing a load of nuts from Kiev on seven carts, each cart driven by a team of three horses," the driver told me, "but the nuts got wet on the way and the merchants deducted their losses from our pay and now we're returning home without any money at all."

"Where are your mates?" I asked.

"My mates," he replied, "have all gone back to their own villages, but I'm trying to find some fares to take back with me."

"Where are you from?" I asked him.

"I'm from the village of Kurakina," he said.

As it happened it was just my way and, "Here," I said, "is your first fare."

We talked it over and he agreed to take me home for one rouble. He said he'd go round the inns to pick up more passengers and that we'd leave the next day after breakfast.

Next morning, one, two, five, eight people came to the yard of the inn, all of them men and every one of them big and handsome. One of them carried a sack, another a satchel, a third a trunk, and one even had a shotgun.

"How will you squeeze us all in?" I asked the driver.

"Never you mind," he said, "you'll get in all right, it's a big cart, carried three and a half ton, it has."

I was in half a mind to stay behind, but I had already given him the rouble and there was no other driver about to take me back to town.

With a heavy heart I clambered into the cart and off we drove. No sooner had we passed the toll-gate than one of our fares shouted, "Stop at the next pub!" So we stopped at the pub and they all got off and had many drinks there and stood the driver drinks, too. Then off we drove again. We had only gone about a mile when another of our passengers shouted, "Stop! Ivan Ivanych Yelkin lives here and I must see him!" and so they kept on stopping about a dozen times, each one at his own particular Ivan Ivanych Yelkin's. It was getting dark and our driver was as drunk as a lord by then.

"Don't you dare to have another drop," I said to him.

"Why shouldn't I dare?" he replied. "I ain't a daring one, anyway. I'm acting like that just because I don't dare to refuse, see?"

"You're a yokel," I said, "just a stupid country yokel."

"What if I am a yokel?" he said. "So long as I can get a drink I don't mind what I am."

"Oh, you fool," I said, "you fool! you'd better look after your horses!"

"I'm looking after my horses, ain't I?" he replied and, raising his whip, he began flogging them.

The cart was jolting terribly and I was afraid that we might be tipped out any minute and killed. The men were all drunk and raising an awful din. One of them produced an accordion, another was bawling a song, a third one was firing his gun, while I was just praying, "Holy Mother of God, save us, I beseech thee!"

Our horses careered along until they got tired, and we were again crawling at a snail's pace. It got dark in the meantime and, although it was not raining, it seemed as if a cold, wet mist was enveloping us as with a blanket. My hands went numb with holding on to the sides of the cart, but I was so glad that we were no longer going at breakneck speed that I sat there quietly, without uttering a sound. The men, I could hear, had begun talking to each other, one of them saying that he had heard that there were robbers on the road who had recently held up and robbed many people, another declaring that he was not afraid of any robbers because he could fire twice from his gun, and a third starting to tell a story about dead bodies. "I'm always carrying about a bone from a corpse," he said, "and if I wave this bone over a man, he straightway falls asleep, just as if he was dead, and he'll never waken again." Another one boasted that he had a candle made from the fat of a dead man . . . I just listened to their talk when of a sudden I had an odd feeling as if somebody was pulling me by the nose and I felt so sleepy that in another minute I dropped off.

But I couldn't sleep soundly because all the time we were shaken up as if we were nuts roasted on a grill, and in my sleep I seemed to hear someone saying, "I wish we could throw that damned woman out! Can't stretch my legs, I can't." But I went on sleeping until I suddenly heard a shout and a scream, followed by a general hubbub, and I woke up. What was the matter? I looked round. It was pitch dark, our cart had stopped and everybody was running about and shouting, but what they were shouting I couldn't for the life of me make out.

"Shirl-mirl, shire-mire," one of them shouted.

Our passenger with the gun pulled the trigger once and it went snap, but there was no report, he fired again, and again the trigger went snap and there was no sound. Then the one who was shouting screamed at the top of his voice again and, seizing me under the arms, swung me off the cart and began whirling me round and round. Goodness, I thought, what's going on here? I peered into the pitch darkness round me, but all I could see were some hideous, black faces and all of them were turning round and round and whirling me round with them, shouting "Shire-mire!" and, lifting me by my feet, they began to swing me to and fro.

"O Lord," I began to pray fervently, "St. Nicholas of Amchen, defender of the three virgins, protector of purity, do not, I beseech thee, let them behold my nakedness!"

No sooner did I utter that prayer in my heart than, suddenly,

The Amazon

I became aware of a great stillness all around me and it seemed to me that I was lying in the middle of a field, on green, lush grass, and near me, just at my feet, was a small lake with wonderfully clear, transparent water and round it, just like a fringe of thick silk, the rushes were waving gently.

I forgot all about my prayer and began staring at those reeds, as though I'd never seen any before in my life.

Then, suddenly, what was that? A mist, a light blue mist rose from the other side of the lake and spread all over the field like a shroud, and under the mist, in the middle of the lake, a little ripple arose, just as if a fish had splashed its tail there, and from the ripple a little man, not bigger than a cockerel, appeared. He had a tiny face and was dressed in a long blue coat and wore a green cap on his head.

"What a funny little man," I thought, "just like a beautiful doll," and I kept looking at him, couldn't tear my eyes away from him. I was not a bit afraid of him, as if he really was a pretty little doll. But as I looked at him, he began to rise and rise out of the water and he came nearer and nearer to me until at last he just hopped on to my bosom. He was not really standing on my bosom though, but over it, hovering in the air and bowing. Raised his cap with such an important air and greeted me gravely.

I felt like screaming with laughter. "Where could you have sprung from, you funny little man?" I thought to myself.

But he doffed his cap again and said, well . . . the things that little mite did say, I declare!

"Let's have a little love frolic together, my dearest Domna," he said.

I couldn't help bursting out laughing.

"Oh, you naughty little thing," I cried. "What kind of love frolic could I have with you?"

Then he suddenly turned his back on me and crowed like a young cockerel : cock-a-doodle-doo !

Everything then burst into loud music : there was the sound of drums, fiddles, flutes and hundreds of musical instruments : my ears rang with the din ! Goodness, I thought to myself, what's all this ? The frogs, the carp, the bream, the crayfish— every creature in the lake began to scrape, pluck and beat fiddles, guitars, drums, while some danced and others just skipped about and others leapt into the air !

"Oh dear," I thought, "that's bad, that's very bad ! Let me say a prayer to protect myself from the evil one !" and I was about to say aloud, "In the name of the Holy Resurrection," but instead I said, "Higher and still higher soar aloft . . ." and at the same time I could distinctly hear a weird sort of drumming inside my belly : tum-tara-tum, tum-tara-tum !

"What's that ?" I thought. "Am I a drum or a double-bass ?" and as I looked at myself, I saw that I was a double-bass and that the little man was standing over me and sawing away for all he was worth.

"Oh dear," I said to myself, "holy saints !" but he went on sawing away with his bow and what didn't he play on me ? Waltzes and quadrilles and everything, while the others were standing round and egging him on, "Scrape away harder," they shouted, "scrape away harder !"

I had a terrible pain in my belly, but there I was droning like anything, and so they scraped away on me the whole night. Yes, the whole night I, a baptised Christian woman, was just a double-bass to them, kept them merry, those damned devils !

"That's terrible !" I said.

"Yes, indeed, it was terrible, but it was even more terrible when I woke up in the morning after they had had their fun with me. I looked round and I saw that I was lying in a strange field and a few yards away from me was a large pool, like a small lake with reeds and everything, just as I had seen it in the night, and the sun was roasting me, streaming down on me from the sky. My bundle with the cloth I had purchased and my small bag were lying beside me. Everything was quite safe, and only a few hundred yards away was a little village. I got up, dragged myself to the village, hired a peasant's cart and arrived home in the evening."

"But are you quite sure, Domna Platonovna, that all that had really happened to you?"

"Why, you don't think I'd be telling you lies about myself, do you?"

"I mean are you quite sure that everything had happened just as you told me?"

"Yes, dear, it happened just as I told you. Now, if there's anything you ought to be surprised at, it is that I shouldn't have uncovered my nakedness to them."

I looked duly surprised.

"Yes, dear, I prevailed with the devil, but I was not so lucky with one fiend of a man!"

"Oh? How did that happen?"

"Listen. I bought some furniture from a merchant's wife: second-hand furniture it was, chests-of-drawers, tables, beds and a child's cot with a kind of braided bottom. I paid thirteen roubles for the lot, put everything out in the passage and went out to fetch a cart. I found a driver with a cart and he agreed to take the furniture for a rouble and forty copecks to St. Nicholas-the-Seafarer's. We put the furniture in the cart and in the meantime the people I had bought it from had gone out and locked their flat. Suddenly, the caretakers of that block of flats —Tartars they were—swooped down on us, shouting, "What right have you to take the furniture?" I tried to explain to them that I had bought it, but they wouldn't listen to me. Meanwhile, it started to rain and the carter did not want to wait any longer. I didn't know what to do! At last I thought of something. 'Take me to the police station,' I said, 'I'm the wife of the police officer!' But no sooner did I say that than the people from whom I had bought the furniture came back and, of course, they said at once, 'We've sold the furniture,' they said, 'we've sold it to her.' Well, so that was that, and the carter, he said to me, 'Get on the cart,' and I thought to myself, 'Why, indeed, waste money on a cab when I can sit in the cot and be taken home for nothing?' They had put the cot very high up in the cart, on top of a chest-of-drawers, but I managed to climb up and sat down in it. Well, what do you think happened? Why, directly we left the courtyard, the bottom of the cot began to give under me. 'Heavens,' I thought, 'I'm falling through!' and I was just about to scramble out when, crash! I did fall through. Lord, the disgrace of it! There I was, sitting astride a piece of webbing like a mounted policeman on his horse. My dress, of course, shot up and my bare legs were left dangling over the chest-of-drawers. The people in the street stared at me and the caretakers shouted, 'Cover yourself up, police officer's wife! What a scoundrel!'"

"Who do you mean?" I asked.

"The carter, of course! Too busy looking at his horse, if you please! Didn't care a fig for his passenger, nearly drove through the whole of Gorokhovaya Street like that, but for a kindly policeman who stopped us. 'What's all this?' he said. 'You can't travel like that,' he said. 'It ain't allowed to show what you're showing!' So that was how I showed my nakedness to the whole world . . ."

CHAPTER SIX

"I SHOULD LIKE TO ASK YOU A QUESTION I've wanted to ask you for a long time, Domna Platonovna," I said. "How old were you when your husband died? You were still quite a young woman, weren't you? Well, haven't you had any love affairs at all since then?"

"Love affairs?"

"Yes, I mean haven't you been in love with anyone?"

"Me in love? Good heavens, the nonsense you do sometimes talk, dear!"

"But why nonsense?"

"Because," she said, "it's only women who have nothing to do who have love-affairs. I'm much too busy rushing about day and night, leading so aggravating a life as I do, never a minute to myself . . . Why, such a thought never crosses my mind!"

"Doesn't it even cross your mind, Domna Platonovna?"

"No, dear, not as much as that even!" Domna Platonovna struck one finger-nail against another and added, "Besides, dear, let me tell you this love business is just a kind of craze : 'Oh, I can't live without him or her! Oh, I shall die!' That's all you hear from them. Now, if you ask me, dear, a man who's really in love with a woman should be always ready to help her, never let her down, that, I grant you, is real love. And as for the woman, she should never give way to temptation and should always behave decently."

"So I can take it, Domna Platonovna," I said, "that you've never been guilty of any such transgression and that in the eyes of God you're as pure as driven snow. Am I right?"

"Mind your own business, dear," she replied, "and don't you go meddling with my sins. For even if I did commit a sin, it's my sin, isn't it? Anyway, it's not yours and you're not a priest to whom I ought to confess my sins, are you?"

"I merely mentioned it, Domna Platonovna," I put in propitiatingly, "because you were so young when you lost your husband and I can see that you must have been very beautiful."

"Whether I was beautiful or not, I can't say," she replied, "but I was never considered a plain woman."

"That's it!" I said, "Anybody can see it even now."

Domna Platonovna passed a finger over an eyebrow and fell into thought.

"I've often wondered," she began slowly, "whether or not I had been guilty of a particular sin. Tell me, O Lord, was I guilty of that sin or not? That was how I'd ask for the Lord's guidance, but I never received a proper answer to that question from anyone. One nun once persuaded me to let her write down my story so that I could give it to the priest at confession. I let her write it down, but on my way to the church I dropped the paper and couldn't find it."

"What story are you referring to, Domna Platonovna?"

"I don't rightly know to this day whether it was a sin or whether I imagined it all."

"Well, even if you did imagine it all, Domna Platonovna, I should very much like to hear it."

"It all happened a very long time ago when I was still living with my husband."

"What kind of life did you have with your husband, dear Domna Platonovna?"

"Not a bad kind of life. Our house was a little too small perhaps, but it occupied a very good position, for it stood on the market place, and we had many market days in our town, mostly for household goods and provisions of one sort or another, only there was precious little of either, that was the trouble. We were not particularly well off, but we were not exactly poor, either. We sold fish, lard, liver and anything else we could. My husband, Fyodor Ilyich, was a young man, but a queer one, aye, a queer one, very haggard he was, but he had a pair of the most extraordinary lips. I never met a man with such lips in my life. He had, God forgive me, a terrible temper, very quarrelsome he was and quick to take offence, but I, too, was a real Amazon, dearly loved a fight as a girl, I did. Having married, I was at first as meek as a lamb, but that didn't please him at all, so that every morning before breakfast we used to have a grand old fight together. I was not very much in love with him, nor did we often agree, for we both were rare fighters, and, besides, you couldn't help fighting with him, for however nice you tried to be to him, he'd always look glum and glower at you. However, we carried on for eight whole years and did not separate. Now and again, of course, we'd have a row, but it was very rarely that we had a real fight. Once, it is true, he hit me over the head, but I was not alto-gether blameless myself, for I had been trimming his hair at the time and I cut off a bit of his ear with the scissors. We had no children, but we had friends at Nizhny to whose children I stood godmother. They weren't well off. He called himself a tailor and even had a diploma from a society, but he didn't earn his living by his needle, but by singing psalms for the dead and being a member of the Cathedral choir. As for earning a living, getting something for their home, it was his wife, Praskovya Ivanovna, who had to worry about it. She was a woman in a thousand, brought up all her children and made ends meet somehow.

"Well, once—it was in the same year that my husband died (everything was going topsy-turvy with us just then)— Praskovya Ivanovna invited us to her place to celebrate her birthday. We went and no sooner did we arrive than it began to pour and, as I had an awful headache at the time (I had had three glasses of punch and some Caucasian brandy and there's nothing worse than that Caucasian brandy for your head), I lay down for a bit on a couch in another room. 'Stay with your guests, dear,' I said to Praskovya Ivanovna, 'and I'll just go and lie down for a rest on the couch here.' But she wouldn't let me lie down on the couch, because, she said, it was too hard, so I went and lay down on their bed and dropped off to sleep immediately. Did I do anything wrong?" Domna Platonovna asked me.

"Why, no," I said, "you didn't do anything wrong."

"Very well, now listen to what happened. I felt in my sleep that somebody was embracing me and, you see, not just embracing me, either. I thought it was my husband, Fyodor Ilyich, and yet it didn't seem to be Fyodor Ilyich, for he was rather delicate, you know and shy, but I couldn't wake up, and when at last I did wake up, it was morning. I found myself in my friend's bed and beside me lay my friend's husband. I sort of scampered over him quickly, trembling all over, and there on the floor, on a feather bed, lay my friend and beside her was my husband, Fyodor Ilyich . . . I nudged her and then she, too, realised what had happened and began crossing herself. 'How did it all happen?' I asked her. 'Oh, dear,' she said, 'it's all my fault, for after everybody went away your husband and mine sat down to finish up the drinks and I didn't want to waken you in the darkness, so I lay down where I had made a bed for you and your husband, well, I just spat, so vexed was I. 'What shall we do now?' I asked. But she said there was nothing we could do and that we'd better keep quiet about it. Yes, dear," Domna Platonovna said, "you're the first I ever told this story to after so many years, but it has been worrying me terribly all the time and whenever I think of it, I'm ready to curse that heavy sleep of mine."

"Don't distress yourself so much, Domna Platonovna," I said, "for whatever happened was against your will."

"Of course it happened against my will! I should think so! Still, it did worry me, I can tell you, and after that I was over-taken by one trouble after another. Fyodor Ilyich soon died, and not a natural death, either. Was crushed to death, he was, under a load of logs which collapsed on top of him on the bank of a river. I had no notion of the Petersburg circumstances then and I didn't know what to do to distract myself, but sometimes of an evening when I'd remember what had happened to me at that birthday party, I'd sit down at the window, all alone in the house, and sing, 'Take away my gold, take away my honours all,' and I'd burst out crying, tears gushing in a flood out of my eyes, so that it was a real wonder my heart didn't burst with sorrow. Oh, I felt so terrible when I'd remember the words of that song, 'My dear love in the dank ground lies sleeping,' that many a time I thought of putting a noose round my neck and ending it all. So I sold everything, gave up my business and left our town, for I decided that it was best to make a clean break with my past life."

"I can believe that, Domna Platonovna," I said, "for there's nothing worse than being depressed."

"Thank you, dear, for your kind words," said Domna Platonovna. "Indeed, there's nothing worse than that and may the Holy Virgin bless you and comfort you for your pity and understanding. But you can hardly be expected to know what I have been through, if I don't tell you how scurvily I was treated once and how shamelessly I was insulted. That my bag was stolen or that Lekanida Petrovna was so ungrateful to me, all that is nothing compared with what happened to me on another occasion. For there was such a day in my life, dear, when I prayed to God to send a serpent or a scorpion to suck my eyes out and devour my heart. And who do you think it was who did that wrong to me? I'll tell you: Ispulat, the Turk, that's who it was, that infidel Turk, in league with my own friends, Christians, baptised and annointed with myrrh!"

Poor Domna Platonovna burst into a flood of tears.

"A friend of mine, the wife of a government messenger," she went on, wiping her tears, "used to live in Lopatin's house on Nevsky Avenue and that Turkish war prisoner began to worry her about getting him a job. She asked me to see if I couldn't find some work for him. 'Find some situation for that devil, Domna Platonovna,' she said to me. But what sort of a job could I find for a Turk? A footman's job was all I could think of. Well, I found him such a place and I told him about it. 'Go there,' I said, 'and you can start work at once.' So they decided to give a party to celebrate the occasion and they got a lot of drinks, for that damned Turk had renounced his religion and could now drink spirits. 'I don't want anything to drink,' I told them, but I did have a glass or two. That's the kind of silly character I have, dear. I always say 'no' at first, and drink afterwards. So it was there, too. I had a couple of drinks and got quite befuddled and lay down in the same bed with that woman friend of mine."

"And?"

"And . . . well . . . that's all there is to it and that's why now I always sew myself up before going to bed."

"Sew yourself up, Domna Platonovna?"

"Yes, dear. You see, dear, if I happen to be spending the night somewhere, I just get my feet into a kind of a sack and sew myself up, and, let me tell you, even when I am at home, I can no longer trust myself, seeing the kind of heavy sleeper I am, so I just sew myself up every night."

Domna Platonovna heaved a deep sigh and let fall her mournful head over her ample bosom.

"There you are, dear," she said after a long pause, "knowing the Petersburg circumstances as well as I do and yet I let such a thing happen to me!"

She got up, bid me good-bye and went back to her flat in Znamenskaya Street.

CHAPTER SEVEN

A FEW YEARS LATER I had to take a poor fellow to an emergency hospital for typhus cases. Having seen him put to bed in one of the wards, I tried to find someone who could be relied on to look after him properly.

"You'd better see Sister," I was told.

"Won't you ask Sister if she will see me?" I asked.

A woman with a faded face and sagging cheeks entered the room.

"What can I do for you, sir?" she asked.

"Good heavens," I exclaimed, "Domna Platonovna!"

"Yes, sir," she said quietly, "it's me."

"How did you get here?"

"It was God's will, I suppose."

"Please, look after my friend," I said.

"I'll look after him as if he was my own son," she assured me.

"What about your business?"

"This is my business now : I gave everything up to serve the Lord. Yes, my friend, I've given up my business. Come along to my room, dear," she whispered.

I went to her room. It was a very little room, very damp and with no furniture or curtains, just an iron bedstead and a little table with a *samovar* and a little painted chest.

"Won't you have tea with me?" she asked.

"No, thank you," I said. "I'm in an awful hurry."

"Come to see me again," she said. "I'm all broken up, dear, done for, finished."

"Why, what's happened?"

"I can't tell you, dear, my heart's aching and I'd rather you didn't ask me."

"But are you sure there isn't anything the matter with you, Domna Platonovna? Why do you look so haggard?"

"Haggard? Good gracious, what are you saying? I'm sure I don't look a bit worse than I did when you saw me last!"

Domna Platonovna quickly produced a small, folding mirror, looked at her faded cheeks and said hurriedly, "I haven't changed a bit. True, I look a little tired, but that's because it's almost bedtime and I've had a tiring day. In the morning I shall be as fresh as a daisy!"

I looked at Domna Platonovna and I couldn't understand what had happened to her. It seemed to me that her face was not only faded and baggy, but also a little made up. And why all that alarm when I told her that she looked haggard? "Can't make it out at all," I thought to myself.

About a month later a soldier from the hospital came to see me and insisted that I should go immediately to Domna Platonovna. I took a cab and at the gates of the hospital I was met by Domna Platonovna, who fell on my neck, crying and sobbing.

"Please, go at once to the police station," she implored me.

"But whatever for?" I asked.

"Try to find out about a man there, see what you can do for him, dear. I'll repay you for it one day, I will."

"All right," I said, "only please stop crying and shivering like that."

"I can't help shivering," she said, "for it comes from inside, my whole inside is shivering, but I shall always be grateful to you for this service, for, you see, everybody has abandoned me now."

"All right," I said again, "but who shall I ask for?"

The old woman looked embarrassed for a moment and her faded cheeks began to twitch.

"A piano-maker's assistant was taken there yesterday, Valerian Ivanov his name is. Try to find out what you can about it, dear, and please, please put in a good word for him.

I drove to the police station. There I was told that it was quite true that a young man by the name of Valerian Ivanov had been arrested. He was an apprentice of a piano-maker, had stolen some money from his employer and had been caught red handed. It was very probable, I was finally told, that he'd be sent away for a long stretch.

"How old is he?" I asked.

"Twenty-one," they told me.

What was it all about, I wondered, and what was that young man to Domna Platonovna?

I went back to the hospital and found Domna Platonovna in her little room, sitting on the edge of the bed with her hands crossed and looking more dead than alive.

"I know everything," she said, "don't bother to tell me any more. I sent one of our male nurses to find out and he told me everything. Oh, even before my death this soul of mine is burning in hellfire!"

I could see that my Amazon had completely gone to pieces; in less than an hour she seemed to have drooped and withered.

"Dear Lord," she said, gazing at the small hospital icon, "let my prayer go up straight to Thee in heaven, take my soul out of this body of mine and bring peace to my wicked heart."

"What is the matter with you, Domna Platonovna?" I asked.

"What's the matter with me, dear? Why, I love him, that's what's the matter with me. I love him to distraction, I love him hopelessly, desperately, old fool that I am! I clothed him and I fed him and I cherished him. He was so fond of a show, poor boy, hated to stay at home with me, always wanting to run off to the theatre or the circus . . . I gave him all I had. I used to implore him on my bended knees, 'Valerian, my dear, my angel, what do you want to run off to the circus for? What good can a circus do you?' But he'd begin stamping his feet,

shouting at me and throwing his arms about! A real circus
turn that was, I can tell you. He forbade me to speak to him,
so I just looked at him and then I'd beseech him from a
distance, 'Darling Valerian, my dear life, my precious treasure,
don't make friends with any man you meet! Don't drink so
much!' But he wouldn't listen to me. If I hadn't paid the house-
porter to find out what had happened, I shouldn't have heard of
this last trouble of his. Oh, Lord, sweet Lord, why has this
happened and what's going to become of him?" she exclaimed
and fell on her knees before the icon, crying more bitterly than
ever and shaking her grey head.

"I gave him all I had," she repeated, rising from her knees
after a few minutes and looking round her dreary little room
with dead eyes. "I gave him everything till I had nothing more
to give. If only I could see him just for one minute . . ."

"Why not go and see him?" I said.

"He told me never to see him again. I daren't go to him!"
she said, shaking feverishly.

I was silent and just to sober her down a bit I said :

"How old are you now, Domna Platonovna?"

"What did you say, dear?"

"How old are you?"

"I don't know really . . . I was forty-seven last January, I
think."

"Where did you meet that Valerian of yours?" I asked.
"Where did you dig him up to your own undoing?"

"He's from the same town as I," she said, wiping her tears.
"A nephew of that friend of mine to whose children I stood
godmother. Sent him to me, she did, asked me to find a job for
him. Tell me," my Amazon turned to me, crying again, "are
you at least sorry for me, silly fool that I am?"

"Yes, Domna Platonovna," I said, "I'm very sorry for you."

"I daresay nobody else will be even sorry for me," she said.

"People will only laugh at me. Anybody who heard my story would just laugh. Yes, of course, they laugh, for why should they be sorry for me? But I can't help loving him, however little joy or happiness that love has brought me. Never mind what the world thinks. People will never understand what a terrible misfortune it is for such a thing to happen to a woman at my time of life. I went to one of those old believers and he said to me, 'It's Satan who's tormenting your flesh. Do not let your soul do aught presumptuously.' I went to a priest. 'Father,' I said, 'tell me what's wrong with me?' and I told him everything. 'Read the hymn, 'O Lord, alleviate my sorrow',' he said to me. So I read that hymn and I got myself this job so that I shouldn't get into greater temptation, but . . . oh, my darling, Valerian, my dearest, my precious one, what have you done to me?"

Domna Platonovna pressed her head against the window frame and began to bang her forehead against the sill.

In that state of utter prostration and grief I left my Amazon. In another month I received news from the hospital that Domna Platonovna had ended her aggravating life. She had suffered a sudden and complete collapse and died. She lay in a black coffin, looking so small and shrivelled that it seemed as if indeed nothing was left of her but skin and bone. Her end was painless, quiet and peaceful. Domna Platonovna received extreme unction and she kept saying her prayers to the very end, and with her last breath she asked that a little chest, her pillows and a pot of jam she had been given, should be sent to me, so that I, if possible, should give it "to the man I know of," that is to say, to Valerian.

A LITTLE MISTAKE

The Secret of a Moscow Family

CHAPTER ONE

ONE EVENING DURING THE CHRISTMAS HOLIDAYS I was in the company of some highly intelligent people who were discussing the subject of belief and unbelief. The conversation, though, did not turn on the higher questions of deism and materialism, but concerned the more popular topic of belief that certain people are endowed with special powers of insight and prophecy and, perhaps, even with the gift of working miracles. There happened to be among us a grave-looking, thoughtful individual, a native of Moscow, who listened in silence for a long time and then suddenly broke into the conversation.

"It isn't such an easy matter, gentlemen," he said, "to determine which of us lives by faith and which of us is an unbeliever, for in life all sorts of unforseen accidents may happen. It is no wonder, therefore, if our reason occasionally misleads us."

After this preamble, he told us the following curious story, which I shall try to tell in his own words.

My uncle and aunt (he began) were great believers in the late miracle worker, Ivan Yakovlevich. My aunt, in particular, did nothing without consulting him. First of all she would pay him a visit in the lunatic asylum where he was confined and ask his advice on any matter that was uppermost in her mind at the time, and then she'd ask him to pray to God to grant her whatever she had set her heart on. My uncle was a very shrewd man and he did not rely on Ivan Yakovlevich altogether, but he, too, would confide his secrets to him and he never interfered with his wife if she wanted to send the saint presents and offerings of various kinds. They were not very rich people, but neither were they poor. They lived in their own large house where they had a warehouse. My uncle was a dealer·in tea and sugar.

A Little Mistake

The Lord did not bless them with any sons, but they had three daughters—Kapitolina Nikitishna, Katerina Nikitishna and Olga Nikitishna, all good-looking girls, very capable, too, and useful about the house. Only one of their daughters, Kapitolina Nikitishna, was married. Her husband, however, was not a merchant like her father, but a painter. Still, he was a good fellow and did well at his trade : he always got good commissions to paint icons for the churches. One thing about him did cause great unhappiness to his parents-in-law. Although engaged on works of piety, his opinions smacked too much of the free-thinker. He liked to talk about such subjects as Chaos, Ovid and Prometheus and he was, perhaps, a thought too ready to make comparisons between pagan legends and stories from the Bible. But for that everything would have been all right. Another thing that worried my uncle and my aunt was that although Kapitolina and her painter husband had been married for three years, they had no children. So far only one of their daughters was married, and the fact that there were no children of the marriage made it difficult for the other two daughters to find suitable husbands, for the rumour had gone round that the girls were barren.

My aunt, of course, kept asking Ivan Yakovlevich why her daughter did not have any children. "Both of them," she used to say to him, "are young and healthy and yet they have no children !"

"The Lord's in his heaven," Ivan Yakovlevich would mutter in reply, "the Lord's in his heaven !"

The women followers who always clustered round Ivan Yakovlevich interpreted the saint's enigmatic words to mean that her son-in-law should pray to God, for Ivan Yakovlevich, they hinted, suspected that he was weak in faith.

My aunt gasped in astonishment. "Nothing," she exclaimed, "is hidden from him !"

121

She thereupon began to badger her son-in-law to go to confession, but he just laughed. He was, in fact, a very easy-going young man and he did not refuse to eat meat in Lent, and it was even whispered that he enjoyed such outlandish delicacies as oysters.

They all lived in the same house, and the painter's in-laws were greatly grieved at the thought that in their respectable family there should be a man who cared so little about religion.

CHAPTER TWO

MY AUNT WENT TO SEE Ivan Yakovlevich and she entreated him once more to say a prayer for his handmaiden Kapitolina that by the grace of God her womb should be opened, and also for his servant Lary (such was the painter's name) that he should no longer err from the true faith.

Both my uncle and aunt beseeched the saint to grant them their request.

Ivan Yakovlevich, as was his wont, again mumbled something incoherently, and his women disciples were as usual eager to enlighten the humble petitioners.

"He's a little confused today," they said. "Tell us what you want and we'll write it down on a piece of paper and tomorrow we shall hand it to the saint."

My aunt told them, and they wrote it down as she dictated it to them. "May the womb of Thy handmaiden Kapitolina be opened and may Thy servant Lary see the light of the true faith."

The old couple left this short petition with the saint's disciples and went home rejoicing, strong in their belief that it would be granted.

At home they told nobody about it except their married daughter and that, too, only after obtaining a solemn promise from her that she would not say a word about it to her husband, the free-thinking painter, but be more loving and devoted to him than ever and watch out for any sign of a change of heart in him towards Ivan Yakovlevich.

The painter, however, was a terrible scoffer, turning everything into ridicule, cracking unseemly jokes, and making fun of the most sacred things. He'd approach his father-in-law in the evening and say, "Let's turn the fifty-two pages of the sacred

Book of Hours," meaning, of course, that they should have a game of cards. Or he'd sit down and say (tempting Providence), "Let's go on playing until one of us passes out."

My poor aunt would be horrified by these dreadful remarks and my uncle would ask him again and again not to upset her. "She loves you," he said, "and she made a promise for you." But the painter laughed and said to his mother-in-law, "Why do you make promises for me? Don't you know that it was because of a promise that John the Baptist's head was cut off? Take heed lest some unexpected misfortune befall your house!"

This shocked his mother-in-law even more and she kept running to the lunatic asylum, where she'd be comforted by the saint's disciples. "Don't worry," they told her, "everything is sure to be all right. The saint, bless him, reads your note every day and whatever is written down is sure to come to pass."

And come to pass it did and in a way that is hardly decent to mention.

CHAPTER THREE

ONE DAY MY AUNT'S SECOND DAUGHTER, Katerina went up to her mother and, without saying a word, fell down on her knees before her.

"What's the matter, child?" my aunt cried in great alarm. "Has anyone offended you?"

"Oh, mother," Katerina sobbed, "dear mother, I don't know myself what it is or how it all happened . . . I promise it won't happen again, only, please, mother, hide my shame from father!"

My aunt just gave her one look and then poked a finger into her belly.

"Is that it?" she asked.

"Yes, mother," the poor girl replied. "How did you guess? I'm sure I don't know how it all happened . . ."

My aunt then threw up her hands in despair. "My poor child." she said, "don't tell me, for I'm afraid it may be all my own fault. I shall go there at once and find out."

So she immediately took a cab and hurried off to the lunatic asylum.

"Show me the note with our petition," she said to the saint's disciples, "the note I left with the holy one to pray for the womb of the handmaiden Kapitolina to be opened. Is there no mistake in it?"

The women disciples immediately looked for the note on the window-sill and handed it to her.

My aunt glanced at the note and nearly went out of her mind. For what do you suppose had happened? There *was* a mistake in the petition, for instead of the name of the handmaiden Kapitolina, the name of the handmaiden Katerina was written on it, Katerina who was still unmarried!

A Little Mistake

The women disciples at once began to console my aunt.

"Dear, dear," they said, "what a terrible thing to happen! Their names are so alike . . . But don't you worry, my dear, *it can still be mended*!"

"Mended?" my aunt thought to herself. "Rubbish! This cannot be mended. Katerina has had our prayer granted!" and she tore the paper into little bits.

CHAPTER FOUR

WHAT MY AUNT DREADED MOST was to tell my uncle about it. For, once roused, the old man's wrath could not be easily assuaged. Besides, it was well known that his favourite daughter was the youngest girl, Olga, to whom he had promised the largest marriage portion, and that Katerina had always been in his bad books and could therefore expect no mercy from him. My aunt did not know what to do, for, however hard she tried to think of some way out of this dreadful dilemma, she could find no way of acquainting her husband with the calamity that had befallen their family. At last she decided that the only chance of saving her daughter from disgrace was to take her son-in-law into her confidence.

"You may be an unbeliever," she said to him, "but at least you are not entirely devoid of feeling, so please take pity on Katerina and help me to hide her shame."

The painter knit his brows and said gravely, "I'm sorry, but although you are the mother of my wife I cannot help resenting, very deeply resenting, your attitude towards me. In the first place, what right have you to regard me as an unbeliever and, secondly, why should you of all people consider that there is anything shameful or sinful about Katerina's condition? Has not Ivan Yakovlevich been praying for just that to happen to her? Now, I love Katerina like a sister and I shall do my best for her, because I for one do not think that she's in any way to blame for what has happened."

My aunt just bit her finger and began to cry. "Are you sure," she asked, "she's not to blame for anything?"

"Of course she isn't! It's all your saint's doing. You'd better call him to account."

"How am I to call him to account? He's a saint, isn't he?"

"Very well then, if he is a saint then you'd better say nothing. Just send Katerina to me with three bottles of champagne."

My aunt gazed speechlessly at him. "Champagne?" she murmured.

"Yes," he replied, "three bottles : one to be sent straight to my rooms and two to be put on ice for when required."

My aunt again looked at him and just nodded. "May the Lord forgive you," she said. "I thought you just had no faith although you paint the images of saints all day long, but I can see now that you've not a shred of decent feeling, either . . . That's why," she added, "I can't bring myself to worship the icons you paint."

"Leave my religion alone, I beg of you," he replied. "It is you who lack faith, for in your heart you're convinced that Katerina is the cause of all the trouble, but I am of the firm opinion that the real cause of it is Ivan Yakovlevich. As for my feelings, you'll see whether or not I have any when you send Katerina to my work-room with the bottle of champagne."

CHAPTER FIVE

MY AUNT THOUGHT IT OVER and decided to send Katerina with the wine to the painter. Katerina, her face streaming with tears, put the bottle of champagne on a tray and carried it to the painter's work-room. As she entered the room, the painter jumped to his feet, grasped her by the hands and burst out crying too.

"I'm deeply grieved for you, Katerina," he said, "but we must waste no time. Tell me quickly all your secrets and, mind, don't conceal anything from me!"

The girl told him everything, and he asked her to remain in his work-room where he locked her in. My aunt met her son-in-law with tear-stained eyes and looked imploringly at him.

"Don't be afraid," he said, embracing and kissing her, "and please stop crying. Maybe the Lord will take pity on you and everything will be for the best."

"But where's poor Katerina?"

"I've pronounced a terrible painter's curse on her and she's vanished into thin air!" he said dramatically, showing her the key at the same time.

My aunt guessed that he had locked the girl in his room to protect her from her father's wrath and she embraced him again.

"Forgive me, dear," she whispered. "I can see that you have human feelings all right."

CHAPTER SIX

MY UNCLE CAME HOME, had his tea as usual and then turned to his son-in-law and said, "Well, let's turn the fifty-two pages of the Book of Hours."

They sat down at the table, while my aunt and her two daughters left the room, shut all the doors, tiptoeing as they did so for fear of disturbing them. My aunt kept tiptoeing up to the door and then tiptoeing back again, listening at the keyhole and crossing herself all the time. At last she heard a terrible noise inside the room and she scurried off to hide herself.

"He's told him the secret," she said to her daughters, "and now hell itself will break loose."

And, to be sure, the door burst open and my uncle rushed out, bawling at the top of his voice, "Give me my fur-coat and my big stick!"

The painter tried in vain to pull him back by the hand. "What are you going to do?" he asked. "Where are you going?"

"I'm going to the lunatic asylum," said my uncle, "to give that saint a damned good hiding!"

My aunt emitted a dreadful groan from behind the door of the next room. "Run to the lunatic asylum," she shouted, "and tell them to hide Ivan Yakovlevich immediately!"

My uncle would have carried out his threat to give the saint a hiding had not his son-in-law prevented him by appealing to his faith in Ivan Yakovlevich's miraculous powers.

CHAPTER SEVEN

THE PAINTER BEGAN BY REMINDING his father-in-law that he had another unmarried daughter.

"Don't be a fool," my uncle shouted, "I know that! Haven't I promised her the largest portion? I want to give that saint the beating of his life. Let them prosecute me if they like!"

"But," the painter pleaded, "I don't want to frighten you with any court action. I'm only appealing to you to think of the harm the saint could do to your daughter Olga. Why, think of the risk you're running of ruining her reputation!"

My uncle stopped and reflected for a moment. "What harm can he do to her?" he asked.

"The same harm he did to Katerina," the painter replied.

My uncle gave him a quick look and said, "What are you talking about? Do you mean to say he really can do such a thing?"

"Very well," said the painter, "if you don't believe he can, then do what you like, but remember don't accuse the poor girls afterwards!"

My uncle now seemed definitely to have given up the idea of punishing Ivan Yakovlevich, and his son-in-law dragged him back into the room and began to entreat him to forget all about the saint.

"Leave the saint alone," he said, "and let's try to settle everything quietly without any public scandal."

The old man acquiesced, although he had no idea how such a thing could be settled without causing a public scandal. His son-in-law, however, came to his rescue even there.

"Happy thoughts," he said, "are not to be found in anger, but in joy."

"Expect a man to jump for joy when his daughter goes wrong, do you ?" said my uncle.

"To begin with," said the painter without paying any attention to the old man's words, "I have two bottles of champagne and I shan't say a word to you before we have finished them. I think you know me well enough to realise that once I set my mind on something, nothing will change it."

The old man glared at him, but agreed. "All right," he said, "let's have the drinks. I wonder what you have up your sleeve, though."

However, he did give in.

CHAPTER EIGHT

THE PAINTER WENT OUT to fetch the wine and he came back almost immediately followed by his assistant, a young painter, carrying a tray with two bottles of champagne and glasses.

As soon as they entered the room, the painter locked the door and put the key in his pocket. My uncle stared at them and—understood. His son-in-law beckoned to the assistant who immediately went up to my uncle, and stopped before him in an attitude of humble contrition.

"I'm very sorry, sir," he said. "Please, forgive me and give me your blessing."

My uncle turned to his son-in-law. "Shall I give him a beating?" he asked.

"By all means," said the painter, "but if I were you I shouldn't."

"Well," said my uncle, "in that case let him at any rate go down on his knees before me."

The painter nudged his assistant. "Kneel before the father of the girl you love," he whispered.

The assistant knelt and the old man burst into tears.

"Do you love her much?" he asked.

"I do, sir."

"All right, you can embrace me now."

It was thus that Ivan Yakovlevich's little mistake was concealed and everything was kept a dead secret, and very soon young men began to compete for the youngest daughter's hand in marriage, for they saw that there was nothing really the matter with the girls.

THE MARCH HARE

*The Life and Opinions of Onopry Peregood
of the Village of Peregoody*

*Pray, Sir, stand on a flat piece of ground and let a hundred mirrors be
placed all round you. You will then perceive that this clod of earth, this body
of yours, has assumed a hundred different shapes : but remove the mirrors,
and those faithful copies of yourself will vanish. And yet this clod of earth
of ours is itself but the shadow of the real man. That ape-like creature repre-
sents in its outward manifestations the invisible and infinitely diversified
divine substance of the Man whereof all our bodies are like unto shadows
reflected in mirrors.*

GRIGORY SKOVORODA
(Ukrainian philosopher, 1722-1794.)

A BRIEF INTRODUCTION

I WAS FOR MANY MONTHS unfortunately obliged to visit a hospital for nervous diseases, usually referred to in common speech as a "lunatic asylum," which, in fact, it was. With the exception of a small number of patients under observation, all the inmates of this asylum were considered "insane" and "irresponsible," that is to say, they were not held answerable either for their words or actions.

Coming regularly to this hospital to visit one of the patients, I little by little got to know many more, including a few who were not devoid of interest in the sense that while their insanity was hardly perceptible, they were most definitely insane. Among them was a hard-working, cheerful and very talkative old man who wore a knotted peasant woman's handkerchief on his head. The old gentleman's name was Onopry Opanassovich Peregood. The medical and domestic staffs of the institution, as well as the patients, had nicknamed him "the sock manufacturer" because he was always knitting socks and giving them away to those patients who were too poor to afford socks of their own. The only time he did not knit was when he was either eating or sleeping.

Onopry Opanassovich did not resent his nickname at all; on the contrary, he seemed to glory in it, finding that knitting socks was his true vocation in life. He was a friend and favourite of everybody and he was not ill-treated even by his Majesty the King of Small Beer, a madman of enormous size and immense physical strength, who strutted about in a tinfoil crown and demanded from everybody to be treated with the proper respect due to his exalted station, tripping up and even boxing the ears of those whom he considered disloyal. He had treated Peregood like that only once, namely, on the first day of

Onopry Opanassovich's admission to the asylum. He never ill-used him again and even rewarded him from time to time for being his "loyal fool" and "Court knitter." I shall come back to Peregood's friendship with the King of Small Beer later on in this story.

Peregood was a man of some sixty years. He was in excellent health, thick-set and of strong build, and his face was round like a water melon. He came of a family of small Ukrainian land-owners, of whom there seemed to have been a great number in his native village of Peregoody, and was never intended for a knitter of socks. He had indeed enjoyed "a singularly choice" education and carried out "the usual duties of serving his country in a way that exceeded all expectations." In all that Peregood had so surpassed himself that it was a matter of constant wonder to himself and he never stopped marvelling at his own accomplishments.

According to his political convictions he was "partly ambiti-ous and partly a conservative," but in private life it was peace and quiet that he liked most and, above all, that "no one should dare to show a haughty cast of countenance to anybody else." However, with all these natural gifts of his, Onopry Opanasso-vich owed his great success chiefly to a religious tract entitled "Rules for the Revelation of Truth," but subsequently he fell on evil days and suffered a most humiliating change of fortune.

It all happened in an extraordinarily sad manner, but Pere-good never murmured against his bad luck, for all his troubles were the direct consequence of his own "amazing" character, which was such that even as a boy he used to chase himself round a barrel in the hope of being able to overtake himself. Now, obviously, a man with such a disposition could not hope for a quiet termination of his career and, indeed, things at last came to such a pass that, after many attempts, Peregood finished up as a permanent resident of a lunatic asylum where, during the many highly fascinating and entertaining talks I had with him, he told me the story of his life, an account of which I shall give presently.

But before addressing myself to the story of Peregood's life, I should like to ask the reader's indulgence for a brief account of his family and the place where he lived and worked.

CHAPTER ONE

THE LARGE AND PICTURESQUE VILLAGE OF Peregoody is situated in one of the more beautiful provinces of the Ukraine. In the opinion of well-informed people, this village should have long ago become a township or even a town, but this cannot be done because old Peregood, the founder of the village, imposed a curse upon everyone who attempted such a change. Who was this Peregood? Well, that is something to bear in mind, for he was a very important personage in his day—a Cossack elder and a knight. He was a gallant commanding officer of a regiment and his name was Opanass Opanassovich. It is in his honour that today all his grandchildren and great-grandchildren who bear the name of Peregood or Peregoodenki make sure that their children of the male sex are called either Opanasses or, at any rate, Opanassoviches. It is the custom among them that a male child is always christened "after grand-dad," for "grand-dad deserved it."

"I can tell you all about it," Onopry Opanassovich Peregood said, pushing back the knotted kerchief to the back of his head, and he went on to tell me a long story, of which I shall recount only the most interesting bits.

I hope no one will find fault with me if his words and my own words get a little bit mixed up in the course of this narrative. I am afraid it cannot be helped if I am to avoid too long-winded an account of a story that was anyway too long, as Onopry Opanassovich himself used to say during our walks in the grounds of the lunatic asylum. Besides, much of what he considered important was not in my opinion of any real importance, and I have left it out altogether as something that had nothing to do with our story, or have retold it in my own words in an abbreviated form, retaining the essence of the story while omitting many unnecessary repetitions and uninteresting digressions, of which my garrulous romantic of a maniac was exceedingly fond. For if I had not done so, his story would have become much too unwieldy on account of its length and would thereby have undoubtedly lost some of its interest.

CHAPTER TWO

COLONEL OPANASS OPANASSOVICH, or, as he is usually spoken of, "old Peregood," was, as I have already mentioned, the founder of the village of Peregoody. Before he came on the scene there was absolutely nothing there, and afterwards someone put up a windmill. You know the Ukrainian song, "He's been here, but he's gone, at the mill you'll find him," or as the Muscovites sing it, "He drank all day and he drank all night, now he's gone to the mill to get tight." A silly old ditty, but everybody will give his own version of it! Well, anyway, afterwards, the hamlet of Peregoody grew up near the mill and in the fullness of time and with the Lord's blessing more and more people were born and, as the population multiplied, it became a village. It was then that grand-dad Peregood gave a twist to his long forelock and began to introduce all sorts of innovations : he dug ponds and filled them with fish from the river Oster, and he began growing vegetables and melons, enlarging his plots and orchards and employing women and girls to weed them, and with their assistance, if you please, he still further multiplied the population so that soon there were so many Christians there that, whether he liked it or not, he had to build a church for them and provide them with a learned priest to make sure that all of them kept the Christian laws and precepts and knew of what origin they were and why their faith was better than any other faith in the whole world. For otherwise, they would not have been able to keep themselves apart from the Lithuanians and the Poles, let alone the Jews and the Lutherans. Old Peregood did everything that was necessary, sparing neither pains nor money: he cut down timber and built a church with a belfry and he brought a priest by the name of Prokop from somewhere or other, to the great amazement of everybody in the village, for Father Prokop was a man of a very imposing presence, being very tall and with a big paunch and wearing red top-boots and, as his face was also red, he looked like a blessed seraph; but the most remarkable thing about him was his voice which was so stentorian that the people in the congregation had to put their hands over their ears every time he opened his mouth.

Whatever old squire Opanass did, he did to perfection and, being an indefatigable and true fighter for the "Orthodox faith," he could not abide any "doubters" and he naturally got for his village a priest who would stand no nonsense from any Lutherans or Jews or (God forbid) Poles. To be quite frank, the squire and the priest had not a very high opinion of the Muscovite gentlemen, either, and indeed they always spoke of them as "the devil's brood"; but to avoid the danger of having Russian soldiers stationed in their backyards, they never openly provoked any hostilities against the Russians, confining themselves to offering up silent prayers to the Highest, beseeching him "to destroy them utterly by His great strength and power."

Grand-dad Opanass was very adroit in his relations with the authorities, especially those of them with whom it was worth while keeping on good terms, but for all that he never sought their company and preferred living with people "of his own kind." Peregood never made a secret of the fact that the only men he truly respected were the Cossacks, and so great was his respect for them and so much did he set his heart upon keeping them always with him that he never hesitated for a moment to assert his power over the Peregoody Cossacks. He thus made sure that not a single inhabitant of the village left for some other place or got himself entangled, as was the foolish custom of that time, with anybody he happened to meet.

Indeed, so fond was Opanass Opanassovich of his Cossacks that he soon turned the whole population of the village into his serfs and proclaimed himself to be their lord and master long before the days of Catherine the Great. Peregood did it at the time when the Cossacks still governed themselves in accordance with their ancient laws, for which so many good Ukrainian patriots today shed bitter tears and fetch deep sighs from the bottom of their hearts. He had managed everything so cleverly with the help of the elders that the Peregoody Cossacks did not even notice that they had become his serfs, and they certainly never knew for what reason they had been deprived of their ancient liberties, and those who refused to be grand-dad's serfs were—if you please—given a good thrashing in the squire's yard just to prevent any unnecessary unpleasantness in the future, some being flogged with Russian whips and others with whips of native manufacture, both varieties having the same sting and virtue. Still, as Peregood's serfs persisted in disliking their new position, Father Prokop undertook the task of extirpating their subversive beliefs and mollifying their hardened hearts. The priest, who always wore his red top-boots in church, read to his congregation every week at morning mass that passage from St. Paul's Epistles which strengthened the belief among the people that they were "servants" and that the whole purpose of their lives was that "they should be obedient to them who were their masters." It was to make sure that this teaching remained inviolate for ever that the curse was imposed on the village of Peregoody which keeps it to this day from assuming the dignity of a market township or a town.

CHAPTER THREE

FINDING LITTLE PLEASURE in being serfs and having, more-over, made the acquaintance of both the Russian and the native whips and realised that there was not much to choose between them, the Peregoody Cossacks decided that it was too danger-ous to start a rebellion in their village; they consequently be-took themselves to the Jew Khaim from whom they wished to borrow fifty golden roubles to defray the cost of sending a trustworthy emissary to the Empress Catherine and her great Russian lords to prove to them that the inhabitants of the village of Peregoody had always enjoyed the liberties of the Cossack Knighthood and had never been serfs who could be sold and bought like Crimean slaves or cattle. But before the Cossacks had time to come to terms with the Jew about the proposed loan, the colonel himself got wind of their plot and he dealt with all those former knights in his own fashion, using for that purpose a whip of native make, and, as he greatly disliked half measures, he had enough sense "to take steps for the future." Knowing perfectly well what would happen if his serfs not only got some sense into their heads, but also some money in their pockets, Peregood decided to avoid all trouble by remov-ing every temptation out of their way. As it is usually free men who put temptation in the way of men who are not free, it was necessary to see to it that those who were not free should never get the chance of becoming friends with those who were free. For that praiseworthy reason, the old colonel raided the Jew's house with his own servants and, demolishing it, drove the Jew himself out of the village, setting fire to all his belongings "so as to leave nothing of the wicked Jewish spirit about," for as is well known "all Jews are the enemies of true Christians and there is little to choose between them."

After that there was no more trouble in the village, and many years passed and the Cossacks never again attempted to regain their lost liberties, and the Lord heaped His blessings upon Opanass Opanassovich and he lived to see his sons and daughters and the sons of his sons and daughters, and he took care of them like a good Christian who knows what is written in the Holy Scriptures, in St. Paul's Second Epistle to the Corinthians, in chapter twelve, verse fourteen, where it is said that "the children ought not to lay up for their parents, but the parents for their children."

Opanass Opannassovich kept this commandment, and when the number of male and female Peregoods had, owing to his own endeavours and the blessing of God, increased mightily, the old colonel had laid up enough treasure for them all. When at last all his earthly affairs had been put in order and Peregood saw that all his grain barns were full and his days were drawing to an end and the time was fast approaching when he was to be gathered to his fathers, he did his best to make his peace with the Lord. When therefore one day he fell ill and got such cramps in his belly that it was a wonder his bowels did not fall out, he realised that "his hour had come" and he said unto himself, "What will happen when my Cossack soul, bit by bit, and then altogether, jumps out of my body? I fear it is sure to meet those dreadful spirits who fly about everywhere, those evil spirits or devils whose hideous images have been painted for the whole world to see on the wall near the very entrance to the Cathedral by the Peshchersky Gates! . . . Oh, I'm afraid I shan't find it so easy to deal with them, nor shall I get off so lightly, for I couldn't possibly bribe them, since I shall have to leave all my money behind . . ." He was a very gallant old gentleman, but, you know, once the thought of so dreadful an encounter enters the head of a man and one who is ill at that, things begin to look black indeed! Peregood, to be sure, tried to seek forgetfulness in drink and did his best to fall asleep, but even then hosts of devils ran after him in his dreams. Peregood saw that with a noise of their webbed wings, which was more dreadful than the noise made by the wings of bats, they were about to seize him by his long forelock and drag him off to hell, while other devils were ready to spur him on from behind with fiery rods . . . . .

"May the Holy Virgin of Pechersk save and protect us from so horrible a fate!"

CHAPTER FOUR

SQUIRE OPANASS THEREUPON WOKE UP and the first thing he did was to summon the priest in the red top-boots and add a codicil to his will, leaving one hundred ducats for a church bell, which was to be cast with a good likeness of himself on it. He then whispered a solemn adjuration in the ear of the potbellied priest so that no one else in the room could hear him, and having done that, his lips twisted into a most hideous grimace, and he gave up the ghost in the presence of all the people.

Such was his end. When they brought him to the church, every man and woman in the congregation wanted to file past his bier to pay their last respects to him and also to see the splendid clothes in which he was to be buried, for he was dressed in a short scarlet coat and a belt in which a spray of golden flowers was stuck. But priest Prokop would not permit any villager even to have a look at the colonel, and ascending the pulpit, he waved his hand in the direction of the open coffin and said, "Can't you smell the terrible stench? Shut it up quickly!" When the lid of the coffin had been hastily closed and Peregood's scarlet coat hidden from sight, Father Prokop raised his voice in praise of squire Peregood and spoke as follows :

"Dearly beloved brethren, you have all known our squire Opanass, but I do not expect you know what his last wish was, for that was the great secret he imparted to me alone with his last breath so that I should reveal it to you over his coffin. And I hope you will all believe me, for, being a man in holy orders, I am forbidden to take an oath, but every one of you must put his trust in my priestly conscience which, as you know, has been sanctified. Well, then, brethren, do you or do you not believe me? I want a straight answer from you!"

The whole congregation replied in one voice, "We believe you, Father, we believe you!"

Father Prokop nodded a few times and shed a few tears, and wiping his eyes with his hands, he said in a shaking voice, "Thank you, my spiritual children, thank you a thousand times for having gladdened my heart, for I know full well how unworthy I am of your love. Not that I have doubted for one moment your implicit trust in me, for I could read it in your eyes, and I know that the respect you show me is free from malice and hypocrisy and is not due to any desire on your part to curry favour with me, and, indeed, my dearly beloved children in God, our mutual trust of each other has borne fruit and has been the cause of a great and ever-growing number of good deeds. Therefore know ye, all the people gathered here in this house of God, know ye that our late squire, the benefactor whom we are now burying, leant over to my ear in his last hour, yea, even fell upon my chest, so that I could verily savour the dust and stench of death, and, as he did so, he said to me . . . Hearken to me, brethren, all of you, and incline your ears to my words, for they can in truth be said to have come to us from the other world . . . He said to me, 'Father, tell all the people at my funeral that I forbid them and any of my heirs and descendants on pain of eternal damnation to permit any Jew or Catholic to settle among us in our village of Peregoody, and warn them that my curse will be on the head of any man who defies this wish of mine, and may it last for ever and ever! Never shall there be a Catholic cathedral or a Jewish synagogue in this village of ours, for it is our duty always to cling to our true Christian faith. Moreover, it is my wish that everybody in the village should go to confession to you, Father, and should reveal to you everything anybody may be thinking about, and he who will not fulfil this sacred wish of mine and conceals something from you and keeps it locked up in his heart, may his fate

148

be the same as the fate of Judas who is with Satan in hell, holding a purse on his knees and being roasted in brimstone'."

Here Priest Prokop raised his hand and swore that he had not invented it all, but that the colonel had indeed spoken thus.

For a long time the people in the village believed him, but afterwards a certain number of sceptics appeared who began to give utterance to the view that Father Prokop did not always speak the whole truth and that sometimes even (the Lord forgive him!) "he tells lies" in quite a shameless way, which, they argued, gave some substance to the doubts entertained by them whether it had really been old Peregood who had imposed such a curse on the village or whether it was Father Prokop (the Lord have mercy upon him!) who had invented the whole thing in order that he should be the only man to intercede to God for all the village.

As soon as this heresy spread among the people, the fear of eternal damnation was somewhat allayed and in a little while nobody seemed to be in the least afraid of the danger of sharing "Judas's fate." It was then that both Jews and Catholics began a regular invasion of Peregoody and started buying up building sites and erecting dwellings in the market place; and very soon they would, no doubt, have begun to make tables, sew trousers, manufacture boots and hats, bake buns and bread-rings and play the fiddle in the pubs, and in this way bring things to such a pass in Peregoody that all the native Christians would get dead drunk and start punching the hooked noses of the Jews and then be called to account by the authorities, as though they had in truth been molesting honest folk. However, notwithstanding all these perils, Peregoody could still have risen to the dignity of a town had not the Peregoody gentry quarrelled among themselves.

What the Peregoody squires were like and how many there were of them, Onopry Opanassovich could not say with any certainty and, indeed, it is hardly possible to describe them all. Suffice it to say that, whatever their numbers, they had all quarrelled among themselves and that all of them did their best to fall out and wrangle with one another.

The chief among them, however, ought to be mentioned. Opanass Opanassovich was his name and he had advanced the fortunes of his family by relinquishing his hearth and home and getting himself a job in the office of the Quartermaster-General of the First and Second Armies. He had thus greatly enriched his homestead and, having only one son, Dmitry, it was perhaps natural that he should wish to give him as splendid an education as it was possible to get in those days. He therefore sent him to the famous Moscow boarding school run by a certain Galushka, where the young lad actually picked up enough French to be able to discourse in that tongue about anything your heart could desire. Thereafter, there was no difficulty at all in providing him with a job in the customs-service where he served so honourably that he not only reached the rank of Collegiate Assessor, but also laid up a decent competency for himself and resigned from the service with a pension.

While still in the customs-service, Dmitry Afanassyevich Peregood entered into a legal contract of marriage with a kinswoman of one of his superiors, a lady by the name of Matilda Opoldovna, about whom, however, it was rumoured that she was not really anybody's kinswoman, but that is neither here nor there, for as soon as Peregood returned to his village, his wife, finding life there not to her taste, left him and went to live in Mittava. Poor Dmitry Afanassyevich thus lost the only person he could discourse in French with, but he soon found a way of mending this matter and there will indeed be some talk about his goings on a little later in this story.

The other important personage in Peregoody was—if you please—none other than Onopry Opanassovich Peregood, whose acquaintance I made in the lunatic asylum, and now I shall let him carry on with the story of his life and adventures himself.

Onopry Opanassovich's education was very different from Dmitry Afanassyevich's, for, to begin with, he never went to the Moscow boarding school of Galushka. Instead, his education was remarkable for something else, something of much weightier import. But let him speak himself. Here he is: he has just adjusted his knitting on his knees and is about to address you.

"Carry on, sir!"

CHAPTER FIVE

THERE IS HARDLY ANYTHING I have not experienced in my life (Onopry Opanassòvich began), which is most of all remarkable for two things : originality and surprise. To begin with, I hardly believe that any educated man ever received the kind of education I was fortunate enough to receive. But for all that I had no difficulty at all in making my way in the world and, mark you, obtaining at one turn of fortune's wheel a situation where I was policeman and magistrate rolled into one. I may add without, I hope, being accused of immodesty, that I conferred great benefits upon my fellow-citizens and should, no doubt, have gone on being of assistance to them as long as I lived but for the fact that, as the popular song has it, "My dreams, perchance, are mad ! . . ."

But then consider, sir, that I was coached in every branch of knowledge in a bishop's choir ! Yes, indeed ! And how I got from there to a post in the civil service, that, too, is quite a remarkable story, but I'm afraid I shall have to tell you first where our village of Peregoody is situated, for otherwise you will never be able to follow what I have to relate to you of my father, the burbot fish and my benefactor the bishop, and how I got mixed up with him and how he got me fixed in my job.

It—our village I mean—is situated, as they say in novels, in a very beautiful and picturesque spot where two rivers either flow into or out of each other, although, I'm sorry to say, neither of them is really worth mentioning, since neither of them is any good for the purposes of navigation. We have everything in Peregoody, though, which makes the Ukraine so famous a country for its natural beauties : we have orchards, we have ponds, we have whitewashed cottages, we have fine, upstanding lads and dark-browed lasses. Altogether, I should

say there are more than three thousand souls there and all of
them live in whitewashed cottages with ample space between
them for gardens and orchards. But great men like Gogol,
Osnovyanenko and Dzyubaty have given us so many descrip-
tions of the Ukraine that after them it is hardly fit or proper
for me to come to you with more. The only extraordinary
thing about Peregoody was that in one village (the Lord be
praised!) we had as many as eleven different squires who,
needless to say, owned eleven estates, and the windows of all
their houses looked out onto a large pond in which the Peregoody squires (the Lord grant them health and happiness!)
used to take a dip in summer. That gave rise to a good deal of
excellent fun, but also to much unpleasantness, which was
chiefly due to the fact that the self-same former student of
Galushka's Moscow boarding school, Dmitry—as I shall call
him from now on, or I may, perhaps, add his patronymic
Afanassyevich—took it into his head to transform part of the
pond into a private bathing-pool by screening it off with white
sheets. For after the departure of his lawful wedded wife to
Mittava, Dmitry always had a pretty housekeeper in his house
and, being of a jealous disposition, he resented it if other people
stole a look at those sweet ladies of his. Goodness gracious,
you'd think something might happen to them if strangers did
have a peep at them! Anyway, the rest of the Peregoody
squires did not trouble their heads about such quaint innovations and were certainly not willing to spend a penny on them,
but went on bathing straight from the bank, choosing the most
convenient place from which to plunge into the water. Neither
did they dream of covering themselves, for why indeed try to
make a secret of whatever the good Lord has endowed you
with? It is true, no doubt, that what makes the male sex so
different from the female sex is one of the great mysteries of
creation which the Lord alone can comprehend, but it would

be foolish either to be shocked at it or philosophise about it, for it is surely not for nothing that Ecclesiastes said, "Be not righteous over much, neither make thyself over wise." For, in truth, there were ladies and gentlemen in our village who, when they stripped and took to the water, did give you something of a shock if you were unwise enough to look at them. But our squires and their ladies did not care a straw whether you looked at them or not. Indeed, there were some among them who not only did not mind appearing naked before the populace, but who, if one of their neighbours whom they had good reason to detest, happened to appear at the time on the balcony of his house with his guests, did not hesitate to station themselves stark naked in front of that balcony and, if nobody would look at them, shout, "My best regards to your grandmother, sir! Pray, kiss her hand for me!"

I'm afraid, sir, the Peregoods and their ladies are a very tough lot, with the single exception of myself, of course, for, as I've told you already, I received a special training, having been educated in a bishop's choir.

Now, if you don't mind, I shall say a few words about my education, for I can see that you're wondering what kind of education I can have received in a bishop's choir, and as I do not want to keep you in suspense any longer, I shall without any more ado acquaint you with the quite remarkable incident which launched me upon my scholastic career, an incident most strange and, mark you, arising from quite an unexpected cause, namely, a burbot.

CHAPTER SIX

I AM VERY SORRY, SIR, but I shall have to beg your indulgence again, for I have to ask you to come back with me once more to those far-off peaceful days of my happy childhood when I was still under my mother's supervision and care. I used to follow my mother about the house and I was particularly fond of eating the sweet froth of jam which she was a past master at making, and she also taught me to knit socks and gloves for myself. It seemed to me then that I wanted nothing more in the world, no riches, no honours, no favours and no worldly pomp. I even thought that it was a sin to ask God for anything else save, "Grant us, we beseech Thee, O Lord, that we may enjoy the kindly fruits of the earth," which is mentioned in the grace before meat. And indeed, if you please, sir, what else does a man want, but to have enough to eat, to live in warmth and comfort and to enjoy good company? There are, to be sure, people who are wicked and ungrateful by nature and who are never satisfied, but there were no such people in our house. Although my mother was not herself born in Peregoody, she came of a good family and as a girl was used to a simple life because her family was poor. She was very fond of my father, but then it was quite impossible not to love him, for he was such a fine gentleman. Yes, indeed, he certainly was that! Not a bit like me. No, sir, there can be no comparison between us. I am, as you see, a man of small stature and rather heavily built, whereas he was as tall as a poplar. An army man he was, retired with the rank of major because he had been wounded in battle, and he received a pension of seven roubles a month which was sent to him straight from the Treasury. I don't mind telling you that without that pension we should have found things a bit difficult, as indeed many other inhabitants of our village did, but with the pension we lived quite comfortably.

The March Hare

"Honour your dear father, my son," my mother used to say to me, "for you can see for yourself how much money we get for the blood he hás shed for his country, and now we can drink real tea while the others can't even afford a lump of sugar for their mint tea."

So, with the Lord's blessing, we lived very comfortably and, as my parents were very pious people, my mother took me to the priest to confession when I was only seven years old! At that time our priest was Father Markel, son-in-law of Prokop, for Prokop was long since dead, and Father Markel was a terribly domineering person and as cunning as the devil.

"You haven't by any chance ever stolen cucumbers or water melons from the vegetable gardens, have you, my boy?" he asked me, craftily.

"Yes, Father, I have," I replied, for my mother had taught me always to tell the truth.

"You're a good boy!" he said. "The Lord will forgive you, for it's just a child's prank." But then he remembered something and asked me again, "Tell me have you ever taken things from my garden, too?"

"Why, yes, Father," I said, "the other boys and I have stolen water melons from your garden, too."

Hearing that, Father Markel at once grabbed me by the hair, gave it a vicious pull and was going to drag me along by it on the floor. I only saved myself from his clutches by punching him in the belly under the cassock and even then it was only by a miracle that I escaped from him. I ran home crying and told my father and mother about it, and my father was so angry that he rushed out of the house vowing to give the priest a good beating. They did not fight when they met, however, but had a friendly talk instead. The reason for that was that just at that time we had got a new bishop who was a schoolfriend of my father's and who was about to visit every church in his diocese. My father thought of boasting about it to the priest.

"I warn you, Father," he said, "I'm going to give you a good hiding, for I have nothing to fear since even if you do complain to your bishop, he'll not hear a word against me and he may even unfrock you if you do say anything."

"In that case," said Father Markel, realising that my father meant business, "in that case, everything's all right and I don't know what we have to quarrel about. If the bishop's really a good friend of yours, I don't mind whether you give me a beating or not. For my part, I can assure you that I haven't the slightest intention of picking a quarrel with you. On the contrary, if, as you say, the bishop is a friend of yours, then both of us ought to derive an advantage from it."

"What do you mean?" said my father. "Of course the bishop is a friend of mine. Why, I slept next to him in the seminary and we always used to go out stealing water melons together."

"I'm very glad to hear it," said the priest, stroking his beard, "and that being so, I'm sure you won't refuse to accept something from me. Now, first of all, here's a lovely piece of cloth which will make you a very excellent coat, and for your wife I have a pound of the best foreign soap which will make her skin as soft as velvet."

So Father Markel handed to my father the cloth and the soap.

"Why are you giving me these things without first telling me what you want in return?" my father asked. "Not trying to bribe me by any chance, are you? All you clergymen are the same: too damned clever by half! Do you think I've forgotten how your father-in-law told us that story about my grandfather's last wish, from the pulpit, too, and over the old man's coffin! A tall story, wasn't it? Wanted to kick the Jews out of Peregoody so that he could practise usury himself without any competition from the Jews and, when the Jews had been driven out, he began issuing small loans at interest, and you're now following in his footsteps, aren't you ?"

"That's exactly what I'm talking about," said Father Markel.

"So that's what you're getting at, is it ?" said my father. "Aren't you ashamed even to mention it ? The Jews used to charge only one per cent. a month, but you ask much more than that, don't you ? That, my dear sir, no soap can wash white."

"Well," Father Markel replied, "if soap won't do it, what about my large brown turkey-cock ? What do you say to that ?"

"I'm afraid even a turkey won't make much difference."

"But if I should throw in two turkey-hens to go with it ?"

"Mind you," said my father, "I never said I wouldn't accept your brown turkey, for such a bird is just the sort of thing I want in my backyard where I've already got a heifer of the same light brown colour, but, all the same, truth is dearer to me than any bird and the truth is that you bring ruin upon the people."

"All right," said the priest, "let truth be dearer to you than anything else in the world. That's your business. I can see I shall have to throw in a heifer to salve your conscience. Take her : she'll soon grow into a lovely cow !"

"That'll take some time, won't it ?"

"Time ? Don't talk such rubbish, man ! How long does it take a calf to grow up ? And think what a lovely cow she'll be !"

"But how long shall I have to wait for that ? How long ? Besides, do you really think I shall enjoy drinking her milk when every gulp reminds me that it is the price I had to pay not only for truth, but also for my child's blood !"

"What blood ? Child's blood, indeed ! I saw no blood."

"You saw no blood ? I suppose the next thing you'll say is that you never pulled my son by the hair. Do you stand there and tell me that a priest has a right to behave like that at confession ?"

"Upon my soul, what's so terrible about pulling a young lad's hair because he's been stealing my water-melons? That should make him grow, that should. And don't forget that he'll be drinking that cow's milk, too!"

"No, sir," said my father, "I can't do it."

"But why can't you?"

"Why? Have you never read the story of how after Joseph had been sold for twenty pieces of silver, not all his brothers spent the money on food, but some of them bought their wives pigskin boots because they didn't want to eat blood-money but to trample on it?"

"I see, so you want something to trample on, do you? Very well, I'll give you something to trample on, just as you say. I'll throw in a young pig and you can make yourself a pair of boots out of its skin. There, does that satisfy you? But let me warn you that you won't gain anything by refusing to defend me against the people, but if you speak well of me to the bishop, everything I promised you will be yours."

"All right," my father said to him, "go and fetch your turkey, your heifer and your young pig and with God's help, I'll do my best for you. But remember, you'll have to pay me for any expenses I may incur on your behalf."

The priest brightened up. He could well afford to pay *any* expenses! He then went on plying my father with questions about what the bishop fancied most in the old days, but my father gave him a playful dig in the ribs and said, "Aha! What a rogue you are, to be sure! Catch me telling you that! There were lots of things we both fancied in the days when we were gay lads together, which the bishop would hate to be reminded of now that he has reached so high a position in the church."

"All right," said the priest, "but surely you can tell me what dish he likes most?"

"As to that," said my father "I suppose that, like most clergymen, he shows a partiality for roast pig. Yes, I remember, he liked crackling in particular, but I daresay he can no longer indulge his appetite that way. If I were you, I shouldn't waste any time, but go up to town and find out from his cook what titbit he now fancies most."

Father Markel didn't waste any time and went to town the very next day and on his return, he said, "Today the bishop shows a marked preference for soup made out of the liver of an angry burbot." So it was at once decided to find and obtain a burbot, bring it alive to our village and, tying it with a thick, tarred line by its gills, let it swim about in our pond and feed it until the bishop's arrival, when it was to be taken out, put in a wooden trough and have its temper gradually roused to a frenzy by teasing it with birch twigs. When the burbot got really angry and its liver swelled, it was to be killed and made into the delicious soup the bishop liked so much.

In the meantime my father wrote a letter to the bishop on a large sheet of paper, showing, however, little civility in what he wrote, for, alas, such was the character he had acquired while serving in the army. The message he sent to the bishop was brief and written in rather a facetious vein. He welcomed the bishop to our village and reminded him that when he arrived in Peregoody he should not forget that an old comrade of his lived there who, in their days at the seminary, "shared the same execution block and had his hair pulled an equal number of times." And in a postscript my father added that he hoped that the bishop would not "disdain our hospitality" and would come to our house "to partake of a dish of soup from the liver of an angry burbot."

Bless my soul, what dreadful consequences that invitation to dinner had !

CHAPTER SEVEN

IT WAS FATHER MARKEL HIMSELF who volunteered to deliver my father's letter to the bishop's house, for in those days it was not considered polite to write to persons of quality by post and, besides, the priest was anxious to glean something else that might be of use to him and, to be sure, he brought back a great deal of information that was highly instructive. It was quite wonderful how many persons of the bishop's retinue he was able to see in so short a time! He even had an opportunity of treating many of them to a meal and, while plying them with drinks, he kept on asking them questions about the bishop. He finally came to the conclusion that the bishop was a man of the most eminent intellect, but rather rough and ready otherwise, which opinion was indeed fully confirmed by the bishop's reply to my father, scribbled on the back of my father's letter and reading more like a marginal note to a petition than a civil reply to an invitation to dinner. The whole contents of the bishop's note was: "Excellent! Get everything ready. I'll be there."

Following that laconic reply, a most remarkable correspondence ensued between my father and the bishop. For my father, rightly proud of his major's rank, was far from satisfied with this lack of civility on the part of the bishop and, having read the message, he straightway let out a strong Cossack oath and wrote on the letter: "Shan't get anything ready. Don't come." He then sent the letter back without even bothering to seal it up. The bishop, however, was really worthy of his exalted position, if only because of his goodness and prudence. Far from being angry at my father's brusqueness, he, in his turn, sent the letter back with a new message: "Don't be an ass. I said I'd come and come I shall."

On reading this second message from the bishop, my father—

if you please—was deeply moved and, flinging the letter on the table, exclaimed, "Blast and damn him! Hanged if he isn't a fine chap after all!"

So father asked mother to give him a large glass of vodka and, having emptied it, said, "That's to the health of a good friend!" and then he told mother to get ready some damson-cheese and sent an urgent message to Father Markel to set about getting the burbot. This was done in good time. Father Markel brought a fish of an enormous size in a cask. He had obtained the burbot from a Jew with the help of the local sub-district police officer, for the Jew refused to part with the fish because he was expecting the arrival of a thrice-blessed Rabbi, famed alike for his piety and his miracles. As soon as the fish arrived, an order was issued to our maid Sidonia to weave a strong line out of a ewe's fleece, and afterwards my father and Father Markel tied the line to the gills of the burbot and placed it in our pond, where it was free to swim as far as the line, the other end of which was securely fastened to a willow, would stretch. The villagers were warned not to dare even to think of stealing the fish, because it had been sanctified and was "awaiting the bishop." And what, sir, do you think was the reply they gave to that solemn warning? Why, they all replied in one voice, "Keep your damned fish! Who'd think of stealing it?" But they did steal it all the same and when, you ask, did they do it? Why, on the eve of the bishop's announced arrival in our village of Peregoody. Dear me, what a rumpus that caused! The very thought of it makes my flesh creep, I assure you, sir, it does!

Well, you'll soon learn how everything was settled in spite of that difficulty and how closely my own fate was interwoven with it all.

CHAPTER EIGHT

THE AMAZING CIRCUMSTANCE of the theft of the burbot became known in this way : when people went to the pond to drag it out, for the time had come for it to be subjected to corporal punishment, which would provoke it to anger and make its liver to swell, the line to which the fish had been fastened was found to have been cut and no fish was attached to it ; indeed, it was just dangling in the water. No clue was left which might have led to the apprehension of the thieves, for we had many smart lads in our village who were crack thieves where food was concerned and did not fear God Himself, let alone a bishop. Inasmuch, therefore, as precious little time was left for the preparation of the meal, all further investigations into the circumstances of the theft and any search for the villains who were responsible for appropriating for their own table that most delectable of fishes, were given up and a net was instantly thrown into the pond and, as good luck would have it, a fairly large pike was dragged out which, it was suggested to my parents, should be prepared "in the Jewish fashion," that is to say, with saffron and raisins, for, as far as my father could remember, the bishop had been rather partial to such a dish in the days of his youth.

But another unpleasant surprise awaited my father. For after the inspection of the church, the bishop was pounced on by Finagey Ivanovich, another of our squires, who hauled him off to have a meal at his own house. My father disliked Finagey Ivanovich intensely for his impudence, as well he might, for just as the bishop was blessing the congregation, Finagey Ivanovich rushed into the church, wearing a uniform which the devil alone must have supplied him with, and made straight for the altar steps where he caught hold of the bishop's outstretched right arm and proclaimed in a loud voice, as though reading a verse from the Bible, "As the Lord liveth and thy soul liveth, I shall not let thee go!" He bore himself with such insolence and dragged the bishop so forcibly after him that the bishop said to him, "Leave me alone, will you? Where are you dragging me to?" and then he seemed to say something else which apparently sobered Finagey Ivanovich a little. But for all that the bishop did go and have dinner with Finagey Ivanovich, and our own dinner, which, albeit without the burbot, was well prepared, was utterly ignored by him. This made my father so wild that he dispatched a messenger to Finagey Ivanovich's house to ask the bishop what he meant by it. But the bishop merely said, "Tell him to wait."

Having had his meal at Finagey Ivanovich's house, the bishop entered his carriage, which did not, however, stop at our house, but at the house of Alena Yakovlevna, who had also clung to him like a leaf from a bundle of birch-twigs with which people switch themselves in the bath-house. My father dispatched another messenger to Alena Yakovlevna's house to find out what the bishop was doing there, and the messenger came back and said that he was again having dinner. That seemed to my father such rank bad manners that he shouted to the servants, "You are not to let him into my house when he comes, do you hear?" Then he told one of them to fetch him a towel and went to have a bathe in the pond to cool off.

On coming to the pond, my father purposely stationed himself in front of the balcony of Alena Yakovlevna's house, where the bishop and three ladies were just having coffee, and began to strip. When the bishop saw the tall figure of my father, he said to the ladies, "However much you pretend not to see anything, I think I'd better go and put him to shame." So he got up immediately, put on his cowl and drove away in his carriage round the pond, making straight for our house.

From Alena Yakovlevna's balcony, her little girls pointed to the bishop's carriage and shouted to my father, "Quick, sir, dress yourself! The bishop's gone to see you!" But my father took no notice and didn't dream of hurrying himself. Standing up to the neck in water, he followed the bishop's carriage with his eyes and even seemed to grin. On reaching the place where my father was bathing, the bishop stopped the carriage and, alighting from it, walked up to the edge of the pond and shouted to him merrily, "What are you showing your nakedness for? Have you no shame left? Fie upon you, you miserable old sinner!"

"Well," replied my father, "I'm glad to see that you at least have some shame left in you! Where have you been dining?"

Then the bishop asked him in even plainer language, "What are you up to, you old fool?"

"Same to you," answered my father.

The bishop just grinned and, sitting down on a bench, said, "So you're angry with me, you unmannerly wretch! Want me to be civil to boors like you, do you?" And having said that, he belched and, raising his eyes to the red clouds which were gathering round the setting sun, he said in Latin, "*Si circa occidentem rubescunt nubes, serenitatem futuri diei spondent.* You see," he went on, turning to my father, "this is rather important to me, for I've still got to dine with you, as I have promised, and I'm in a hurry because tomorrow I have to sanctify a whole pile of stones. So come out of the water, there's a good fellow, and send them word to get ready that marvellous burbot which you've been bragging about so much!"

Hearing that scathing reference to the burbot, my father just laughed and said that there was no burbot. "While you were thinking out your quotation in good Latin style," he said sarcastically, " the godfearing people here stole the fish in good Russian style."

The March Hare

"Oh, well," said the bishop, "I hope they enjoy it. I've had plenty to eat already and the poor beggars are probably hungry. Come on, sir, let's go to your house and have a talk about the good old days and, as for the food, I don't mind what I eat, for the important thing is not what you eat, but with whom you eat it."

My father felt rather flattered by this remark, but what particularly pleased him was that the bishop was ready to dine again. So he got quickly out of the water and for the rest of the evening the two of them behaved with the utmost cordiality towards each other, my father's amiability being, I am afraid, chiefly due to the fact that the bishop was dining once more, never once refusing any dish placed before him. During dinner the bishop cracked merry jokes with my father, recalling all sorts of agreeable things they had shared together, such as some extraordinarily fine Kiev pasties they had eaten at the Katkov hostelry and also pig's crackling. As the meal drew to its close, my father, perhaps as a result of having applied himself too liberally to the bottle, asked the bishop a somewhat delicate question.

"Why do you recall with such evident relish the innocent pleasures you enjoyed while still in the world, if you yourself have renounced the world and put on that black cowl on your head?"

"Never mind that, my dear fellow," the bishop replied, not in the least cross with my father, "and don't even attempt to find a reason for it. What's the use of talking about something that cannot be helped? I will say this, though: I do not regret having renounced the world, for it is full of vanity and vexation of spirit and is, like ours, far removed from the sacred serenity of a life devoted to the study of philosophy, but in our calling, at any rate, the Spirit of Grace descends much more gently upon the bosom."

"That may be true enough," said my father, "but then you leave no issue after you," and he went on to say that he himself had seen in the Greek monasteries where they had "gerontes," how they, the "gerontes" that is, sometimes beat the monks with a slipper . . .

But here my mother, who was following the conversation with growing uneasiness, said, looking rather shy, "Of course, my lord bishop, everything's just as you say!" And turning to my father, she said, "You'd better leave your preaching alone, dear, for is it not written that they that have wives be as though they had none? Besides," she added, turning to the bishop again, "if the Spirit of Grace does descend upon your bosom, there's nothing anybody can say against it, for I suppose it has to descend both according to law and the Holy Writ. You'd better not listen to my husband, but instead I should be obliged to you, sir, if you'd comfort me about a question of religion which has been greatly worrying me!"

"I expect, dear," said my father, "it's just some silly nonsense!"

"Not at all, dear," replied my mother, "it isn't silly nonsense, but something anybody might be glad to know, for it might happen anywhere."

She then told the bishop what had been worrying her. It seemed that when the dust was being swept from the ceilings and particularly from the corners before Easter, the icon of the Blessed Saviour had fallen off the wall of our parlour and that ever since my mother had been greatly worried, afraid lest some calamity should befall our house, and she wanted to know what it really signified and what she was to think of it.

The bishop heard her out patiently and, after a moment's reflection, said, starting "from the end":

"I shall reply to your query by dealing first with your last question, for we find some mention of it in history books : the

167

belief that the fall of an icon signifies some impending calamity
comes to us from Rome and from the pagan days of Rome at
that, where it became widely held ever after the falling down
of the *lares* during a sacrificial offering shortly before Nero's
death. It is, as you see, a pagan superstition really, and it is not
meet that Christians should pay any heed to it. As for the cause
of the icon's fall, I should advise you to examine at least once a
year the cords upon which your pictures and icons are hung and
do not forget to tell your maids not to apply the brush too
vigorously to them when dusting the rooms. If you do that, no
icons will fall off the walls in your house. Tell this to everybody,
pray."

But this explanation of the bishop threw my mother into
an even greater perplexity, for she was a woman of quite
exceptional piety and what she desired most was that her superstitions should be considered by everybody as the most sacred of
truths. I'm afraid, sir, it is usual for women, whatever their
station in life, to regard their foolish beliefs as articles of faith.
The bishop, of course, knew how hopeless it was to argue with
them and for that reason he suddenly changed the subject and,
from the superstitions of ancient Rome, he plunged straight
into a discussion of household matters and asked, "Do you
know how to pickle tomatoes for the winter?" Having discussed this matter thoroughly, he fixed his gaze upon me and
his attention, apart from throwing me into terrible confusion
at the time, had a most important bearing on the whole of my
subsequent life.

I'm telling you all that because but for the aforementioned
accident with the icon, there would have been no talk about it,
and the unexpected events which were presently to engulf me
would never have happened.

CHAPTER NINE

BEING BY NATURE not only a theologian, but also a realist, the bishop was not fond of contemplation and he did not like people to lose themselves in the realms of abstract thought. He therefore readily turned aside from a discussion of a philosophic nature to one dealing with everyday necessities. So it happened here : the fact that my father was not exactly well off did not escape his well-disposed notice.

"Well, my dear colleague," he said, "I hope you don't mind my saying so, but it certainly strikes me that you're not exactly a millionaire !"

"How the deuce do you expect me to be a millionaire?" asked my father. "On my hard-earned pennies I can't even afford to buy a new psalter every year."

"That's what I thought and I suppose it's not only a question of a psalter, either. I expect you find it jolly hard to educate your children, don't you?"

In reply, my father remarked that, fortunately, he did not have many children, but only one son.

"But your only son, too, must be trained for some career, mustn't he? He has to be educated, hasn't he?"

When told that I had already finished my schooling with our church-beadle, the bishop turned to me and asked me to tell him what were the objects placed in the Tabernacle. I replied that they were the Tables of the Law, Abraham's staff and a basinful of thick gruel made out of mannah.

The bishop laughed and said, "You needn't be so shy, my boy, for you know more than the headmistress of our girls' boarding school," and he told us that when he had asked the young ladies of the boarding school which of the forty-two articles of the Orthodox Church began with a "T," not one of them could answer that question and the headmistress said, "They know the articles of the Creed only in their proper order."

Everybody laughed again and mother said, "I'm sure I don't know anything about tea, either."

When the bishop learnt that I had a pleasant singing voice, he asked me to sing something for him, either a hymn or a song, and I sang rather a stupid song, the words of which were :

> I curse and I swear, I swear and I curse,
> O, dear bishop, the devil take thee,
> O, dear bishop, won't you give me
> A little money for my purse?

My parents were terribly embarrassed that I should have sung that particular song, but for my part, I sang it because I had learnt it from my teacher, the church beadle. The bishop knew nothing about that and he laughed even more merrily and, after praising my voice, said, "Don't blame the child. I most definitely like the cast of his countenance and, bless my soul, if I haven't also grown fond of him because of his innocence ! Now you'd better tell me what kind of a career you have in mind for him."

"There's no hurry about that," said my father. "Let him grow up a bit and then I shall present my humble respects to Dmitry Afanassyevich and ask him for a letter of recommendation to admit the lad into the customs-service : as a customs officer it shouldn't take him long to get rich."

"God forbid !" the bishop replied. "Can't you think of anything better for your son than making him into an apprehender of smugglers? Read what's written in the Book of Enoch on this subject : 'These guards are terrible to behold and they stand like unto monsters : the fire is extinguished in their eyes and their teeth are bared.' Is it that kind of glory you wish for your son? No, my dear fellow, this won't do, and to prove to you that I'm not talking in vain, I'm going to repeat to you what

I've already said : I like the cast of his countenance and I should be glad to take this boy of yours for a choir-boy in my Cathedral choir. Can you wish for anything better for him ?"

The bishop further promised to provide me with food, clothes and boots, and to have me coached in all the subjects in accordance with a specially abridged curriculum "like a prince," for it seemed he had a special tutor who went through this shortened course of studies with all his choir-boys. Mother did not quite grasp it, but my father did and when he had explained it to her, she liked it very much, but what she liked most was that the bishop promised that I should wear an alb, which meant that I should take part in all the religious services. This seemed to have wrought so wonderfully upon my mother's imagination that she burst into tears of happiness, for she already saw me dressed in a brocaded alb and no doubt imagined me to be only a small degree removed from the blessed angels and as near as I could possibly get to heaven, whence I should be able to assist my family by tossing them down something every now and then.

So while my father was still revolving in his mind the bishop's offer, my mother was the first to agree to let me follow the sacred calling. My father, however, could not make up his mind even then.

"Believe me, my dear fellow," the bishop said to him, "a career in the church is the best possible thing for a man, and indeed there are no more fortunate men than those who occupy ecclesiastical offices, for whether the people are afflicted or whether they rejoice, the clergy still manage to get something from them. Be wise, my friend, and do not throw away such a golden opportunity for your son, for Russia is a country which will remain like that for a long time to come."

But my father still insisted on having his own way. "And where" he asked, "are we to get new generations of guards from?"

"What do you care?" answered the bishop. "It isn't your business is it?" And he again quoted from the Book of Enoch: "'He saw guards standing there, and they were terrible to behold, and the fire was extinguished in their eyes and their teeth were bared.' Just compare it with the life of the clergy," he went on, "who lack nothing of bodily comforts! I promise you that I shall myself keep a fatherly eye on your son's career and shall personally guide him from one honour to another and bestow upon him any office you care to suggest. I'll give him the office of the Bearer of the Holy Book or the Candle, and I shall appoint him Holder of the Bishop's Staff, and he'll walk in procession in the Cathedral, carrying the lighted candle and spreading the light of faith among the entire congregation! Isn't that a far better career for your boy than a customs officer or a frontier guard?"

Well, here my father could hold out no longer and my mother raised her hands aloft and exclaimed, "O Lord, O Lord, praised be Thy name, for I'm sure I don't deserve it and I wonder if I shall live long enough to see it. Pray, my lord bishop, do not say another word about it, for I can feel already that I am chosen and exalted above all other mothers. Take my son! I want it to be as you said: let him stand in front of everybody else in church and spread in broad daylight the light of the candle and let him, please, also hold the book you read from. You wouldn't mind that, would you, sir?"

The bishop smiled and said, "Of course not!" and my mother, who looked very pleased, went on, "I know that everything is possible in this world and I shall go now and collect his linen so that, God willing, he could leave with you at once." Then she bent over my father and, smoothing the mop of hair that hung over his forehead, said, "Please, dear, do not interfere any more!"

"Very well," said my father.

172

So she at once set about to prepare everything for my journey and ran off to pack my clothes, while my father shouted after her, "See the great vanity of women! Never thought of asking the lad, have you? For all we know he might have preferred to be a clerk at a court, for then one day, God willing, he might even have become a sub-district police officer!"

The job of sub-district police officer was held in great esteem by my father, because, you see, a sub-district police officer has the right to order a flogging and he rides about with a sabre dangling at his side and you could not tell him from an army officer.

"Well, as to that," said the bishop, "I assure you that any time your son shows a preference for a secular post, I could easily accommodate him. I have only to ask the Vice-Governor of the province and he'll be registered as a clerk and later on he can easily become a sub-district police officer. Why, if it comes to that, he can even become a frontier guard and beget a whole generation of frontier guards, but I still say that as a police officer he'd be much more useful than as a frontier guard, for a sub-district police officer merely tries to catch murderers and horse-thieves, and that's something that has to be done."

His doubts now set at rest, my father, who never expected the bishop to be as generous to him as that, did not know what to say in reply, and instead of expressing his thanks in words, he fell upon the bishop's neck, while the bishop himself stretched forth his consecrated arms and so the two of them embraced and their happy tears commingled, while I, unhappy wretch, about whose future they had come to so amicable an understanding, stole quietly out of the room and, running into the hall, hid myself in a dark corner and, embracing my favourite dog Gorilka, kissed him on the muzzle and shed bitter tears.

CHAPTER TEN

BUT, AS THEY SAY, Moscow does not believe in tears, and neither did I help myself by weeping, for presently I was told to ask my parents for their blessing and left for our town with the bishop himself, or rather not with the bishop, but with his staff-bearer, who sat in a little two-wheeled cart which was attached to the bishop's carriage.

So it came about that while the burbot either got away and escaped or was stolen by our wicked neighbours, I was caught on the line instead of it. Nor do I believe that there was any talk between the bishop and my father about Father Markel and his usurious transactions, but for me the happy and carefree days of my childhood came to an end and a new life began in the bishop's house. It was there that I was brought up and educated in accordance with the abridged method, in the manner of a prince, and took part in the most colourful religious ceremonies, occupying the most conspicuous place in them. It is here that a natural break occurs in my life, for hitherto I had grown up in the bosom of my family, while now began my mental and moral development, a development that, as it were, forms the second part of the story of my life, which was afterwards to enter upon a third phase.

CHAPTER ELEVEN

FROM THE VERY OUTSET the bishop proved himself to be a very simple and kindly person. He remained the same all through the time I spent in his household and deserved every bit of the affection he got in return. It is true that some people did not seem to find in him that devotion to religion which they expected to find in a bishop, but he made up amply for it by his great love of peace and his deep understanding of farming. Indeed, he was so experienced in, and entered so deeply into, all the details of a countryman's life that whenever people came to him with some request or other, he could not help discussing the produce of their fields or the condition of their flocks and herds, and much of the advice he gave was quite remarkable. Thus, for instance, he'd advise a farmer about the best way of finding out the thickness of fat on a pig by piercing its back with an awl, which made the pig scream only a little ; or, on another occasion, he'd tell some villagers, whose domestic fowl had been stolen, about the wonderfully cunning methods employed by gypsies to keep the birds silent when stealing geese, adding the warning that, generally speaking, it was best to exercise great care when gypsies were about. He knew many more things and he was, of course, famed for his knowledge of the many vain and false pagan superstitions spread about and even invented by all sorts of boorish persons. So that when a cow, which had been bought to provide him with milk for his tea, began to bellow at the top of her voice, and the steward and those with him said that the cow would have to be exchanged for another because the colour of her coat did not match the colour of the bishop's cattleyard, the bishop just smiled and said at first in Latin, "*Tu deorum hominumque tyranne, Amore!*" that is to say, "O, what a tyrant of gods and men thou art, Cupid!" and then he went on to upbraid the steward in Russian, saying, "Aren't you ashamed to believe in such nonsense, or don't you whose duty it is to dissipate darkness in people's minds understand that when a cow moos loudly it is most likely because she's dreaming of a meeting with a bull?"

To prove that he was right, the bishop told them to send the cow to the deacon who kept a pedigree bull, and when the cow came back entirely satisfied with life, it was seen that the bishop was much more far-sighted than all the superstitious folk. It could indeed hardly be otherwise, for he was a man of immense erudition and great mother wit, and in many things he even agreed with the philosopher Skovoroda, and he usually met all suggestions about improvements in his diocese with the words : "What boots it to be constantly turning this way and that, when what we have to do is to drive a road through the mountains of unbelief and across the treacherous swamps of slavish superstition?" which, as you will remember, is a saying of the never-to-be-forgotten Grigory Skovoroda.

The bishop saw it all so clearly that he could not help laughing at the people who travelled abroad and came back as wise as they were before they left, "mocking with their eyes, talking big with their mouths and showing off like monkeys, while being as fickle as the moon and as fidgety as Satan himself. He who is blind in his own house will never see anything when he goes a-visiting."

The bishop preferred to stay at home in his own small monastery, which in no way limited his thorough understanding of men and affairs. He knew the works of Plato, Plautus, Seneca, Terence and many other ancient philosophers and poets and, goodness me, what else didn't he know and read! Indeed, I shouldn't be a bit surprised if it weren't his intention to teach me, but, alas, he just could not manage it because he was always so busy. It is gospel truth I'm telling you, sir! You may not believe me, but it is true all the same : he just could not manage it! It was my good fortune that, as he had said, he had taken a liking to the cast of my countenance and he verily took pity on me like a father and he would not permit the precentor to hit me on the head with his tuning fork. He treated me like the son of his best friend, being fonder of me than of any of the other choir-boys, and, as I was a very affectionate boy and sang most sweetly, it soon came about without any effort on my part, that I became a constant visitor to the Vice-Governor's house and a special favourite of the wife and daughter of that State dignitary and was employed by them in a certain business of which I shall tell you presently.

As regards acquisition of knowledge, that, I'm afraid, was something that none of our choir-boys particularly distinguished himself for. You could hardly expect anything else, for we, the choir-boys, were expected to acquire all that learning in the shortest possible time and that, too, from one person only, namely, our master, who for some reason was known as "inspector." He, too, was in a way a most remarkable individual and at first his name was Eugraph Semyonovich Ovyechkin, but afterwards he saw fit to change his surname because he had the misfortune of being suspected of having hastened the demise of his most excellent wife, after which he was forbidden to celebrate mass and he had voluntarily to resign his priestly office and take up a secular calling. It was then that he had made himself a waistcoat of an enormous size with leather pockets which he always kept well replenished with snuff. He never used a snuff-box, but helped himself to the snuff with all his fingers straight from those pockets and so conveyed it to his nose ; for the clerks in government offices were supposed to take snuff that way, and our master was very fond of imitating them, wishing to convey the impression that he was really one of them, and in that way make sure that people

were afraid of him, suspecting him of being a Government
informer.

That the bishop should have employed a man like that as
instructor of his choir-boys was a thing, mark you, for which
he could hardly be blamed, for was not Regulus as big a rascal
as our master and were not the Romans mortally afraid of
Regulus, who combined great piety with a talent for playing
the informer? Eugraph Semyonovich was highly successful
with his denunciations even while he was a real school inspector, when he became also known far and wide as a man
who did not believe in sparing the rod. He was, moreover,
thoroughly versed in the ways in which Government business
was transacted and that was why the bishop, who needed such
a man to advise him on the conduct of official business, valued
him so greatly and appointed him inspector for the education
of his choir-boys. But to make sure that his former wickedness
was entirely erased from the memory of men, Eugraph
Semyonovich decided to change his surname, and instead of
being known as Ovyechkin, an appellation that bore so close a
resemblance to the Russian word for sheep, he began to be
known as Vyekovyechkin, which has a much more ecclesia-
astical connotation, putting one in mind of the Russian word
for eternity. Thus all his acts of violence were discreetly covered
up by the change of his former name, whose verbal association
with the meek sheep did little justice to this veritable wolf in
sheep's clothing.

But I suppose you must be wanting to hear what it was he
taught us. That, indeed, is quite a story by itself. Vyekovyechkin must have won his reputation as a theologian
because he knew by rote all the holy days and the hymns to be
sung on each of them. For our instruction he had special note-
books, out of which he extracted all the knowledge with which
our youthful minds were to be stuffed. So, for instance, after

the benediction, to make sure that our faith would remain unshakable for the rest of our days, he made us learn by heart, the following injunction : "Doubt not your faith, O man, for there is not one, nor ten, nor one hundred witnesses of the faith, but countless multitudes of people are witnesses thereof." So, you see, there can be no question here of any intellectual discussion or any bandying about of words or opinions, but everything, so to speak, is based on accounts of eye-witnesses. That statement was so cleverly supported that no one could even attempt to cast doubts upon it. "For the first witnesses are the prophets who themselves believed and who handed down their faith to us." Well, sir, can you think of anyone who would have the courage to say a word against such witnesses? Furthermore : "The second witnesses are the apostles : they sat at the same table with our Lord and wrote about Him." Just try to refute that, if you please ! And so he went on and on, piling up evidence right up to the Councils of the World Church and the Fathers of the Church and the Abbot Dorotheus, and he gave us the number of the participants of all those councils. "At one of them alone there were present four hundred and eighteen saints . . ." How do you like that? And how many real saints were there altogether? Well, I bet if you ask any of our present academicians, "How many?" not one of them, not even the inspector himself, would give you a straight answer, and if he did, it would be sure to be the wrong one. But our Vyekovyechkin knew it all exactly, month by month ! Yes, indeed, he knew the correct number of saints for each month by heart and he made us learn it so well that even if an arch-bishop were to ask me now I could tell him that "in September there are 1,100 saints, in October 2,534, in November as many as 6,500, and in December even more, namely, 14,400, while in January the number reaches the truly amazing figure of 70,000. Now, in February, the number of saints falls to just 1,072, in

March there is a further drop to 535, while in June there are only 130 saints." But, taken as a whole, just think of it, sir, how convincing it all is and what, pray, is one to say against so countless a multitude of such witnesses! Then, in addition to these proofs based on the evidence of eye-witnesses, there were the most exact statements concerning the day and the hour when a certain Biblical event had taken place and once again, "Humble thyself, O man, and acknowledge that thou are naught."

I have met many people who express their amazement that our historian Karamzin should have dug up and copied out so many historical data, though goodness only knows whether what he tells you is true or not; but in the note-books of our inspector Vyekovyechkin it was plainly stated that the Holy Virgin was born in the summer of the year 5,486 and that the Annunciation took place in the summer of 5,500 on a Sunday at ten o'clock in the morning when she was twelve years and seven months old. Our Lord was born in the summer of the year 5,550, at seven o'clock in the evening. And so everything else to the minutest detail. And indeed as soon as he began to adduce evidence, he'd remember not only these, but also much less important facts : "Remember, dearly beloved, this and that, remember Moses, who chained himself as if he were a mute beast of the field, remember Athanasius whose body became paralysed like unto dead wood from the feet to the waist, remember Dmitry who tasted nothing but water, and Alexander who fed upon wool, or Simon from whom all reptiles ran away . . ." In short, he knew absolutely everything that had happened on earth and he could even gaze heavenward and tell the kind of passion a man was possessed of and whence it came and which man wrestled with it : "Men of little faith and those who doubt wrestle with religion and they are in the clutches of the devil of doubt ; men who fight against love and are given to anger and malice are in the power of the devil of anger ; and those who fight against mercy are at the mercy of the devil of cruelty ; and those who are against virginity and purity are in the hands of the devil of lechery." And so on, "in whomsoever whatsoever devil dwelleth, where he spendeth his time and how he arouseth passion," and "how certain spirits enter the body of a man without his knowledge and how others both enter and leave the body of a man without his knowledge," and "what man must do to thwart them."

All these subjects we had mastered and, indeed, excelled in ; but, in addition, the bishop himself would sometimes call me to his room and very often taught me Latin and I, well, I proved to be such an intelligent lad that we not only translated Cornelius Nepos together, but he would often read to me some of his own translations of Ovid ! Oh, if you had only heard that, you would have realised that you were not dealing with an Ovyechkin and you would have been amazed what real poetry could do to a man ! Take, especially, that passage about the herds : "What have the peaceful herds, born for man's sustenance, done to deserve death ? O ye, who give us sweet nectar, ye who clothe us with your wool, ye who are of greater use to us when alive than when dead, what have you done to deserve such base ingratitude from man ? What has the ox done (Mark this passage about the ox, sir. How full of tenderness it is !), what has the ox done, an animal of so trustful a nature, born withal to bear its yoke so meekly (Oh, how true, how true !), an animal which knows neither deceit nor cunning ? Truly, that man is bereft of all gratitude and unworthy of enjoying the fruits of his labours who, having taken off the yoke from the neck of the steer, decides to slaughter him . . . who with his knife inflicts a grievous wound upon a neck already sore from the hard work of bringing new life to the cruel soil . . . (Don't mind my tears, sir !) Whence doth man obtain the desire for this forbidden food ? O mortals, how dare you to feed upon your friend the ox ? Desist, I pray you, flee from the bloody feasts at which you devour those who feed you ! . . ."

Having concluded this quotation from Ovid, Onopry Opanassovich Peregood spent two minutes in sighing piteously at the thought of the cruel fate that dogs the steps of the ox, and then he added that whenever the bishop used to read to him that passage from Ovid in those far-away days of his youth, he could not eat any meat for the next few days, except perhaps the meat in sausages in which, of course, there was nothing to remind him of the ox, but afterwards everybody used to laugh at his pagan fancies, and Ovid's influence "left him by and by" and he would once more revert to his routine of daily life and study.

The most noteworthy thing about my education (Onopry Opanassovich went on, feeling much relieved by his tears) was not that I was taught by Vyekovyechkin according to the abridged method and that all the teaching was done from his note-books, but that we were never examined, for we had no time for preparation. I have told you already how we were taught religion and church history and, as for secular history, it was taught in an even more amazingly abbreviated form. So, for instance, I have frequently noticed that in quite a large number of books the French Revolution is mentioned more than once, several pages being devoted to the subject, but with us the whole thing was compressed into a few lines so that I can still remember the whole passage by heart : "This dreadful and most shameful event, worthy of eternal damnation, is hardly worth mentioning, except perhaps that it was brought about as a result of the senseless and pernicious demands for liberty and equality and that it ended in the utter destruction of everything that was good and meritorious in France and in the death of the French king on the scaffold, after which France was declared a republic ; Paris was subsequently taken and restored to the French only because of the generosity of the victorious nations. Since then, France has become a country of no importance."

However, although this was summarised in a few words, it did, you know, all the same, give us some idea that it was something disgraceful and when later on, during my visits to the Vice-Governor's house I heard about our poet Zhukovsky's proposals for the execution of felons, I loved to listen to the stories of what those desperate villains of Frenchmen had done during their revolution.

You see, sir, they gathered together a band of cut-throats and began to sing their *Marseillaise* and—just imagine it, sir!—marched off to the sound of those dreadful words, "*Allons enfants de la patrië,*" and demolished with their own hands that most terrible fortress, the Bastille ! What can you do with a people like that ? Then off they went to slaughter the loyal servants of the King of France, having first released all the felons by taking off their heavy chains which alone prevented them from committing the most horrible crimes !

Vyekovyechkin always referred to the Frenchmen as "those damned Frenchies," but the bishop was less severe on them, agreeing with our playwright Fonvisin that "the French are a nation of brutes and are easily induced to do the most unspeakable things."

I'm afraid, sir, that I've been anticipating a little in mentioning capital punishment according to Zhukovsky's ideas, for which the time has not come yet. I shall go back to that later. At present, let me continue from where I left off and let me tell you everything in the order in which it took place.

CHAPTER TWELVE

BARELY SIX MONTHS HAD PASSED since they tore me from my mother's arms and I knew already the order of the church services in their smallest detail, and I managed everything so well that I did not even have to ask the senior deacon to instruct me in my duties as he did the other boys. I accomplished it all simply by learning by heart the thirty-nine ways of bowing before a bishop during divine service and I knew when to bow once or three times as well as I knew the Lord's Prayer. It was not surprising therefore that I was soon deemed worthy of wearing an alb. I was taught how to walk in it with my eyes fixed humbly on the ground and my hands, too, crossed with proper humility and the cast of my countenance decidedly grief-stricken.

Henceforth I embarked upon my religious career about which I shall now relate everything in order. To begin with, I was the one chosen to stand in front of the choir and sing the verse welcoming the bishop on his entry into the church, but later, when I lost my voice owing to a certain unhappy accident, I became the bishop's staff-bearer. How I lost my voice is something that is closely connected with Zhukovsky's proposals for carrying out executions and I shall tell you about it in its proper place, but about my job as the bishop's staff-bearer I shall tell you now. The chief duty of that office consisted in putting down a small, circular cloth with the image of an eagle under the knees of the bishop every time he knelt during divine service and, of course, removing it from under the bishop's knees when no longer required. This, sir, is one of the most tedious jobs imaginable, but it is also one that demands the closest possible attention, for if you don't take care, you can easily make a slip and spoil the whole business. It was also part of my duties to carry the bishop's staff surmounted by the image of a cherub, hold up the Bible before the bishop and carry the candles, and in the performance of all these multifarious duties I again excelled everybody else. No one, for instance, could lay out the sacred garments on the salver better than I, for they have to be placed in the right order, such as the long robe first, the cassock on the robe, the cowl on the cassock and, finally, the beads on the cowl, while on another salver the bishop's mitre has to be placed and, on either side of it, the small icon the bishop wears round his neck and the cross, and on top of the mitre all the bishop's decorations and stars and, behind it, the comb "for my lord bishop's beard."

Yes, indeed! Young as I was, I had already obtained as thorough a knowledge of all the decorations as any true-born prince and I had quite an extraordinarily fine grasp of the differences between one decoration and another, how, for instance, one enjoyed a certain preference over another in the way of honour, and which, consequently, had to be placed before which. The decoration which was worn lowest I put on top of the salver, the one which had to be put on afterwards being underneath it. You may think, sir, that no great knowledge is required for that sort of thing, but all the same I learnt it all very thoroughly and, in case of any mishap, I always had on me, as indeed it is laid down in the primer on this subject, needles and pieces of silk material as well as threads, pins, scissors and cords ; for, the bishop's robing procedure being so complicated, all that might be required suddenly. The bishop, of course, took note of the accurate way in which I performed my duties and he tried several times to persuade me either to enter the angelic order or to get married and become a priest by joining "the white priesthood," but I—mark that well, sir— I did not want to do either and that for a reason that I'm sorry to say has very little to commend it. My reluctance to take holy orders was, in fact, due to a most unusual event in my life which I'm rather ashamed to mention. For, imagine, sir, I had fellen in love with two girls at once, one of whom was the Vice-Governor's daughter! Just like in a story by Gogol!...

I dare say you must be wanting to know how it all happened and how I dared even to think of such a thing. Well, it all started because the Vice-Governor's wife was a lady of the most tender feelings that one would expect of a lady who had finished a boarding school for gentlewomen with the highest mark of distinction, having been awarded the much-coveted diploma adorned with the Empress's monogram, which entitled her to the rank of lady-in-waiting to her Majesty. She also had a talk once with the poet Zhukovsky, who was exceedingly kind to her and who did his best to console her for the tragic end of her brother's career. The poet succeeded in comforting her and later she got very fond of reading his works and particularly his Proposals for the Execution of Orthodox Christians. Zhukovsky pleaded that Orthodox Christians should be put to death in a way that would be shorn of the coarseness that attended public executions and would be morally uplifting to everybody, while being easy on the condemned persons themselves and beneficial to their souls. Zhukovsky's dearest wish was that executions in Russia should not be carried out as they were carried out in foreign countries. There should be no brutality, no unnecessary humiliation. An execution should be "a means of redemption instituted by God Himself." And, dear me, how charmingly he puts it all! The "mystery" was to be enacted at a special church which was to be built in a special way behind a high wall. The executions, which were to take place inside that church to the accompaniment of the most melodious singing, should be witnessed only by a select band of people, while the common people were to kneel round the high wall and listen to the singing of the choir and, as soon as the singing stopped, they were all to go home in the knowledge that "the mystery had been consummated."

The Vice-Governor's wife was very anxious to see such a church surrounded by a high wall built in our town and kept ready for the performance of the "mystery." She even began to collect funds for the erection of such a church, but she was too impatient to wait for the money to be collected and she started holding "rehearsals" of "the mystery" in her own rooms. At these rehearsals her fourteen-year-old daughter hovered over the condemned man dressed up as an angel while I, covered by her tunic, sung hymns composed for the occasion by his reverence, my tutor Vyekovyechkin. It was generally thought that I had strained my voice while singing those hymns, but the real reason was quite different. What happened was that I had fallen in love at the same time with the angel and the condemned felon, represented, by special command of her mistress, by a very young and pretty parlour-maid, a girl with hair that waved naturally and with a pair of eyes that blazed like the devil's own ... It was she who in truth was more than anybody responsible for the loss of my voice, for, first of all, I learnt to embrace her and press her to my heart and later I used to wait a long time outside the gates for her to be sent for biscuits ... How foolish one is when one's young! One sings with the voice of an angel and falls in love with a devil! But, thank God, everything turned out well in the end, for at the very time when we were rehearsing the "mystery" of execution, my father died and my mother, who by that time had probably had her fill of joy at seeing me at divine services, suddenly and quite unaccountably changed her mind and began saying to me, "Haven't you had enough of playing deacon? I've seen everything now, how you walk in procession with downcast eyes and with a grief-stricken cast of countenance. I think we've done our bit and the Lord ought to be satisfied with our contri-

bution. You'd better come home now and be a comfort to me
in my old age.''

The bishop, as he had promised, asked the Vice-Governor to
do something for me, and the Vice-Governor, who was contemplating starting divorce proceedings against the authoress
of the rehearsals of executions, immediately registered me as a
Government clerk and after a few days summoned me to his
office and told me to go and tell the bishop that I had been
appointed sub-district police officer at—where do you think?—
my native village of Peregoody! As our village was at that time
suffering from an epidemic of horse-stealing, the Vice-
Governor warned me that he depended entirely on me to put
down the mischief and get rid of the horse-thieves.

Well, so there I was entrusted with a task about which I knew
nothing, having been trained only in spreading the little eagle-
embroidered cloth for the bishop to kneel on.

Hearing of my new appointment and the trust reposed in me,
I was about to refuse it, but knowing the wonderfully practical
mind of the bishop, I first went to see him. Falling down on my
knees before him, I told him everything and asked for his
advice.

"First of all," said the bishop, "get up, my son, for you are
no longer within my jurisdiction. Now," he went on as I stood
up, "this is what I'd advise you to do: never refuse the offer of
a good job just because you don't think you're fit for it, but
accept everything you are offered, for you ought to know that
other people, too, accept offices for which they are not suited
either by education or ability. To be quite frank with you, my
boy, even bishops, although, as a rule, we at first refuse the
offer of a bishopric, do so merely to uphold an old custom, for
afterwards we accept and say naught against it. It is thus that
we show our obedience. As for the question how you are to
proceed in your new job, why worry about it? Let's call in

Vyekovyechkin and he, good man, will tell you everything you want to know."

When Vyekovyechkin came and heard what my trouble was, he at first refused to do anything, but after being given a rouble by the bishop, he at once put all his five fingers into one of the leather pockets of his waistcoat and, producing a handful of snuff, he immediately conveyed it to that terrifying nose of his and then delivered himself as follows :

"If you treat criminals according to the civil laws, you'll only make a fool of yourself, for criminals are not citizens, but enemies of every law-abiding citizen in the country, for it is they who have declared war on society ! . . . You must and you can prevail against them only by the application of the spiritual laws."

"Are you sure you've understood it ?" the bishop asked, turning to me.

"No, sir," I replied, "I haven't understood anything, for, to tell you the truth, having been taught with the other choir-boys according to the abridged method, I haven't learnt anything at all."

"What are you complaining about, you idiot ?" Vye-kovyechkin said to me. "Are you the only one to be educated like that ? Besides, it's of no consequence, for no one has ever learnt anything according to the easy way. However, many people educated in this fashion get on very well in life. You've been taught the easy way, well then, learn to judge things the easy way, too. Our people know nothing of human justice and the thing they esteem above everything else in the world is the word of God. Very well, then, keep that in mind !" And having said this, his reverence went off to his room and after a short time he returned with a little book published by the Holy Synod and bearing the title : *Rules to be Observed for the Revelation of Truth in cases of Litigation between Two People.*

"Take this book," his reverence said to me, "for in it you'll find all the rules laid down by God for every occasion you may need and, by applying them, you will rid your village of horse-thieves, and I hope you will remember me on holy days."

I took the little book from Vyekovyechkin, and receiving at the same time the bishop's blessing and fortified by it, I went to the Jewish tailor and ordered my uniform and a hat with a cockade and then I left for Peregoody, having made up my mind to accomplish two things : to reveal the truth and to comfort my dear mother, who, however, soon after my taking over the post of police officer, followed my father to the place where there is neither sorrow nor sighing, but life everlasting, each being rewarded according to his own deserts. So, as you see, I, poor orphan that I was, had now been left alone on this earthly planet and, moreover, one against a whole multitude of the fiercest and most fearless malefactors and horse-thieves, of whom I had to rid our district according to the "Rules for the Revelation of Truth."

Imagine my position!

CHAPTER THIRTEEN

HOWEVER, AS THE HOLY SCRIPTURES SAY, "God was with me," for although I had taken over my post quite unprepared for it by my education, I firmly resolved to devote myself wholly to the service of the law-abiding citizens exposed to the never-ceasing machinations of one sort of malefactor or another. Very soon I was as good at my job as anyone else and, indeed, the common people worshipped me and many even bragged about me. Yes, sir! The first thing I did, of course, was to sit down at the table with a lighted candle and go over the *Rules for the Revelation of Truth* line by line until I knew them inside out ; for, as you have no doubt gathered already, I had great faith in the bishop's practical mind and Vyekovyechkin's all-conquering impudence. Besides, I had no other source to consult about questions of law than these "Rules." In the end I got to know the *Rules for the Revelation of Truth* as thoroughly as I had earlier got to know the order of genuflections and the way of putting down the embroidered cloth under the bishop's feet. Everything, you see, is really simple, not at all the same thing as Cicero or any other Roman author, and why indeed should we toil and moil over those pagan Romans?

What I liked most about the "Rules" was their utter reliance upon the efficacy of the spiritual approach to the problem of larceny. Thus, in case of "the loss of any object" the "Rules" laid it down that the authorities should put the fear of God into the suspect and expose his guilt in a subtle manner so as to leave him in no doubt as to God's attitude towards the act of appropriating property belonging to other people. The "Rules" indeed give the most precise directions about the way of dealing with such a situation. "The delinquent," they state, "should be fetched and put against the lintel of the door and then you should get up and, after shedding a tear about his wicked and unrepentant spirit, read aloud the following prayers : "Heavenly Father," "Thrice Holy," "The Lord's Prayer," and "O Lord, have mercy upon me," and in the last prayer repeat several times with feelings such passages as "I beseech Thee, O Lord, teach them the iniquity of their ways and may the wicked be converted," or "O Lord, O Lord of my salvation !"

Oh, what fine medicine this is for the soul ! While reciting these marvellous prayers, I used to lower my voice for greater effect and, then, coming to a particularly telling word, I'd raise my voice and so enunciate it that it seemed to be coming straight from my heart, so that—believe it or not—some rogue would listen and listen to me until, poor chap, he'd suddenly burst into tears and lift up his voice in most piteous lamentations, or if he happened to be made of sterner stuff, I'd watch him growing weaker and weaker until, completely exhausted, he'd not know what to do and would just say in a hoarse whisper, "I've had enough of it ! Finish it for God's sake !" But seeing the state of mind he was in, I would not pay any heed to his words and, raising my voice, I'd intone still more fervently, "Hearken unto my voice, O Lord, and spread out Thy protecting arm over my office !" (I was of course referring to my job of sub-district police officer, a fact which the poor fellow realised very well !) And I'd follow that up by another prayer, namely, "Thou art a God that condemneth all evil-doing . . . and Thou destroyest all who tell lies . . ." Here again I'd repeat the same words three times : "Destroy them who tell lies, destroy them, destroy them, destroy them !" and I'd go on, "May the thought of the grave open their mouths . . . Judge them, O Lord, and spew them out . . . I call upon Thee, O Lord, for I know Thou wilt not forsake me, and may my flesh flourish !" (Ever since I was a boy, my flesh has flourished exceedingly.) Then I'd turn to the malefactor and, looking sternly at him, say once more : "May my flesh flourish and may the wicked perish!" Well, any man, however stouthearted a felon he might be, would get frightened by such a mode of address and, trembling with fear, be ready to say, "Guilty, sir." Having got that confession of guilt out of him, I'd sit down at my table and, picking up a goose quill, begin to clean it and then to sharpen it and then to press it against a bit of paper to see whether it had been properly nibbed. I used to do it with great deliberation and afterwards I'd begin to write very slowly and, as my hand fashioned the letters, my lips would utter each word aloud. I'd begin by saying, "Let's try this pen and ink . . . Let's see what is the nature of the power that resides in it : 'Pen writeth as fly breatheth.' Now then," I'd say, turning to the prisoner, "what's your name?" and I'd write his name down and then say, "Listen to me, you poor wretch, as the Holy Writ teaches and commands us, confess whether or not you have possessed yourself of a horse or a bull which does not belong to you, or whether you've carried off some hay and how many stacks? And if you've been unjustly slandered, tell me so on your oath, saying 'I swear by Almighty God that I've not driven away any horse or bull or anything that does not belong to me.' Remember, though, tell the whole truth and nothing but the truth and do not try to prevaricate or to lie, for there are invisible angels in this room and they will take down your words and great will be the torment you will endure on account of them during the Second Coming and the Last Judgment. Why, my good man, should you dare to tell a lie, you will condemn your soul to eternal perdition! Tremble, you wretch, tremble!" Well, here the poor fellow would start shaking in every limb and I'd just add fuel to the flames and say, "Yes, the earth will swallow you up as it did Dathan and Abiram, and may you be stricken with leprosy like Uzziah, and may you meet the same fate as Judas!" You should have seen how terrified they were of being strangled like Judas! Uzziah's leprosy, I'm sorry to say, did not always produce any effect on them, for in truth they were terribly ignorant and did not even know what leprosy was, but hanging and being swallowed up by the earth, why, everybody was terrified of that! For, you see, they would ask themselves, "What is there under the ground?" and, of course, that would make them shudder, for what else is there but hell?

When things got as far as that only the most desperate characters would persist in refusing to confess, but the rest would just scream, "Stop! For mercy's sake, stop! Don't read such dreadful things any more. I don't want to listen to them. I'm willing to confess anything you want rather than to listen to such horrors!"

There's legal practice for you, sir! That's the way to get a villain to talk! Would you ever be able to make a man confess anything you wanted him to confess if you proceeded according to our civil laws?

Now as for the desperate characters who remained unmoved by the fear of being swallowed up by the earth or hanging, they would be treated to a stronger dose of the same medicine. I'd say, "The earth will swallow you up and the fate of all heretics will overtake you and eternal hellfire will be your last abode," and if they still persisted in their refusal to confess, I'd turn to the end of the book where there was a glorious chapter dealing with the subject of kissing the cross. It said : "Any man who persisted in telling a lie and who kissed the cross and committed perjury should be chastised with the lash for three consecutive days and then put to prison for a year and should even then no proof of his guilt be forthcoming, he should be made to speak by being put to torture . . ."

At this point, dear reader, I, the humble author of this story, permitted myself to interrupt Onopry Opanassovich by remarking respectfully that I questioned whether the people he had been interrogating would have accepted his authority, since he had no legal right either to flog them or to put them to torture.

"How do you mean they wouldn't have accepted my authority?" Onopry Opanassovich asked. "Why shouldn't they have believed me? Isn't it printed in the book?"

"That book," I replied, "was no doubt published long before the abolition of slavery or torture or flogging."

"I'm afraid, sir, you are mistaken," said the ex-sub-district police officer and, producing from the drawer of his table the book in question, namely, the '*Rules for the Revelation of Truth,*' he showed me that the last edition of it was published "in the Holy City of Moscow, on March the Sixth, in the year of our Lord 1864."

Having produced this evidence, Onopry Opanassovich said that there was nothing to prevent him from "putting the fear of God into men and exposing their guilt in a subtle manner," and he further claimed that it was a highly efficient way of making thieves talk and that nobody had ever challenged his right to proceed in such a way, but that, on the contrary, since it seemed to have had such a beneficent effect on horse-thieves, the villagers got a great liking for that "law" and esteemed it higher than "all the volumes of the Civil Code." Furthermore, every law-abiding citizen was eager to show his appreciation to Peregood for "knowing such a law," while the malefactors trembled before him. But his success in ridding the village of horse-thieves did not turn out to be so great a blessing after all; for in the end it brought about his undoing, since, on the one hand, it encouraged him in the hope that he would not only be able to bring every miscreant to heel by means of the "Rules," but also rule over everybody else with their help for ever and, on the other, he was overtaken by evil fate inasmuch as he began to entertain so high an opinion of himself that his soul was filled with an unquenchable desire for glory. It was then that Onopry Opanassovich, of the village of Peregoody, was fired with ambition to bring off a coup of the greatest moment, and as a consequence of that ambition "he perished utterly" and had in the end to hide himself from the eyes of men in a lunatic asylum where I was now talking with him.

After this brief digression, let Onopry Opanassovich again continue his story in his own words.

CHAPTER FOURTEEN

I DON'T KNOW, SIR (Onopry Opanassovich went on), what is your opinion of Father Prokop who so many years ago had driven the Jews out of Peregoody and become an even worse usurer himself, an occupation he had bequeathed to his son-in-law, Markel. So far as I'm concerned, I'm sorry to say that I can't quite make up my mind about him. Many people, no doubt, would tell you that there were no worse villains than Prokop and Markel, but I'm afraid I can't agree with them. Quite likely one ought to live differently and walk before the Lord in a different way and not as the priest Prokop did in his red top-boots, but does any man live as he should? For my part, I can only say that no sooner did Markel die (he died suddenly while sitting over his open money-chest), than we witnessed something which was a hundred times worse than usury. For a large number of students, not only from the seminary, but also from the religious academy, turned up at the funeral of the usurer-priest Markel and all of them began to cast such insatiable glances at his daughter, the poor orphan girl Domassya, or Domna Markelovna, and shoot such arrows at her over her father's coffin, that they made everybody in church feel very uncomfortable on account of that battery of blank shots they fired at the young girl. The intention behind that unseemly behaviour of theirs was, of course, quite clear : each of them wanted to inspire so great a passion in the girl that she would agree to marry him and thus make him the possessor of her father's renowned and much-talked-of money chest. Not that I blame them for that, for

> Money happiness procures,
> In money truth resides and pow'r,
> All for money man endures,
> All that's sweet and all that's sour.

This was the song we choir-boys used to sing, and who can withstand the attractions of so potent a spell-binder as money? But unhappily one of the cleverest of all those wooers of the fair Domna Markelovna was a fellow called Nazarko, a poet and a dreamer, who waited for the right moment and then ruffling his hair over Markel's coffin and twisting the locks that fell over his temples, he stretched forth his hand and—damn him!—launched forth into an oration; and so wonderful an oration did that rascal deliver, so deeply moving and so richly garnished with the most extravagant figures of speech, similes, metaphors and synechdoches, that he straightway sailed into Domassya's snow-white bosom. So the poor wretch fell head over ears in love with him then and there, like a cat; and soon afterwards he was ordained and became a priest. He took the name of Father Nazary and settled in Peregoody. Now he was not a bit like his wife's father or grandfather, for those two were just country bumpkins and only cared for their ill-gotten gains, while this one began to thrust his nose into everybody's business the moment he was inducted priest of the parish of Peregoody; and, most of all, he began to meddle in my own affairs, and that in a way that was quite astonishing. For instance, he suddenly began to question people who came to confession not, mind you, whether they had any intention of stealing a horse, but what they were thinking about, putting such nonsensical questions to them as "Are you quite sure that nobody is bothering you?" or "Is there anybody in the village who's inciting you to expect better things?" or "Are you satisfied with the way the sub-district police officer collects your taxes?" Now, I ask you, sir, what did he mean by that? But when my own maid Christina, a young woman who—to be quite frank with you—was . . . well . . . as comely a wench as ever came my way, went to him to confession, that rascal of a priest treated her worse than I'd have treated the most hardened malefactor according to the *Rules for the Revelation of Truth*. He left her so limp by his questioning that the poor girl came back home in tears and burst out sobbing, for, she said, "People are already laughing at me! Why, they ask, did the priest keep you so long in the confessional?" She kept on wondering who could have told the priest all those stories about her, until I said to her, "Leave it alone," I said, "let him think what he likes!" But the silly fool kept on crying and asking herself, "How did he find it all out? How is it that he knows everything, as if he'd lived in the house with us?" And, needless to say, she began blaming me. "No," said she, "thank you very much, never again will I carry on with you as before, and I don't want to live in this village any more, either. I shall go away to the town and live there as long as my good looks last."

"Go to the devil for all I care," said I. "Go to town if you like!"

But all the same, you know, I could not help being mad at that priest for not minding his own business and interfering with the freedom of a gentleman's private life. However, all this domestic upheaval did not last long, for Christina was an affectionate soul and she soon got tired of sulking and asked me to forgive her. "Let him say what he likes," she declared. "I'm afraid to be alone, for if I sleep by myself I always dream of dead bodies, so I'd rather everything was as before, for I'm sure the good Lord will forgive me."

But the priest Nazarko carried on in the same way and his inquiring mind delved deeper and deeper into the minds of the members of his congregation and things went so far that he not only investigated all their current transgressions, but also attempted to anticipate their future ones. "Are you quite sure," he'd ask, "that you're not thinking of doing something else?" Well, naturally, all the people in the village got frightened and began to complain to me about his unprofessional behaviour.

'What does he think he's doing?" they said. "Why, so long as a man does not commit any crime, there can be nothing against him, even according to God's laws. You yourself are a man of education, sir," they said to me, "you used to stand before the bishop himself and hold up a candle to him and you ought to be able to see into things that are hidden from the sight of ordinary folk, so, pray, tell us what is it this new priest of ours is up to, or we shall go and live in another village!"

So you can see how far things had gone : they were even talking about leaving the parish! One more step and they'd be committing murder!

CHAPTER FIFTEEN

WELL, AS YOU CAN IMAGINE, all this made me think, for I could see that it was something against which I myself might sooner or later be called upon to take action. But what kind of action? I could find no mention of it in the *Rules for the Revelation of Truth* and, indeed, what book could be expected to provide an answer to all the manifold problems of life?

As far as I could see, I was faced with one of two alternatives : either I should have to go and see Nazarko himself and ask him to stop sowing dissension among the people, or I should have to warn the authorities that Nazarko was a man who wanted watching carefully. Now, as to my first alternative, it occurred to me that I couldn't possibly ask Nazarko to mind his own business, for, in the first place, he would at once ask me what right I had to presume that he didn't mind his own business and, secondly, he'd immediately let loose on me all his similes, metaphors and synechdoches. As for the second alternative, I was rather apprehensive of informing the authorities against him in writing, and while I was wondering what I had better do, I myself was urgently summoned to town by no less a person than the Governor of the province himself, who, as soon as we were alone in his office, asked me this sort of thing : did I know the Ukrainian song, "Sweet and pleasant was life in the Ukraine in the days of old?"

"Yes, sir," I replied, "I know that song very well."

."You do, do you? How do you come to know it?"

"Quite simply, sir," I said. "I know it because the people in our village are always singing it."

"Are they? And did it never occur to you to send in a report about it?"

"No, sir," I replied. "Never."

"But why not?"

"Why should I send in reports about such trifling things?"

"But what about the words of the song? 'Life was sweetly spent, when to the Muscovites our fathers their knees ne'er bent!' Isn't that how it goes?"

"Yes, sir," I replied, still unable to overcome my astonishment, and I told him that we had many such songs and that even now people composed new songs of the same kind.

The Governor inclined his head in sign of agreement. "You are right," he said, "and as you seem to know all about it, I hope that in future you will remember what it is you ought to pay particular attention to."

Good Lord, as if I didn't know before what I had to pay attention to! And, really, what was there to remember? Was it not clear that the people I had to keep an eye on were those who stole horses and not those good-for-nothings who sang songs? Why even talk of such silly nonsense and, above all, why summon me to town and face me with such a ridiculous conundrum? If the bishop who had educated me according to the abridged method of studies in the manner of a prince had been still alive, I should have prostrated myself before his immaculate feet and he, as a man of the world, would have explained to me what it was all about; but he had already been gathered to his fathers or, to put it more plainly, he was as dead as a doornail. Yes, indeed, a man of great piety though he was, he, too, died and I forgot to tell you that on his deathbed he showed no trace of fear and that from his last words it was apparent that he regarded himself as "a personified idea," this being the will of God Who Himself "breathes the spirit of life into us, feeds us, tells us what to do, repairs us and takes us to pieces again." He comprehended it all and it was, therefore, all the more surprising that he should not have bequeathed the same spirit to anyone and although he, no doubt, obtained eternal salvation for himself, the only clear-headed man left after him in the whole of our province was undoubtedly the universally respected Vyekovyechkin, and it was to his reverence that I went in the hope that nothing was hidden from his powerful intellect, and, having arrived at his house, I put on the table two bottles of Madeira wine and I said to him, "How do you do, much beloved sir, and first of all do me the honour of accepting this German wine for the better preservation of your health and, secondly, tell me what is the meaning of the hints I've been given and what am I to do in such a situation?"

Vyekovyechkin did not give me a straight answer, but he spoke to me as if in a parable.

"There can be no doubt at all," said he, "that Madeira wine comes from the German city of Riga, but it is not itself a German wine, but it is a Greek wine. As for the thieves and bandits, the world has always been full of them and, let us hope, will continue to be full of them. So it was before the deluge, for Cain killed his brother Abel and Joseph, too, was sold into bondage by his brothers who bought boots with the money they had received for him. But today a new kind of villain has arisen. Men go about wearing long hair and hats from the same country of Greece where the Madeira wine comes from and women cut their hair short and walk about in dark eye-glasses and they all call themselves Socialists or, which is the same thing, underminers of foundations, for it is they who shake the thrones of kings! So if you wish to deserve well of your country just grab one of those long-haired males or short-haired females and then the authorities will show quite a different regard for you."

But I said that unfortunately such a thing was only possible in civilised countries and not in our village of Peregoody where no one had ever heard of any such underminers of foundations.

The dear old fellow, however, swept away my objection as of no consequence whatsoever.

"They are now to be found everywhere," he said, "and all you have to do is to keep your eyes open. Even if you caught every horse-thief in your district, you wouldn't earn any credit thereby, but just catch a man wearing a hat from the Greek country or a woman with cropped hair wearing eye-glasses and you'll get an even better decoration than the one conferred on Nazary."

"Nazary, sir?" I exclaimed. "Why, has Nazary been recommended for an honour?"

But my greatly beloved ex-tutor assured me that not only had Nazary been recommended for an honour, but that he had already obtained one.

"When?" I asked.

"Do you remember," his reverence replied, "the fall of snow we had the other week? Well, it was during that week that a decoration also fell upon Nazary's chest."

Dear Lord, where in the world was one to look for justice after that? I, who had caught hundreds of horse-thieves and returned hundreds of horses to their rightful owners, had got nothing to show for it, but that priest Nazarko, who must have told them a pack of lies, had snatched a decoration for himself!

Such base ingratitude on the part of my superiors threw me into the deepest melancholy and I found myself suddenly in the clutches of an irresistible desire to prove my worth and it was thus that I became the helpless slave of my own ambitions. I could not possibly go on as before: I just had to obtain a decoration! So I went to the cathedral and prayed fervently at the shrine of the saint—I swear to you by the Lord's cross, sir, that what I'm telling you is true—and it was by the saint's relics that I took a most solemn vow not to rest until I had discovered at least one underminer of foundations and, having obtained my decoration that way, thrust such a fig under the bulbous nose of the priest Nazarko that he could smell it, aye, and suck it, too, for all I cared, for the rest of his life!

CHAPTER SIXTEEN

HOWEVER, AS YOU KNOW, it is written in the Holy Scriptures, "Thou shalt not take the name of the Lord thy God in vain," and, believe me, sir, that is true, for no sooner did I take that vow than a sudden change took place in all my thoughts and in the whole manner of my life : I gave up the *Rules for the Revelation of Truth* and left off altogether looking for horse-thieves and devoted all my life to one thing only, namely, to discovering in my sub-district one of those terrible fomenters of civil strife and underminers of foundations, so that I could immediately lay my hands on him and in that way earn a decoration which was at least as high as, if not indeed higher than, the one Nazarko had been given.

Dear Lord, when now after my great fall and bereft of the glory that was practically within my grasp, I recall those mad dreams of mine, I am—believe me, sir—petrified with terror ! I became so worried that I could not sleep a wink at night and on the rare occasions when I did fall into a slumber, I would almost instantly wake up in a cold sweat and scream at the top of my voice, "Where are they ? Where ? Catch 'em !" Every time my maid, the young woman I have already mentioned to you as getting into hot water with the priest Nazarko, heard my blood-curdling screams, she'd tremble all over and say, "My goodness, Onopry Opanassovich, have you gone off your head completely ? You are as mad as a march hare, you are, and I'm afraid to be alone in the house with you !"

And, to be sure, I got her into such a state that she'd sit on the edge of the bed and be too frightened to go away, but instead would start plaguing me with her foolish questions.

"Please, tell me, my sweet angel, what's the matter ? Why do you toss about in your bed and scream like that ?"

"Go to your room, Christina," I'd say, "and don't worry me. It's a matter beyond your comprehension."

But as she was a very determined young woman, so sweet and plump, too, she'd just shrug her pretty shoulders and would not leave me alone.

"It's true, sweetheart," she'd say, "that I'm a foolish woman and don't understand a lot, but if you tell me everything, I'll do my best to understand."

Well, how do you like that? To be alone at night with a young woman and to have to put up with such tricks from her! But, of course, I couldn't get rid of her as easily as that. She'd start nagging me and nagging me.

"All right, sweetheart," she'd say, "don't tell me if you don't want to and may the Lord help you to catch whoever it is you want to catch, but please tell me, darling, who are you so afraid of?"

"I'm afraid of a bandit," I'd say to her.

But she'd just pout and reply, "Well, I never! You, such a brave gentleman, and afraid of a bandit? Why, you were never afraid of any bandit, so why should you begin to fear one now? No, darling," she'd say, "I know it isn't true, I know you're just telling me lies."

She was right, of course, for I was never afraid of any thief or murderer. Indeed, I'd often summon one of those malefactors to my office and sit there with him all by myself, reading the prayers and exhortations to him from my little book and putting the fear of God into him, frightening him with being swallowed up by the earth or coming to a bad end like Judas. While talking to him, I'd purposely be laying out my razors on the table, dip them in warm water, drop some olive oil from a little bottle on my strop and begin to strop them very slowly, then wipe them on a towel and, by and by, begin to shave. And all the time that one, the guilty one, would be standing beside me until he was completely worn out, his mouth parched, his feet too weak to support his body and his knees knocking together.

"Why," said Christina, "I sometimes thought that the fool would get hold of one of your razors and cut your throat, my sweet. But no! you were so brave then and now you're even afraid to tell the truth to a poor girl like me. Do tell me who it is you are always trying to catch in your sleep? And why are you so scared of him? If you don't tell me at once, you'll make me cry."

So I said to her, "Oh, all right!" and I told her everything: what strange new men had appeared in the world and how they were walking about in hats from the Greek country. But just imagine it, sir, that damned girl was not a bit frightened. All she said was, "What sort of men are they? Are they young or old?"

"Old?" I said. "Why, you stupid creature, of course they're not old. In fact, I shouldn't be surprised if they weren't in the prime of life, full of pep and vigour, and for all I know they may even be young, handsome fellows."

"Oh?" said Christina. "Well, I'm glad they're young and handsome, anyway, and I wish they were here so that I could have a good look at them."

"Have a look at them, would you?" I said. "One can see at once that you're a silly fool. Never thought of those horrible clothes they're wearing, have you?"

"You don't expect me to be afraid of that, do you? So long as they're young, their clothes don't matter, for all they have to do is to take them off and everything'll be all right."

"But they wear hats of the Greek country, you fool!"

"And what," Christina asked, "is a hat of the Greek country like?"

"Well, you see, the trouble is that I don't know myself what it's like. I expect it must be one of those shaggy ones."

"What if it is a shaggy one?" said Christina. "That's not so terrible."

"Not terrible? Why, my dear girl," I said, "what if he should pounce on you suddenly in such a hat? You'd get such a shock that you'd faint on the spot."

"Well," said Christina, "maybe I will and again maybe I won't."

"Oh, no, my dear girl," I said, "I know perfectly well that they've been created to undermine foundations and shake thrones, so you can imagine what there'd be left of *you* once they got near enough to lay a hand on you."

"That is as it may be," she said, calmly. "We're all in the hands of God and perhaps God will make it so that nothing will happen to me and I'll remain just the same as I am now and they won't do me any harm at all."

I got angry with her. "Oh, you little baggage," I said. "If that's what you're after, then I hope he'll maul you with that hat of his!"

"What are you trying to frighten me with a silly old hat for?" she said, spitefully. "You don't think his hat is nailed to his forehead, do you? Goodness, I'm sure they take their hats off when necessary and don't go mauling people with them!"

That, sir, seemed so brazen a piece of impudence to me that I couldn't help exclaiming, "But they're murderers!"

Christina, however, said that she was sure that they would only kill men. "The young women," she said, "they won't touch."

I just pushed her away from me and said, "Get out of here!"

"With the greatest pleasure," she replied. "And I'm not a bit afraid of a man in a Greek hat, see? I'm not afraid of him, so there!"

CHAPTER SEVENTEEN

I PUSHED THE IMPUDENT CREATURE out of my room, but for a long time I couldn't get over her insolence and it was then that I realised in a flash what a heavy burden I had taken upon myself, chiefly, it seemed, because of some idle dream. "My dreams, perchance, are mad . . ." and " . . . my tears and yearnings all in vain . . ."

But whether my dreams were mad or not, it could not be denied that they were responsible for my mood of the most agonising depression, and who could tell what awaited me in the future? It would, no doubt, have been a big piece of luck— God alone knew *how* big—to have caught an underminer of foundations and brought him to town, but where, oh where was I to find him? And . . . and, goodness me, what a little she-devil that Christina had turned out to be! Just think of it: she, if you please, was not afraid of them and indeed she seemed anxious to find out whether their hats of the Greek country were nailed to their foreheads or not and whether or not they could be taken off. What a devilish woman! But what, I asked myself, if the others were like her?

Oh, if only I could have laid my hands on that blessed underminer of foundations, I should have taken good care not to let him out of my clutches! Let me only get hold of him . . . But where was he to be found? Perhaps he had to be enticed, lured on like a bird by strewing some hempseed for him? But how was I to set about it? What was the right way of going about it?

The thought would not leave my mind and I worked myself into such a state by brooding over it that I felt completely exhausted, and I began to look just like a frontier guard and the fire in my eyes became extinguished and my teeth were bared . . . Ugh, what a piece of damned witchcraft! And, on top of it all, Christina could not sleep at night and fidgeted about in bed like a mangy cur . . . I'd ask her what was the matter with her, and she'd answer that she had a queer feeling as if hundreds of cats were miaowing and scratching in the house.

"What's all this silly nonsense?" I'd say. "What do you care whether there are cats in the house or not? Don't let me hear of it again. Go to sleep at once!"

She'd promise to go to sleep, but next time I woke up, I'd find that she was not asleep, but was looking out of the window instead.

"It's all your own fault,"she said. "Why did you tell me such horrors about men who're trying to shake everything up in their hats of the Greek country? You've frightened me out of my wits and now they're not coming. No wonder I seem to hear cats scratching all over the house."

I told her that I was just teasing her and that there were not such people and that no one would be coming in a strange hat. "That happened a long time ago," I said, "and it didn't happen in our country, either, and I shouldn't be a bit surprised if the whole thing never existed, but had just been invented by some Government clerk."

But she no longer believed my denials. "No, no," she said, "I'm sure they're scratching about somewhere : my heart tells me so."

"You're a silly fool," I said, and I couldn't help mimicking her, "My heart tells me so!"

And suddenly she became so odious to me : so fat! And such a strong odour of sweat came from her body, just as if she were a young nanny-goat !

Those women are indeed the limit, sir, and no wonder we pray not to be led into temptation, but to be delivered from evil.

One day, running across Father Nazary, I asked him whether

he had heard anything in town about any underminers of foundations and I added that, for my part, I did not believe that such men existed.

"What right have you not to believe in their existence?" Father Nazary asked me rather scornfully.

"But where are they?" I asked. "You can't expect me to believe in them, if they're not to be found anywhere, can you?"

"I'm surprised to hear you talk like that," said Father Nazary. "Do you mean to imply that the authorities are telling lies?"

See, how he snubbed me!

"Come, come," I said, "you know very well that I'd never imply anything of the kind about the authorities. I just said it because I've never seen any of those underminers of foundations."

"Have you ever seen China or America?"

"No, sir, I haven't."

"And I suppose you've never seen St. Petersburg, either, have you?"

"No, sir," said I, "I've never seen St. Petersburg and I've never seen Moscow for that matter, but what does that prove? Where's the comparison?"

"The comparison, sir," said Father Nazary, "is simply this: you don't, I take it, doubt the existence of China or America or St. Petersburg or Moscow just because you haven't seen them, do you?"

"Pardon me," I said, "but there's a world of difference between one thing and the other: we get our tea from China and we drink it, don't we? And America was discovered by Christopher Columbus who had been slandered and put in chains by his ungrateful compatriots, and I've seen pictures depicting it and plays are performed about it in our playhouses. As for Moscow, that was where Ivan the Terrible lived, who, I daresay, would not have hesitated to order even you to be flogged, and St. Petersburg was founded by Peter the Great and they have a fish there, the lavaret, which is mentioned by Gogol in one of his stories. As for those underminers of foundations, I don't see them anywhere and, for all I know, we may never see them here, at least I can't see any sign of them."

"How do you mean you can't see any sign of them?" Father Nazary asked, flushing with anger.

"Well," I replied, "I'm not aware of any such sign, for the state of utter ignorance that prevailed here at my birth, still prevails here today."

"Ah-h," said he, "so that's what you're driving at, is it?"

"Yes, sir. I suggest that for many more years to come everything will remain here in the same state of crass ignorance! And," I said, "if I'm wrong, then show me just one sign of their coming. I bet you anything you won't be able to do that."

I thought that I had got him there, but he pointed calmly at the decoration hanging on his chest by his cross and said, "What other sign do you want?"

But there I proved myself a much craftier man than he, for I instantly crossed myself and, bending down, kissed his cross.

"This I honour and believe in," said I.

It was then that he, pricked by his youthful vanity, failed to realise that I was merely having him on and he began to tell me that it was impossible to discern the underminers of foundations all at once.

"But," I pleaded, "how is one to discern them? Tell me, please, for I'm very curious by nature and I like to know everything."

"Their appearance," he said, "is preceded by rumours."

"Rumours?" I asked. "What kind of rumours? What form do these rumours take?"

"They take the form of a keen desire to criticise the authorities and to express opinions about them."

"Do they? And what else?"

"This is usually followed by talk that is subversive to the well-being of the country and it is only then that those enemies of mankind arrive, those whose dearest wish is to undermine the very foundation of the State, the men wearing hats of the Greek country and the women looking like frogs with their cropped hair and dark eye-glasses."

"Still," I said, "I can't for the life of me see what such people can hope to achieve in a place like ours? We haven't got a really educated person within miles and there's nothing for them here to undermine."

But Father Nazary who was itching to enlighten me, said,

"Don't you be so sure about it, sir, for you'll find that they penetrate everywhere with the sole aim of sowing distrust and disaffection, of undermining family life and exalting a state of society where there's neither money nor marriage, and thereafter they suddenly begin to speak disparagingly about those on whom the very foundations of the State rest, and all with the idea of supplanting them themselves and, generally, destroying the souls of men."

"But that's exactly what I've been saying," I cried. "We haven't got anyone here upon whom the foundations of the State could be said to rest!"

"Oh, haven't we? And what about you and me, sir?" Father Nazary asked rather sternly. "Aren't we the foundations of the State, sir?"

"Do you mean us? Why, surely the foundations of the State must rest on something more solid than us!"

"Why do you think so? I, my dear sir, am the foundation of Faith and you . . . well . . . you, I suppose, are the foundation of law and order."

"I grant you," I said, "that you're the foundation of Faith, that, sir, I'm quite ready to admit, but me . . . why, I'm just the

merest bottle-washer and only carry out the orders given
to me."

But Father Nazary—can you imagine it, sir?—suddenly revealed an extraordinary talent for persuasion, and the rascal
began to count on his fingers the reasons why I represented one
of the foundations of the State and with such good effect, too,
that upon my soul I soon began to look upon myself as a very
solid foundation indeed, and I was consequently beginning to
be greatly concerned about my own safety. What else would
you expect? Before I used to live a quiet, humdrum sort of
existence, eat and drink, go to a public bath-house and give
myself a good steaming and, occasionally, go galloping after a
horse-thief, making the very earth tremble under my horse's
hoofs, and, having caught him, I'd put him through a thorough
interrogation in accordance with the *Rules for the Revelation of
Truth*, and I never gave a thought to the dangers that threatened
my own life ; but now all my thoughts and feelings seemed to
be groping in a thick fog of doubt and terror. The first thing I
did was to get myself a big revolver, which I could always keep
near at hand, and I also provided myself with a good supply of
bullets, and I kept the gun under my pillow at night, intending
to fire it at the first man who entered my room.

The revolver, which a Jew had procured for me in town, was
just the kind I wanted. It was called "Bulldog" and it had six
chambers. I put plenty of powder in each of the chambers and
rammed in the bullets, but I did not put in the percussion caps
for fear that I might fire it in good earnest. It was a good thing
I had taken that precaution, for the same night I dreamt that the
underminers of foundations had crawled under my bed and
were shaking it. I woke up in a cold sweat and, seizing my gun,
I aimed it under the bed a few times and I began to yell for
Christina and I would have killed her, too, were it not that my
gun would not fire, for the skin had grown so dry on her that

it made a kind of rustling noise when she moved, as though she really were a nanny-goat who wished to go off with a he-goat to browse on the bark of trees.

But make a note of that dream of mine, sir! For while there are dreams which are of no significance whatsoever, arising out of a full belly, there are dreams which are of tremendous importance, coming to us from the angels. It is these dreams that are so remarkable.

CHAPTER EIGHTEEN

I BELIEVE I HAVE TOLD YOU already that among the somewhat large number of squires in Peregoody there was the highly honourable and universally beloved Dmitry Afanassyevich, who was, in a way, a relation of mine. Now let me tell you, sir, that he was a most excellent fellow, and he is the man I have mentioned briefly before as having had a very superior education at Galushka's Moscow boarding school for the sons of gentlemen and as having subsequently amassed a considerable fortune while serving as a customs officer. Now, I believe I also mentioned the fact that Dmitry Afanassyevich had got a separation from his wife and, being rather fond of female company, he kept his wife's *boudoir* always in readiness to receive certain persons of the fair sex who were expected to carry out not only domestic, but also marital duties, and with whom he conversed in French. To lend those various duties of theirs an air of respectability, Dmitry Afanassyevich adopted a niece of his, a scrofulous child of six, and it was under the pretext of his niece's education that he employed those persons of the fair sex. Dmitry Afanassyevich, however, had rather a mean habit of not explaining all their duties beforehand to the governesses he employed, with the result that rather unpleasant scenes would now and again occur in his household and, indeed, some of the girls left his *boudoir* after only a few days and ran away from him . . . Why, one or two of them even came to me as the representative of the law to demand protection, but I always did my best to calm the poor creatures and talk some sense into them.

"Now, listen to me, my dear," I'd say, "you won't achieve anything by quarrelling, will you? The best thing you can do if you'll take my advice, is to go back to Dmitry Afanassyevich and perform any duty you can perform as a woman."

Some took my advice and did as I told them, but one—if you please—got so enraged that she spat in my face, but for all that the poor thing did not escape her fate . . .

Dmitry Afanassyevich was naturally very grateful to me for my help and he'd let me into some of his secrets. He'd bring his governesses to see me, for instance, and he'd say to me, quoting my own words, "Let's try this pen and ink : now what is the power that resides in them ?" or he'd say, "What's your opinion, my dear fellow, will this Columbine please our Harlequin or not ?" And later he'd tell me frankly, "I'm afraid, old man, that Columbine was a real wash-out. She didn't please our Harlequin at all !" So there would immediately be a change —and there was no end to such changes !

At that time, too, his Columbine happened to be a complete wash-out and the reason was that the Polish girl who lived with him—such a big-mouthed wench she was !—suddenly quarrelled violently with him and threw the bunch of keys at him with such violence that he walked about for many days with a bruised face. What are you to do with women, if they refuse to recognise either rank or good birth ? But because of that bruised face of his, poor Dmitry Afanassyevich could not go to town to engage a new governess for his niece and he had to engage one at random by replying to an advertisement in the papers and, of course, he got a terrible frump with a potato nose, cropped hair and spectacles who, it seemed, had been educated at a Teachers' Institute in St. Petersburg.

Now, what struck me about that ugly creature was, of course, that she appeared in our village in the highly suspicious guise I have just described, and I wanted to put a few questions to her before Dmitry Afanassyevich had a chance of casting his eyes on her.

"Well," I observed to Dmitry Afanassyevich, "I don't know what anybody else would say, but I wouldn't mind betting that this Columbine of yours will prove highly unsatisfactory to your Harlequin."

But instead, as was his habit, of quoting my words, "Let us try this pen and ink : what is the nature of the power that resides in them?" the poor fellow answered sadly, "I'm afraid you're quite right. I seem to have made a slip this time. In fact, I don't think I have ever made such a terrible mistake before. Why, my dear fellow, I can't even see her eyes behind those dark glasses of hers!"

"Well," I said, "that certainly seems to be a piece of rotten luck."

"What I can't understand," he said, "is how our censorship allows such frippery-frapperies to publish advertisements in the press. If I'd been the chief censor, I'd never have permitted it."

"Ah," I said, "that's most probably what it is! A man's eyes are the mirror of his soul and she, you say, refuses to take off her glasses, does she?"

"Yes, imagine it : she just won't take them off!"

"Have you asked her to?"

"No, I can't say that I have. You see, I don't know what reason I could very well give for such a request."

"Would you like me to make her take them off?"

"I'd consider it a great favour."

"I'd do it with pleasure," said I.

The plan I had devised then and there was really brilliant; in fact, it was nothing less than an inspiration!

CHAPTER NINETEEN

I MADE UP MY MIND to lose no time and find out everything I could about that mysterious female, and from her own person, if possible. To get acquainted with her, I pretended that I was suffering from eye-strain and was contemplating purchasing a pair of dark glasses, but not knowing how much glasses cost or how strong they ought to be, I wished to consult her about it. You can see what my plan was, can't you? As for her fine education, that didn't worry me in the least, for having taken part in the rehearsals of executions according to the poet Zhukovsky's proposals in the Vice-Governor's house, I had got so used to the society of educated people that I could talk with my tongue in my cheek as well as anybody.

Revolving these thoughts in my mind, I went in the afternoon to pay a call on Dmitry Afanassyevich. I was in no hurry, hoping to come across that frippery-frappery of the female sex and engage her in conversation by asking her where Dmitry Afanassyevich was.

So it had been before with the Polish governess. I asked her where Dmitry Afanassyevich was and she immediately replied, "There he is, the swine!" For some reason all the young ladies Dmitry Afanassyevich employed sooner or later conferred that title upon him and that after the shortest possible time, too, which made the poor man shake his head and say, "The dear ladies, God bless 'em, are starting their small talk again!" Anyway, you can imagine my surprise when I could not find the new young lady anywhere, so that I had to look for Dmitry Afanassyevich myself, and on finding him, "My dear Dmitry Afanassyevich," I said, "do you know the saying that when the whole world goes crazy about some new fashion, even the face has to adapt itself to it?"

"Yes," he said, "I know it, but what are you driving at?"

"What I'm driving at," I replied, "is that now I, too, want to buy myself a pair of dark glasses to relieve the strain on my eyes, but I have no idea how strong they should be, how much they cost and where to get them."

Dmitry Afanassyevich apparently failed to realise the real purport of my words, for he answered rather surlily, "I'm not a Jew; old man, and thank God I don't trade in glasses."

"I know that," I replied, "but that new lady of yours is wearing just the kind of glasses I'd like to buy for myself."

"Well," said he, "what do you want me to do about it? I told you I loathed the sight of them, didn't I?"

"I can well believe it," I said. "Fancy, having a young lady so close to you and not be able to make out what she looks like! I've come here today on purpose, you see, for I want to give you a chance of seeing the young woman without those charming glasses of hers."

"How splendid of you, my dear fellow! But how are you going to do it so that I could see what's hidden behind those damned glasses of hers?"

"You'll have to conceal yourself," I said, "and watch me do it."

"An excellent idea, my dear fellow! She's in the dining-room now, at the tea-table. Go in and tell her that I shan't be coming for a while and I'll hide myself in the passage and watch everything through a chink in the wall."

"Yes, I suppose that'll do, but tell me quickly her name."

"Julia Semyonovna."

"Thanks. Now what exactly is her social position?"

"Nothing special, I don't think. Belongs to the learned professions I believe. You can talk freely with her and you needn't be afraid of bullying her a little!"

So I went into the dining-room and there she was, nothing

at all to lose your head over, you understand. Just picture to yourself a creature undoubtedly of the female sex sitting at a large table by the *samovar* in a large, white room and not a bit like any of the other young ladies who had before her had to go through a trial period in their manifold duties. I saw at a glance that she couldn't possibly have been Dmitry Afanassye-vich's personal choice, but just something he had picked up without looking. I will say, though, that the dress she wore was very neat and clean, but there was nothing special about it, just an ordinary dress, and her hair was certainly cut very short, just like a court clerk's, and brushed back from the forehead, and you could see at once that she was of a poor physique, for her lips were pale and her nose was rather thick and short, and as for her eyes, they, of course, could not be seen behind those large, dark spectacles of hers with their potbellied glasses which reminded you of the bulging eyes of a toad. Say what you will, but there certainly was something suspicious about them!

I studied her closely and I saw that she was sitting at the table, knitting something. Not, mind you, anything delicate and lady-like, but just an ordinary pair of woollen socks like the ones I'm knitting now myself. There was a book lying in front of her and, while she was knitting, she read something from it to the little girl, the orphan child adopted by Dmitry Afanassye-vich. It must have been a very entertaining story, for the little girl clung to her knees and gazed at her face, looking very happy.

I couldn't help saying to myself as I beheld that domestic scene, "Are those underminers of foundations really such awful hypocrites that, while assuming a look of innocence, they keep on plotting the destruction of the mightiest empires?" Anyway, I introduced myself to the young lady without wasting much time.

"I have the honour of being the sub-district officer of police,"

I said, "but please do not for a moment think, madam, that a sub-district officer of police must necessarily be a brute. I'm a very ordinary fellow and a most loyal citizen and I've come to ask you, frankly and openly, to do me a great favour."

"I don't know what you're talking about, sir," she said

"Never mind, madam," I said, "I shall presently explain myself. You see before you," I said, "a man who is somewhat impaired . . ."

She drew further away from me.

" . . . in health," I went on. "My eyesight, you see, has been badly affected by my official duties which involve a great deal of writing and I should like to acquire a pair of dark spectacles, but I don't know where to purchase them, nor have I the faintest idea how much they might cost, nor, what is perhaps even more important, how strong they ought to be, that is to say, madam whether they'd suit me or not. I should therefore like to ask you, dear Julia Semyonovna, to be so good as to let me examine your glasses."

"With pleasure, sir," she said and she took off her glasses without any more ado.

I pretended that I didn't know what to do with them and kept asking her how to put them on, while looking straight into her eyes and, as a matter of fact, what I saw was a pair of grey eyes, rather sweet eyes they were, and the whole expression of her face was rather pleasant, except perhaps for a certain redness round the eyes.

I tried on her glasses, but took them off almost at once and said, "Thank you very much, madam, but I don't think they quite suit me."

She said that one had to get used to them.

"Did you, Julia Semyonovna, get used to them a long time ago?"

"Yes."

"And why, may I ask, did you start wearing them?"

She was silent for a moment and then she said, "If you really must know, it was because I was ill."

"I see," I said. "And may I ask what was the nature of your illness?"

"I had typhus," she said.

"I'm sorry to hear that, ma'am," I said. "Typhus is indeed a very serious illness and it makes your hair fall out, doesn't it? So I suppose that's why you cut your hair off, isn't it?"

"Yes," she said and smiled.

"Well, ma'am," I said, "that is certainly much wiser than to be left with a bald head. I certainly don't fancy baldheaded people, especially ladies."

She smiled again and resumed her reading to the little girl, but I interrupted her again.

"Incidentally," I said, "I hope you won't mind my saying so, but I don't think that a cropped head suits a young lady of poor circumstances like yourself."

She didn't seem a bit put out by my remark, but just asked me, rather disdainfully, I thought, "What have my circumstances got to do with it?"

"Why, ma'am," I said, "people belonging to the well-to-do classes can do what they like and if they take it into their heads to introduce new fashions, no one can prevent them, but people like you and me, ma'am, can't do as they please, can they?"

"Excuse me," she said abruptly, "I haven't the honour of being acquainted with you, sir, and I do not wish to reply to your remarks."

"But why not, ma'am? Don't you think they're just?"

"I do not," she said, "and, besides, I find them totally uninteresting."

"What is it you're knitting, ma'am?" I asked. "Not a pair of coarse socks? Rather unlady-like, don't you think?"

"It is a pair of socks, sir."

"Yes, of course, I can see it now. But why should you be knitting socks, Julia Semyonovna, and such coarse ones, too? Who are they for?

"For those who haven't got any."

"For the poor, you mean? . . . Ah, what a fine thing charity is, ma'am! I'm afraid it is part of my duties to collect taxes from the peasants and it sometimes happens that I have to sell the so-called "effects" of a peasant's cottage and you can't imagine the heart-rending scenes that usually occur at such a public sale! It's too terrible for words!"

"Why do it if it's so terrible?"

"Aha," I said to myself, "so I've started you talking at last, have I?" And drawing nearer to her, I fetched a deep sigh and said with a sad mien, trying to look as sympathetic as possible, "Oh, ma'am, if you could only see the injustices and inhumanities that are being perpetrated daily here in this village, you'd be unable to restrain your tears!"

She said nothing to that and, turning to the little girl, began to teach her how to knit socks. Well, I could see, of course, that she was a very clever girl, so after another little pause I cast an admiring look at her and said, "May I ask, dear Julia Semyonovna, what your opinion is about the rich and poor?"

At first she seemed rather offended at my words, but a moment later she seemed to have pulled herself together and said, "The deceitfulness of riches chokes the word."

"Excellent, excellent, ma'am!" I cried. "Oh, if every man and woman only thought like that!"

"Yes, sir," she said, "everybody in the world ought to think like that and everybody ought to tell people that they ought not to wish to be in the place of those who despise the poor and oppress them and draw them before the seats of judgment and blaspheme the worthy name by which they are called."

225

"What fine sentiments, Julia Semyonovna, what wonderful sentiments! Would you mind if I wrote them down, for I fear I shan't be able to remember those beautiful words of yours?"

Well, you know, she just swallowed the bait, hook, line and sinker!

"By all means, sir," she said, "write it down."

Seeing how guileless she was, I said, "I'm afraid, my dear Julia Semyonovna, I've got a splinter in my finger and I find it rather painful to write. Would you be so good as to write down those words in my note-book?"

"With pleasure," she said.

Those were her very words, "With pleasure!" and, having said it, she took my note-book out of my hand and, without the ghost of a suspicion, wrote down in a large and firm hand, rather like a bishop's, I thought at the time, first in one line: "The deceitfulness of riches chokes the word," and, then, beginning with a new line, "The rich oppress you and draw you before the judgment seats and blaspheme the worthy name by which you are called."

Put down every word in her own hand, she did, so that, you know, I couldn't help feeling sorry for her.

"Thank you, dear Julia Semyonovna," I said, "thank you very much indeed!" and I even wanted to kiss her hand, which, incidentally, was a very beautifully-shaped hand, but she withdrew it quickly.

I did not insist, but rushed out to Dmitry Afanassyevich and said, "Seen it?"

"I saw it," he replied.

"Well, what do you think of it?"

He made a wry face and I couldn't help agreeing with him.

"The cast of her countenance isn't so bad," I said, "and I suppose one could get used to it, and her hand is certainly very white and of a beautiful shape, but I'm afraid her political views and her whole moral outlook are such that I shall have to report her to the authorities which, I'm sorry to say, will most probably lead to her utter undoing and, in fact, she's as good as done for already."

Dmitry Afanassyevich could not help expressing his admiration of me.

"A fast worker, aren't you?" he said.

"Why, what else did you suppose I was?" said I.

"I didn't expect you to be such a devil with the ladies," he remarked.

"Oh, that's nothing," I laughed. "I've had much trickier situations to handle, I assure you."

And, you know, when we joined her in the dining-room I really let myself go and I gave the young lady a most graphic description of the iniquities that take place in our towns and cities, not omitting to mention the scandalous ways in which our schools were run and what scurvy knaves our rich citizens were. I also told her how terribly expensive everything was there and how confoundedly crowded it was, neither room to turn round, nor any peace or quiet.

She remarked quietly that I ought not to forget that it was in our big cities that learning flourished and the biggest strides in science were made.

"Oh, well," I said, "I don't consider that of any importance. What I did like there, though," I went on, "were the many well-dressed ladies taking a stroll on the promenade in the evening and filling the air with the scent of sweet peas." And when she remarked that there were hardly any trees in our steppes, I replied, "What does that matter, ma'am? It is true we have no woods where we can roam, but instead Dmitry Afanassyevich has a lovely garden where one can not only roam, but also go astray much better than in a wood."

Dmitry Afanassyevich was highly tickled by my little speech

and he pressed my foot under the table, but Julia Semyonovna just raised her glasses at me and asked, "Pray, sir, what language are you talking?"

"Russian, ma'am," I replied.

"I'm afraid you're mistaken, sir," she said. "It isn't Russian at all."

"Oh?" I looked questioningly at her. "What is it then?"

"If you must know, sir," she said, "it's the language of a stupid and boorish man!"

Having said that, she got up and walked out of the room.

"Well, how do you like that?" I said.

But Dmitry Afanassyevich, seeing the sort of person she was, began to entreat me to help him to get rid of her.

"Please, save me from her," he implored me. "I want her out of my house as soon as possible."

"Don't you worry, my dear fellow," I said, "she won't stay long in your house, you may be sure of that!"

Directly I returned home that evening, I sat down at my table and, having uttered a prayer, wrote a most secret and confidential report concerning the appearance in our village of Peregoody of a suspicious young lady, and I enclosed the page from my note-book on which she herself had written down certain of her views, and I sent it off the same evening with a special messenger, who had to bring back a reply to my request for instructions what to do with her.

But it seemed it was not only I who did not sleep that night, for the girl, too, got up very early, packed her things, sent to the Jewish innkeeper for horses, and told Dmitry Afanassyevich that she was leaving his house immediately and that if they did not give her any horses, she'd go to town on foot and lodge a complaint with the President of the Noblemen's Chamber.

Dmitry Afanassyevich was so glad to get rid of her that he said, "Why complain to the President of the Noblemen's

Chamber? I have no objections to your going anywhere you like!"

For Dmitry Afanassyevich disliked the President of the Noblemen's Chamber, who at that time was a certain Prince Mamura, whose father was a freemason who had spent some time in exile and had instilled such ideas into his son's head that the prince could have but little respect for Dmitry Afanassyevich, but of him more later.

The young lady left our village, and I was rather surprised to learn from the Jew who had driven her to town that she had gone to stay at the house of the President of the Noblemen's Chamber! So that was where the underminers of the foundations went to when they wanted to cover up their tracks, and the honour of that discovery would be entirely mine! . . . However, things did not turn out exactly as I had anticipated. The song I spoke of before, you know, was right : my dreams *were* mad! For I received a sudden summons to present myself before my superiors in town and the same official who would in the normal course of events have recommended me for a decoration, began to bully me in a most unmerciful manner as a result, it seemed, of a complaint he had received from the President of the Noblemen's Chamber. Why, he asked me, did I make indecent suggestions to the young lady? And he went on to lay it on thick, chiefly, it appeared, because of the information I had included in my report concerning Julia Semyonovna's dangerous views, which, he said, proved that I was the biggest ass on earth. And producing the page from my note-book on which the young lady had written down the sentences she had used in her conversation with me, he told me to read the remarks made in red ink under them. Under the first sentence was written : St. Matthew, xiii, 22, and under the second : St. James ii, 6. Now, what do you think of that, sir? She got it straight from the New Testament! Why, I'd like to know, are they taught all those things? Even the Governor's aide-de-camp said to me, "It was a good thing my clerk recognised where those words came from, or we should have sent it on to St. Petersburg and they'd have accused us all of being the greatest dullards in Russia!"

He went on blowing off steam for some time, but he had the decency to commend me for my zeal and, as for the decoration, he said that no doubt my desire to obtain such a distinction was highly praiseworthy, but that I should have to try again and hope for the best.

CHAPTER TWENTY

SO THAT WAS THAT! I was so upset that I went straight to my old tutor Vyekovyechkin and asked his reverence to tell me what I'd better do now.

"You must help me, your reverence," I said, "for I find that I've got myself mixed up in politics and, believe me, sir, politicians are much worse than horse-thieves whom I managed very well with the help of the *Rules for the Revelation of Truth*. Say what you like, sir, but politics (may it vanish from the face of the earth!) is something that completely baffles me. So, pray, sir, tell me what I have to do to deserve the approval of my superiors in the service?"

"I'm afraid I should find it very hard to tell you what to do in every single case," Vyekovyechkin said to me, speaking very composedly, as he did before, "but, as a general rule, keep your ears open for any newfangled ideas that are abroad nowadays and try to trace them to their source where you're sure to come across one or another of the underminers of foundations, and then it will be your turn to grab him."

"Oh dear," I said, "if only I could lay my hands on one of them!"

So I drove home in a much calmer frame of mind, and the thought that there was still a good chance of mending matters cheered me up no end, and I arrived in our village feeling refreshed in spirit. I said my prayers and went straight to bed from where I directed an earnest appeal to the underminer of foundations to come forth out of the mirk of night.

"Come on, my friend," I whispered to him, "for what's the use of carrying on this miserable existence of yours? Sooner or later, dear friend, your fate will be sealed and you'll have to pay for your iniquities. So why surrender just to anyone or, maybe, to a man who lacks the most elementary human feelings or to one who has already got a decoration? Why not," I pleaded, "surrender to me instead? I promise, dear friend, to treat you well and to give you plenty of strong vodka to drink and take you to the bath-house to have a good wash and after your death, after they have hanged you, I promise to keep your memory alive in my heart . . ."

But there was no sign of him and once more I began to worry about how I was to find and apprehend him. I couldn't sleep for thinking about it, and I'd begin to pray and everything would be hopelessly muddled up in my brain and I did not know whether I was praying or dreaming. I'd be murmuring a prayer, "I humbly beseech Thee, O Lord, mercifully to look upon my infirmities and, whether I wish it or not, to deliver me from evil and whether my dreams be mad or not . . ." and then I'd suddenly come to my senses and stop muttering my prayer and begin to commune with myself, turning over in my mind again and again the advice given to me by my old tutor. I had been warned not to respect anyone who might harbour new-fangled ideas, but how could I, a police officer of humble rank who had received his education with other choir-boys only according to the abridged course, not respect a university man, such as the President of our newly-established Court of Justice, an institution so gladly welcomed by all? How could I do that? It was true that Vyekovyechkin, who was not daunted by anything, had made it abundantly clear to me that civility cost nothing. "Remember," he had said to me, "that if necessary you need not hesitate to nod and smile and scrape and bow, but do not on that account hesitate to put a spoke in the wheel of the man you've been polite to and, indeed, make it your business not to lose any opportunity of making him look foolish. It is only thus that we shall in the end prevail against them, for it is indeed the height of folly to offer equal justice to everybody, and although this has now become the law of the land, it is our duty to see to it that this state of affairs does not last."

So far, so good.

But there was something else my old tutor told me. Now, what was it? . . . . Ah, yes! "Try to find out what the people are thinking," he said. But gracious me, what could the good people of Peregoody be thinking? Still, I made up my mind to find out. One evening, therefore, as I was driving along in my carriage with my coachman, Stetsko, I tried to find out what he was thinking.

"I say, Stetsko," I said to him, "can you tell me what the people of Peregoody are really like?"

"What's that you said, sir?" Stetsko asked and I must admit he sounded a bit surprised.

I repeated my question.

"Why, sir," he said, "ain't you found out that by now yourself?"

"But," I insisted, "can you tell me what they are thinking about?"

"Lord, sir," he replied, "what makes you ask me such daft questions?"

"These are not daft questions," I said with a touch of asperity in my voice. "These, my good man, are matters of high policy."

"You mean, sir, what other folks are a-thinkin' of?"

"Yes."

Stetsko was silent.

"Why don't you speak? Answer my question, please!"

"What do you want me to tell you, sir?"

"Well, to begin with, tell me what you are thinking of?"

"Me, sir? I don't rightly know, sir."

"How do you mean you don't rightly know? I told you something this minute, well, what do you think of it?"

"Well, sir, if you must know, I'm a-thinkin' you must be daft."

"I see. But let me tell you, my good man, that if you really think that, then you must be daft yourself!"

"Mebbe."

"But just try to think for a minute, please. Do you know if there's anybody in Peregoody who's thinking differently from anybody else?"

"I told you, sir," Stetsko replied sullenly, "I don't know nothin'. How's a man to know what another man's a-thinkin' of?"

"But suppose you did know, would you have told me?"

"No, sir."

"But, confound you, why wouldn't you?"

"Why should I be tellin' you what other folks be a-thinkin' of? I ain't no informer, aye, and no blackguard, neither."

"If that's what you really think, my good fellow, then let me warn you that you're in for a good flogging."

"Why would they be floggin' me?"

"Why? Because you have no right to call such people blackguards!"

"Well, sir, blackguards or no blackguards, it's agin the law to flog people nowadays."

"Oh, you rascal," I exclaimed, "so you expect the law to protect you, do you?"

"O' course, what else?"

"What else? You just wait, my good man, I'll show you how much help the law will be to you!"

"Talkin' a lot of wicked nonsense, you are, sir," Stetsko replied calmly, shaking his head.

"Don't you dare to speak to me like that again," I said, grasping him by a shoulder and turning him round to me. "I order you to listen carefully to what the people of Peregoody are saying to each other and to report it to me afterwards. Understand?"

"I understand," he said.

"And try to remember particularly those who're dissatisfied with things."

"No, sir," Stetsko said firmly, "I tell you aforehand I shan't say a word about them what be dissatisfied with things."

"Why, damn you, won't you tell me anything about them?"

"I shan't tell you nothin' about it, sir, 'cause I ain't, the Lord be praised, one of 'em plain-clothes men, nor no damned police informer, neither, and 'cause heaven forbid I should cause trouble to any man."

"I see, so that's the kind of man you are, are you?"

"Yes, sir, and 'specially 'cause if I did tell on somebody, I'd be properly beaten up, anyhow."

"Oh, so that's what it is: you're afraid that the peasants might give you a beating! But, my dear fellow, don't you be afraid of that."

"I can see, sir, as how you're sayin' that 'cause they never gave you a beatin' yet."

"Not at all, not at all! I'm saying that because even if the peasants gave you a good thrashing, you'd still keep your present job, but if you let any suspicious person dart past you like a bird and fail to stop him by catching hold of him immediately, you'll be sent to Siberia at once!"

"But why should they be sendin' me to Siberia, sir?"

"Because the man you let slip through your fingers is one of those underminers of foundations, that's why!"

"But, Lord, sir, what business have I with him? Let him go in peace, I says."

"Well, aren't you just a damned fool? An underminer of foundations and he says, 'Let him go in peace!' What an ass!"

But Stetsko got offended and began to grumble at me.

"What do you keep on callin' me names all the way for?"

"I'm calling you names," I said, "because, fool that you are, you should not be concentrating all your attention on the horses, even while you're driving me, but be keeping a sharp look-out to see if any underminer of foundations is coming along the road, for if he is, you must instantly go in chase of him. Mind you do it, or it is Siberia for you and me, too, I shouldn't wonder."

Stetsko heard me out carefully, although without losing for one moment that famous native phlegm of his.

"And what's goin' to happen afterwards?" he asked.

Well, I just told him anything that came into my head on the spur of the moment about what things would be like after all the underminers of foundations had been apprehended. We should not go on living as we had in the past, I explained, but everything would be different.

"How different?" he asked.

"That's quite simple," I said. "Now, you see, we're driving in a carriage and four with all the four horses between shafts, but then we shall be driving a team of three horses with only one horse between the shafts and a shaft bow over it and with bells."

"Anythin' else, sir?"

"Why, yes," I said, "we shall no longer be singing Ukrainian songs."

"What songs shall we be singin', sir?"

"We shall be singing Russian songs, of course," I explained, "for instance, 'On the bridge, on the bridge, on the wayfaring-tree bridge . . .'"

"What would a wayfarin'-tree bridge be like, sir?"

"Oh, it's just a merry song, a Russian song . . . 'The skirts of our coats, they fly up in the air and swell out . . .'"

"Why do they fly up in the air and swell out, sir?"

"Don't you understand it?"

"Can't say I do, sir."

"Well, you will!"

"And why will I, sir?"

"You'll see!"

"Will I, though?"

"Yes, you will. When the time comes you'll see it all right."

Here Stetsko said suddenly, "Whoa!" and, abandoning his famous Ukrainian phlegm, he stopped the horses, got off the box and handed me the reins.

"What's all this?" I asked.

"Take them reins, sir."

"What are you talking about?"

"Take them reins, sir," Stetsko repeated stolidly.

"Why?"

" 'Cause I ain't goin' to drive you no further."

"What do you mean?"

"I means, sir," Stetsko said, "that I ain't goin' to be a-listenin' to them horrors o' yourn no more and I ain't goin' to be a-drivin' you no more, neither. Drive yourself, sir."

He placed the reins on my knees and just walked off the road and struck across a field, disappearing presently in a wood.

I kept on calling after him, addressing him as "my dear old fellow" and by other ingratiating names, but I couldn't get him to come back. Only once did he turn round for a second, but only to shout at me, "Don't waste your breath, sir! I shan't be a-comin' back. Drive them horses o' yourn yourself for a change!"

Well, so off he went, leaving me stranded at night miles from anywhere. So that's, sir, what comes of talking politics to such people! "Beg pardon, sir, drive them horses o' yourn yourself for a change!"

My horses, I don't mind admitting, were first-rate, for, not being married, I could afford showing off a little, but I wasn't much of a driver myself and, besides, you know, to return home without a coachman and driving your own horses meant cutting rather a poor figure in our village. I found it indeed a confoundedly hard job to get home at all and I got in such a panic on the way that I promptly fell ill with stomach trouble and afterwards something even more provoking happened, for that fool Stetsko could not really make head or tail of what I had been saying to him and he went about telling everybody that any man taking on the job of my driver would have to act as a police informer or spy or else go to Siberia. The upshot of it was that not a single lad in the village would consent to become my coachman or my stableman and I had nobody to groom my horses or feed them or harness them and, on top of it all, they were stolen one night, all four of them, after Christina and I had filled their mangers with oats and locked up the stable!

That, of course, was the last straw, for what could be more disgraceful for the man who had rid the village of horse-thieves than to have his own horses stolen!

CHAPTER TWENTY-ONE

I FELT TERRIBLY EMBITTERED and infuriated. My reputation had suffered a grievous blow, for, as I said, what could be more humiliating for a sub-district police officer than to have thieves break into his stables and steal his horses? It was a piece of the rankest effrontery. The horses, the four of them, had cost me seven hundred roubles, not to mention the harness which had also been stolen, but the main thing, of course, was that I could do nothing about it, for how could I run after the thieves without horses? I couldn't very well do it mounted on a stick!

I should have got the thieves for all that if everything had gone on as before, and I could have conducted the investigation according to the *Rules for the Revelation of Truth*. Unfortunately, the investigation into the theft had been placed in other hands, and the man in charge would not listen to me and refused to arrest the suspects I mentioned to him. I was, therefore, forced to detain them for interrogation myself and I proceeded against them in accordance with the *Rules for the Revelation of Truth*, but one of the rogues had the impertinence to lodge a complaint against me, with the result that I myself had to appear in court and defend myself against a common horse-thief! What do you say to that? It was I, mark you, who had been robbed, I, an honourable man, and it was I who had to rush to town and appear in court as a defendant! I daresay every kind of lawlessness known to man has at one time or another happened on this sin-ridden earth of ours, but such a thing, I'm sure, has never happened before!

Having no horses of my own, I had to hire a Jewish coachman to take me to town, where, incidentally, I intended to buy myself a pair of horses.

As you can imagine, sir, my nerves were in a terrible state

and I simply loathed the idea of appearing in court in an action of so unusual a nature. Who, I asked myself, wanted those modern courts of theirs? Before, things were quite different in our town : the court decided each case according to the documents placed before it, and whatever the heads of the different departments and their clerks decided was carried out ; the man who was found guilty would cross himself and bend over in accordance with the time-hallowed customs of our forefathers, while another miserable sinner would let him have as many strokes across his back as had been prescribed by law and everything would be settled without any fuss and, I might say, with the utmost goodwill on the part of all present. But now they had to change all that and introduce such equality and fraternity that—if you please—every rogue was permitted to lodge complaints and address the court! What an amazing state of affairs ! Why, a decent man felt deeply humiliated even to be present in such a court : one moment the judge addresses the court, next moment the malefactor himself, if you please, is allowed to make a speech and after him his counsel has his say ! How could I even hope to out-talk them all?

So I went to see my old tutor, Vyekovyechkin, and I asked his reverence how I was to behave in court. "Tell me, my dear Eugraph Semyyonovich," I said, "what am I to say in court when my case comes up for a hearing?"

Well, the old boy (may he live for many more years !) gave me a piece of excellent advice.

"In addressing the court," he said, "affect as flowery a style as possible. In fact, try to speak as if you were reciting poetry, and, above all, don't you let them bully you !"

"Thank you, sir," I said. "I shall do as you say."

So when they asked me, "What do you know about it?" I straightway began to frame my reply in the style my old tutor had recommended.

"What I know about it, your Honour," I said, "is that everything in our village was quiet, it was a fine day and the sun had been shining high in the sky all day long and, while Phoebus was driving his chariot across the sky, I had been awake, but soon the day began to incline towards evening, the sun still shining, though its refulgence was somewhat dimmed, but in a little while it began to sink below the horizon and everything then looked even more splendid, both on earth and in the heavens, and absolute peace reigned until night descended upon the world."

Here the presiding judge interrupted me and said, "Aren't you digressing a little?"

"Not a bit, your Honour," I replied.

"Keep to the point," he said, "and tell us how your horses were stolen."

"I was coming to that, your Honour."

"Very well, carry on, please."

"I had mushrooms cooked in cream for supper and then I sat down at my table to transact some official business, after which I said my evening prayers and was about to go to bed when I suddenly felt very sick, just as if I had been poisoned . . ."

"I suppose," a member of the court interrupted me, "the mushrooms must have disagreed with you."

"I don't know what the reason was, sir," I said, "but I got a terrible pain just here in my stomach and a cold shiver ran down my spine and I writhed in my bed and could not fall asleep."

There was loud laughter in court.

"What kind of night was it?" a member of the court asked me. "Was it a light or a dark night?"

"The night," I replied, "was neither light, nor dark, but sort of betwixt and between, the sort of night when the water nixies like to come up from the river beds and go abroad in search of young men in the rushes."

"What you mean is, I suppose, that there was no moon."

"No, your Honour, there certainly was no moon or, maybe, there was a moon, but a kind of roving, inconstant moon, appearing one minute and another minute hiding herself behind some fleecy clouds. It would peep out, have a look at the earth and again dive into the clouds. Well, so I went back to bed, covered myself well up with blankets and suddenly felt so irresistible an urge to go to sleep that I couldn't help thinking that even God's angels were just then lying down to sleep on little clouds as on pillows. As for our villagers, they were tired out after a day's work in the fields and they were raising such a snoring that they made the earth itself tremble and shake. So I, too, put my head on my pillow, shut my eyes tightly and .."

I could see that the people in court were listening to me with great pleasure and, indeed, somebody among the public even began to cry, but the presiding judge again began to find fault with me and he told me sternly to tell the court how my horses had been stolen.

"But I'm leading up to that all the time, your Honour," I said. "All of a sudden," I went on, "the people who were sound asleep in the village became aware of some mysterious scratching and at first some of them thought that it might be cats, I mean, your Honour, cats who were out on the tiles, in a manner of speaking, while others, however, definitely thought that those were not cats or dogs, but the sons of . . ."

"Please do not use obscene language in court!" the presiding judge interrupted me again.

"I'm not using obscene language, your Honour," I replied. "I was merely going to say that all the people in the world are the sons of their mothers, just like you and me, sir."

There was renewed laughter among the spectators in court and the presiding judge said to me, "That'll do!"

But feeling that the public was on my side, I said, "Yes, sir, but I did not really wish to cast aspersions on the mothers of those who were responsible for the suspicious noises on that night. No, sir. Now, if I had in any way suggested that their mothers were unmarried, then, I admit, sir, it would have been rather an unwarranted attack on the honour of those excellent ladies, but all I said was sons-of . . ."

"No more of your philosophising, if you please!"

But I could see that the presiding judge himself could hardly restrain himself from laughing and, besides, the public were having a most enjoyable time, too.

"Go on with your evidence, sir," the presiding judge said to me, "but cut it short and keep to the point or I shall have to ask you to stand down."

"Yes, sir," I said. "All I have to say, sir, is that those were the sons-of . . ., but as you object to my referring to them by that name, I shall simply call them the bandits who are now sitting on that bench behind the constables, but who really ought to be sent to Siberia."

But here the presiding judge nearly jumped out of his skin.

"You have no right," he thundered, "to make suggestions to the court where anybody's rightful place is or where he should be sent."

"I'm very sorry, your Honour," I said, "but I must beg to differ from you, since my horses were excellent horses and those sons-of-bitches stole them, and if you won't send them to Siberia at once, they'll go on stealing horses till one day, God willing, they may even steal your horses, which indeed the Lord grant they may do."

Here the entire public in court began to clap their hands, as though I had been the actor Shchepkin himself, and the presiding judge ordered the court to be cleared and he ordered me out, too. In the crowd outside the court I heard all sorts of opinions expressed about myself and I even overheard one young fellow saying, "Here's that blackguardly fool." But during dinner at the inn, many people congratulated me and wished to drink my health and, finding myself in the company of such friendly strangers, I yielded to their wishes and I'm afraid I got so tight that I found myself in heaven knows what kind of a place, and I even began to dance with some young ladies, and when I woke up in the morning I said to myself, "Good Lord, if I don't get out of here quickly, I shall lose what's left of my reputation," and inside my head a voice seemed to say very clearly (fancy that now!), "You know very well what you have to do : in the first place, you must go immediately to the public bath-house and have the attendants there give you a good steaming, then you must go to church and say your prayers and then you can go where you like again."

In the meantime, however, the strangers kept on asking me whether I had ever met a real underminer of foundations. I told them frankly that I hadn't and that once I even mistook a girl with cropped hair for one of them, but that I had good hopes of unmasking and apprehending them one day, for I knew all their identification marks.

"But," the strangers persisted, "do you really think such a person would find anything to do in Peregoody?"

"Why, of course," I said, "he'll find plenty to do, for while the people there are law-abiding citizens, they do sometimes fall silent and refuse to talk, or again they go to the woods, or they sing, 'Sweet and pleasant was life in the Ukraine in the days of old.' In fact, things have come to such a pass in our village that the people there think nothing of challenging the authorities and refuse to take on a job as my coachman although I'm the only representative of the authorities there."

"Dear, dear," they said, "that is bad."

"It is indeed!" I exclaimed.

"But why's that?"

"I think I'm right in believing that they want to make quite sure that I never succeed in catching the underminer of foundations and so never get a decoration from the Government. You see, one of the reasons I came to town was to find a coachman for myself, one, particularly, who does not know anyone in our village and preferably one of those fierce Russians from the province of Ryazan who knows how to whistle at a team of horses and who loves everything Russian and about whom I could be sure that he would stand no nonsense from any Ukrainian yokel."

"So be it!" a man shouted at me, and with a great effort, for I was still dazed from my last night's carousal, I recognised in the man who was talking to me one of the strangers who had stood me drinks at the inn the night before and, in fact, it was he who had taken me to the bath-house and later sent me to church for early morning mass. "When you get back home, sir," he said to me, "you'll have a coachman and I assure you he'll be an excellent coachman and he won't ask for much pay, either, and you can depend on him to do all sorts of things . . ."

And, true enough! No sooner did I enter my house than I was met by a fine, strong fellow who welcomed me with a *samovar* in his hands and an ear-ring in his ear.

"The blessings of the Lord upon you, sir," he said, "and may you always feel as fresh as when coming out of a steam bath!"

"What's your name?" I asked him.

"Terenka Nalyotov, known as Terenka the Daredevil, of the province of Orel."

"Well,". said I, "pleased to meet you, Terenka. It is true that I was really looking for a Ryazan man, but it's well known that some of you Orel chaps are men of great pluck and initiative and heaven help anyone crossing their path. Now, what I want you to do is to know everything that's going on in our village and to help me to apprehend traitors and thieves."

"Don't you worry about it, sir," he said. "That's as easy as spitting to me."

"Excellent," I said, "that's the kind of fellow I want!"

So I hired him on the spot.

CHAPTER TWENTY-TWO

EVERYTHING WENT SWIMMINGLY NOW. Terenka was never seen in the company of any Ukrainian peasant and yet he seemed to know all about them. He did not live in my house, but—stout fellow!—preferred to live alone in the stables with the horses. For any other man the stables would have been a confoundedly cold place in winter, but Terenka did not mind. When driving, he'd sing Russian songs, such as "Swiftly along the highway a *troika's* outstripping the wind," and so well did the rascal sing that it made my heart leap with joy . . . Oh, how thankful I was to have got such a man! Now I had no doubt at all that we would not only find the underminer of foundations, but would not let him slip through our fingers. Imagine my consternation, therefore, when I was informed by the authorities that they had been flooded with secret reports, which certainly did not emanate from me, that there was growing dissatisfaction among the peasants, and I was urgently instructed to find out who was responsible for sending those alarming reports. Personally, I confess, I was rather inclined to put the blame on Dmitry Afanassyevich, who walked in perpetual fear of being beaten up by the lads of our village for taking too great an interest in our village maidens, but to make quite sure I questioned Terenka about it while out driving with him one day.

"I say, my dear fellow," I said to him, "do you think it is Dmitry Afanassyevich who's been kicking up such a hell of a row with the authorities lately?"

"No, sir," Terenka replied without a moment's hesitation, "I don't think it's him."

"What makes you think so?"

"I think so," Terenka replied (the dear fellow certainly had his wits about him !), "because he's too stupid to know the truth."

"Is it true, then?"

"Of course, it's true !"

"Well, I'm damned !" I exclaimed. "Tell me about it."

So he told me that the peasants were indeed beginning to grumble about how things were getting worse and worse for everybody, their chief complaint being, it seemed, that people no longer lived as they ought to, not, that is, according to God's laws.

"The dirty rascals !" I said. "What do they know about how one has to live according to God's laws?"

"You see, sir," Terenka said, "there are all sorts of rogues and vagabonds knocking about the village with Bibles in their pockets and they read it to the people on the threshing floors and in pits."

Well, of all things ! I never dreamt even of the existence of such pernicious mischief-makers, and Terenka (stout lad !) seemed to know all about it, while I, who represented the authorities, knew nothing !

Terenka, it is true, said to me, "This isn't your business at all, sir. It's the priest's business : let *him* look to his flock !"

"True enough," I thought to myself, "what has this got to do with me?"

I did ask Christina, though, whether she had not been running about with any rogues and vagabonds and listening to their Bible readings in pits, but the silly fool misunderstood me.

"Who do you take me for?" she asked peevishly. "What kind of a slut do you think I am to go to a pit with a vagabond?"

"Oh, go away !" I said.

"Go away yourself," she said, "and the sooner, the better."

"Is the priest," I asked her, "still pestering you with his silly questions?"

"Of course he is!"

"But you don't tell him everything at confession, do you?"

"My goodness," she said, "what kind of a fool do you take me for?"

"Oh well," I said, "that's all right then."

I put the same question to many other people in our village and all of them gave me the same answer as Christina and to all of them I said, "Well, that's all right then."

For, indeed, why should the priest Nazarko know everything if he already had a decoration from the Government? However, it never rains but it pours, and I had hardly time to recover from the shock of Terenka's disclosures when I was apprised that a serious accusation had· been lodged against me with the authorities, namely, that I was persuading people not to go to confession and that I, mark you, was spreading all sorts of Protestant heresies among them. Merciful heavens, what are Protestant heresies, anyway? I've never heard of them! But the thing that worried me now was whether it was I who was trying to catch someone or whether somebody was trying to catch me? It was a devil of a problem and no wonder I grew more and more distraught and the light was extinguished in my eyes and my teeth were bared.

In the meantime the storm-clouds were gathering more and more and within a week or so a printed pamphlet, full of the most pernicious opinions, was discovered at our inn. In this pamphlet people were exhorted not to put up with their miserable existence any longer and told that "everybody who believes in God should learn to read and write and not listen to potbellied priests." Yes, that was the expression they used: "potbellied!"

Everybody in our village who could read, read that leaflet aloud to the rest, and afterwards they burnt it by rolling it up for cigarettes. It was not long after that another leaflet was found which said all sorts of things about our "rotten, pampered gentry," and in that connection there was a far-from-flattering reference made to the "thieving police." The people were then told that they were as good as their betters and that they ought to live as well as their masters, and they were advised to take no notice of the police and to refuse to obey their orders and, generally, to live in peace with each other in accordance with God's laws! The whole thing was a real nightmare! Oh, if I only knew who was responsible for bringing that pernicious stuff to our village and spreading it among the people!

"Dear Terenka," I said to my coachman, "you promised to help me when I needed your advice and assistance, but I'm afraid, my dear fellow, you don't seem to be doing anything. If only I could lay my hands on the man responsible for spreading those abominable pamphlets, I'd get a decoration from the Government and I swear to give you three roubles."

He told me again that he did not know for certain who that man was, but it did occur to him that it might be those fiddlers who were staying with the priest Nazary and who were scraping away on their fiddles all through the night to the accompaniment of the miaowing and barking of all the cats and dogs in the village, while spending all day among the peasants.

I was simply staggered by that piece of news. "Heavens," I said to myself, "who else could they be but some of those underminers of foundations!"

"Dear Terenka," I said to my coachman, "promise me that you will keep an eye on them."

"Well, sir," said Terenka, "I have a strong suspicion that it's them all right and I'd advise you to get up at midnight and listen to them scraping away on their fiddles."

I did that : I wound up my alarm clock and set the alarm for midnight. I woke up at the right time and immediately opened the windows into the garden, and the first thing I was aware of was the fresh breeze and the fiddlers were indeed scraping away for all they were worth and, whether it was because of that or not, the cats were rushing about like mad all over the village and two tomcats jumped down from the roof under my windows and immediately engaged in a fight with each other. But that's by the way.

Next morning I went to Father Nazary and asked him who those fiddlers in his house were.

"Fiddlers?" he repeated and burst out laughing. "Why, man alive, they're not fiddlers, they're virtuosi. They're writing down our folksongs and they're going to send them off to the opera. Lord, what a nitwit you are! Fiddlers, indeed!"

Well, I let it pass.

CHAPTER TWENTY-THREE

THERE HAPPENED TO BE A HORSE FAIR at that time about five miles from our village and I went there and walked about among the people just to keep an eye on things, this being, of course, part of my regular duties. The two fiddlers or virtuosos were also at the fair and I saw them walking about with notebooks in their hands in which they would from time to time scribble something. I kept them under observation for some appreciable time, until I felt very tired, but I couldn't make head or tail of what they were really up to. But when I went back to my carriage to help myself to a glass of vodka and have a bite of whatever Christina had prepared for me, I saw at once one of those subversive leaflets lying inside my carriage . . . How do you like that? A subversive leaflet lying about in my own carriage, if you please, in the carriage of a police officer! And, mark you, it was no longer printed entirely in prose, but there was a little poem included, all about how our peasants were being bled white by constant tax collections.

"Terenka, my dear fellow," I said, "you haven't seen anyone walking up to my carriage, have you?"

"I've seen nothing," he replied. "I haven't got eyes at the back of my head, have I?"

"A piece of paper has been put in there, so there must have been someone who did it. Are you quite sure nobody's been here or has anyone passed by recently?"

"Sneaky and Seedy, the two fiddlers who're staying at the priest's house, passed by a short time ago. They were the only people I've noticed."

"Are you sure that's what they are called?"

"Of course I am. Sneaky is always sneaking about and Seedy is always scattering seeds."

"It's them then!"

"Yes, sir. I expect, sir, you'd like me to get friendly with them and treat them to some drinks, wouldn't you?"

"Yes, yes," I exclaimed, "do it by all means. Here's fifty copecks for you and—er—remember, as soon as I get my decoration I'll give you three roubles as promised."

Next day I saw Terenka coming out of the priest's house with a little wooden board in his hands.

"I'm doing my best, sir," he said. "I've just been to the priest's house to get acquainted with those fiddlers."

"Tell me quickly what happened," I said.

"Well, sir, I took this little board with me and I said to them, This must be part of a holy icon, I said. I found it in the stables covered up with a swallow's nest, God forgive me. Whether because of it or not, I said, I've been having dreadful dreams, all of which seemed to point to some strange event taking place shortly. Then during a thunderstorm, I said, the nest fell down and under it was the icon, just as foretold in my dreams. I'm afraid no sign of the painting can be seen on it now because the entire image of the saint has been rubbed off. I then asked the priest to sprinkle it with holy water."

"Damn clever, my dear fellow, damn clever! What happened afterwards?"

"The priest, sir, commended my action highly. 'It does you credit,' he said, 'to have discovered a sacred object which our sub-district officer of police had so shamelessly neglected.'"

"Are you quite sure he said that?"

"I swear he did, sir. I wouldn't tell you a lie, would I?"

"Well," I said, "I suppose he'll report me for that, but I'm going to get ahead of him and report him for sheltering Sneaky and Seedy."

So I sent in my report in which I stated that two unknown men, Sneaky and Seedy by name, had appeared in our village and that it was quite impossible to find out what Sneaky was sneaking about or what seeds Seedy was scattering. The only suspicious circumstance connected with their visit was that illegal leaflets were now cropping up everywhere. I would therefore most respectfully submit to the never-to-be-trifled-with authorities that some steps ought to be taken immediately, and I assured them that I was ready to take them as soon as I was authorised to do so.

But imagine my distress, sir, when the whole thing was again turned against me! For nothing of a compromising nature was found on the two fiddlers after they had been taken into custody and subjected to a thorough search, and they had to be set at liberty again. As for me, I became known far and wide as either a trouble-maker or a fool and I was hated and despised by everybody and, on top of it all, I found myself in the midst of a veritable shower of illegal leaflets which seemed to be dropping from a cloudless sky.

Well, if in the past I did, as I told you, plague those villainous horse-thieves according to the *Rules for the Revelation of Truth*, and if I did wear them down until they were glad to confess their crimes, then that, sir, I assure you, was nothing in comparison with what I myself had to endure now. Moreover, it became absolutely necessary to seek out and apprehend the underminer of foundations who was responsible for broadcasting those leaflets, for even my own district police commissioner got very angry with me.

"It is you," he said to me, "who are a damned trouble-maker and confounded villain! Everything used to be so peaceful here and we never had any disturbers of the peace except a few horse-thieves, but ever since you began talking about those underminers of foundations, there's been no end of trouble in your village. Today everybody's convinced that we've got those damned throne-shakers among us. Very well, in that case, produce them! I give you one week and if by the end of it you don't get me one underminer of foundations, I shall have you cashiered!"

That was the sort of hell I had brought upon myself for taking all that trouble! Oh, the bitter tears I shed after that talk in the loneliness of my room at night! It was raining cats and dogs and bright flashes of lightning lit up my bedroom. I couldn't sleep, so I either sat on my bed or walked up and down the room and then I knelt and prayed. "Merciful Father," I said, "I beseech Thee, deliver into my hands only one of those sons of Belial!" And again my head was filled with those mad dreams of mine, and so many times did I seem to see that underminer of foundations and was about to grab him, that it was just as if I had really gone off my head. In the end I collapsed on the floor and lost consciousness. But a most terrible roll of thunder brought me back to my senses and, raising my head, I saw through the window a real and quite unmistakable underminer of foundations, surrounded by a kind of hellish light, driving past in a carriage and pair. I recognised him at once, for he was wearing a hat of the Greek country and a cloak and the cast of his countenance was that of a real bandit!

It was quite impossible to describe what I felt at that moment: after so many dreary months of rancour, sorrow and despair, there he suddenly was, sent in answer to my prayer, delivered into my hands and revealed in thunder and lightning and a most prodigious downpour of rain at night.

There was no time to be lost: he had to be apprehended immediately!

CHAPTER TWENTY-FOUR

I YELLED AT THE TOP OF MY VOICE: "Christina! Christina!" but the damned girl was fast asleep and did not answer my call. I rushed like mad to her room and shouted again, "Christina!" for I wanted to send her at once to Terenka to get ready my carriage so that I could go in pursuit of the underminer of foundations without wasting a precious minute, but Christina Ivanovna, if you please, was not in her bed, and, looking out of the window, I saw her, undeterred either by the thunder or the rain, coming surreptitiously out of the stables where she must have been spending her time with Terenka. She didn't even have her dress on and she looked very pleased with herself . . .

You can imagine, sir, what a frightful shock it was to me to discover such a thing happening under my own roof and at such a time! But I pretended to take no notice, and merely shouted at her, "Go back where you've come from, you little baggage, and tell him to harness the horses this very minute!"

But the false creature replied, "Terenka will not harness your horses at this time of the night!"

"What did you say?" I bellowed to her. "How dare you speak to me like that?"

"Why shouldn't I dare to speak to you any way I like?" Christina said. "What do you mean by ordering people to harness your horses when all good Christians are asleep. Terenka will never harness your horses in the middle of the night!"

"Never?" I mimicked her. "In the middle of the night when all good Christians sleep! Well, why aren't you asleep, you baggage? What were you wandering about the yard for?"

"I know what I was doing," she replied.

"So do I!"

"I went out to listen to the fiddlers."

"Oh, so that's what you were doing, were you? Listening to the fiddlers! As if you could hear anything in such a thunderstorm!"

"I could hear them all right from where I was."

"You could, could you? You're a shameless trollop, that's what you are!"

"You can call me any names you like," she said, "only Terenka won't harness your horses because he isn't feeling well."

"I'll show you! Not feeling well, is he? Go and tell him to get me my carriage at once, do you hear?"

"He's got toothache . . ."

But here I raised such a clamour that my carriage and Terenka were waiting outside my house in no time. Terenka, it was true, had his face wrapped round in a kerchief because of his toothache, but I said to him :

"Well, Terenka, look sharp now. Don't spare the horses and don't spare yourself, either, and drive as fast as hell, for I've found the underminer of foundations and all you have to do is to overtake him before he gets out of our district and when you overtake him, don't hesitate to ride him down and trample on him."

"I think it would be best to overtake him on the bridge across the Gnilusha, sir," said Terenka. "I could easily throw him into the water there and we'd grab him that way."

"Yes, by all means," I said.

And off he drove as fast as anything, and then damned if I didn't see right in front of us that pair of horses I had seen through the window, and in the carriage for all the world to see sat that self-same real and unmistakable enemy of the Empire !

"Shall I throw him off the bridge?" Terenka roared.

"Yes," I roared back.

So directly the underminer of foundations drove on to the bridge, Terenka emitted his shrill whistle and our horses hit the side of his carriage and threw him, bag and baggage, into the stream and we had no trouble at all in apprehending him in the water . . .

He was quite a young fellow, you know, of middle size and with the most horrible cast of countenance you can imagine, and he didn't waste any time, either, I assure you, in telling us the most absurd yarn about himself.

"You don't know who I am or what you're doing," he said.

"Don't you worry about that, my lad," I said, pinioning his arms.

"I'm a Government secret agent," he said, "and I'm on the trail of a desperate criminal and if you don't let me go at once, I might lose him."

"All right, my good man," I said, "let me first put you into an empty cask at our brewery. You'll be safe there for the time being and then we'll see whether I had any right to detain you."

He was furious and he told us all sorts of things about who he was and what trouble we were letting ourselves in for, trying all the time to frighten me, but I said, "Never mind, my good man, let me deal with you first and then you'll deal with me," and I put him in an empty barrel and put a guard over him. Then I drove off straight to the town with my report : "Now give me what I deserve, for I've caught the underminer of foundations !"

CHAPTER TWENTY-FIVE

BUT JUST IMAGINE IT, SIR, I never reached the town and I bet you'll never guess what happened to prevent my reaching it. As I told you, it was raining cats and dogs at the time and the rain showed no signs of stopping even though I had realised my fondest dream and caught the first authentic enemy of the Empire.

So there I was, soaked to the skin and trying to keep warm as best I could under my Caucasian felt cloak, dreaming just like Gogol's Dmukhonetz of the decoration they were going to bestow upon me and wondering what kind of ribbon they'd send me from St. Petersburg, whether a dark or a light blue one. Sunk in those blissful meditations, I didn't notice that I had dropped off into a heavy slumber while the carriage was axle-deep in mud and the rain came pouring down and drenching me. However, I slept like a real hero of the Russian folk-tales under my Caucasian cloak and I dreamt of my victory over the forces of evil and was re-living those moments of triumph again and again. I saw the underminer of foundations sitting tied and gagged, trying all the time to bite me and—in the end he did bite me! This made me wake up and, looking round, I saw that day was already breaking and that we were in a wild, dark wood, where I had never been before, and that for some reason we were no longer travelling, but standing still, and that Terenka was no longer on the box, but was doing something in front of the horses or clambering on top of something, having already unharnessed one of my mettlesome horses and knocking something into the hoof of the other, and every time he hit the hoof, the horse bucked and snorted, shaking the whole carriage.

"What's the matter, Terenka?" I shouted to him. "What's the horse shying and shaking the carriage for?"

259

"Shut up!" he replied.

"What do you mean : shut up? Where are we?"

"Don't know."

"What nonsense is this? Why don't you know?"

"I took a short cut through this wood and now I've lost my way."

"You must have gone off your head," I said, "and I shouldn't be surprised if you didn't want to kill me now."

"It's hardly worth while dirtying my hands on you," he said calmly.

"You damned Russian," I said, "to you everything is worth while. You'd kill a man for one copeck and a hundred men for a hundred and there'd be a rouble for you! But take all my money, only please don't murder me!"

He said nothing, but just led out the side-horse and shouted at me, "Good-bye, you idiot! Sit here and wait for the Order of the Mad Dog!"

And with those words he mounted and galloped away. Fancy, being spoken to like that and without any previous warning, either! So I was left alone in an unknown wood with just one horse and I could not tell where I was or what that damned bandit had done to me.

What he had done was something so awful that it could be explained only on the assumption that the man had gone off his mind suddenly, unless, indeed, he had some ulterior motive, for, as I have just told you, he had galloped off on the side-horse, leaving behind his tattered driver's overcoat and Christina's kerchief with which he had wrapped up his face, evidently because of his pretended toothache. As for the remaining horse, the villain had knocked two nails under one of its hoofs. Now, I ask you, wasn't he a real brute, that confounded Russian rascal? Dear God, what a position to be in! The rain still continued to pour down and the horse was jerking its injured foot and knocking it against the ground so that the poor beast's sufferings made my heart bleed. I thought to myself, 'Let's see if I can find a pair of pliers under the seat, for I might at least have a shot at drawing the nails out of the poor creature's hoofs. But no sooner had I taken off the upholstered seat than . . . Well, what do you think I saw there? Why, the box under the seat was stuffed full with those seditious leaflets which told the peasants that they did not live as they should and went on to tell them how they should live and, in short, overflowed with the most outrageous sentiments!

I fell upon my knees and spread out my arms to hide from my sight the evidence of that unheard-of treachery. For now, of course, it became clear to me that Terenka was none other than that damned underminer of foundations I'd been trying to catch! Yes, indeed, Terenka and no one else! Terenka who seemed to have been nicknamed Daredevil with good reason! And it was I myself who had assisted him in scattering those accursed leaflets all over the district. Yes, there in front of me was the most damning evidence of my own stupid incapacity and shortsightedness!

I thought to myself: What kind of profit can I expect for myself from sitting on top of those leaflets in my carriage and looking dazed and shedding tears? The rain's bound to stop sooner or later and someone's bound to come along the road and I shall be caught redhanded and accused of being a political criminal! I must pull myself together and get rid of those leaflets . . . Yes, I must do it at once! . . .

CHAPTER TWENTY-SIX

WELL, I SPRANG TO MY FEET and began feverishly to collect all those incriminating pieces of paper. You see, I wanted to throw them all into a ditch or stamp them into some swamp and cover them up with something so that they should all disappear and leave no trace behind. But as I seized hold of all those small slips of paper in that most awful rain and amid those blinding flashes of lightning, I did not know myself whither I was going, and suddenly I found myself on the very brink of a deep ravine, and before I knew what was happening, a huge lump of clay gave way in a most frightful manner under my feet and I was precipitated to the bottom of it. In my fall all the pamphlets slipped out of my hands and were carried off by the raging torrent into which I had fallen and in which I was being tossed about and sucked under, being in imminent danger of drowning . . .

But my life was saved and you can imagine my surprise when, on recovering my senses, I found myself in a beautiful room which at first I was inclined to think was a heavenly abode. I lay between two spotlessly clean sheets in a soft, clean bed and near the top of the bed was a little table and on it were bottles of medicine and not far away, just opposite the bed, was another table with a lighted lamp covered with a green taffeta lampshade, shedding a most pleasant light . . . I looked and looked and I seemed to see something darting about quickly in the circle of light. "What on earth can it be?" I asked myself. "Looks just like the paw of a grey cat, or can it be something else?" But I couldn't make out what it was or indeed where I was or how I got there. I just lay there, all sorts of thoughts racing through my mind, but I felt very peaceful and happy. I suppose, I thought to myself, that's what it must be like in the

262

Kingdom of Heaven. Yes, I reflected, that was what it was : a
long time ago I had been a man who was guilty of every kind
of wickedness and then I was swallowed up by a torrent and
died and I could only suppose that, owing to some strange
mistake, I now found myself in paradise. Still, it was also quite
possible that I deserved to get into paradise, considering that
for some time I had been in the service of a bishop. Again, it
was quite likely that even my services to the church did not
entitle me to a seat in paradise and that it wasn't paradise at all
in which I found myself now, but in some kind of Ovid's pagan
metamorphosis. Indeed, that seemed most likely, for in paradise
they all sat about and sang, "Holy, holy, holy," whereas nobody
was singing here. Then my memory returned to me and
thoughts began to flash through my mind like lightning, and I
remembered that I had been a sub-district police officer in Peregoody, and that I had striven to obtain honours, and that my
ambitions had filled me with mad dreams, and I had begun to
look for non-existent underminers of foundations in my district,
and that I had gone in chase of some man and been for a long
time in a state of the most dreadful alarm, and then I must have
suddenly been metamorphosed into something, into a most
gentle creature, and placed in that enchanting room where I
could see something dancing before my eyes, something very
mysterious, some curiously tiny creatures, the size of pea-pods,
just like the dwarfs children sometimes see in their dreams,
and these dwarfs seemed to be fighting with one another and
waving steel spears about which flashed so brilliantly that they
almost blinded me. Then I lost consciousness again and I came
to once more just as someone entered my room from
somewhere and whispered, "How's our patient today ?" And
another voice replied as softly, "He's better. The doctor says he
should regain consciousness today."

The first voice was quite unfamiliar to me, but the second

voice I did seem to have heard somewhere. They went on whispering and I tried to make out what they were saying to each other, but I couldn't, and the grey dwarfs with the steel spears had hidden themselves away; and then again, after some indefinite time, I saw that pleasant room, but now it was day-time and at the table where the cat's paws were darting about there sat a young lady in dark spectacles, knitting socks. I could not help thinking that it must again be that cunning pagan Ovid who had metamorphosed somebody else into Julia Semyonovna whom I had so wickedly deceived in Peregoody while I was still among the living on earth and who had com-plained about me to the President of the Noblemen's Chamber.

"Dear Ovid," I addressed myself to the Roman poet, "thank you for showing me somebody I want to see so much and whom I can now ask to forgive me for my wickedness." And not wishing to put it off any longer, I said to the young lady, "Please, forgive me, ma'am!" but as those words escaped my lips, I could hardly recognise my own voice.

The girl at the table, however, got up quickly and, raising a warning finger, whispered, "Don't talk, please. You're not allowed to talk!" and she adjusted something near my face and went out and after her there came into the room—who do you think?—why, the President of the Chamber of Nobles himself!

Here I remembered not only Ovid, but also Lucian and his meetings and conversations in the world of the dead and, fixing one eye in astonishment on the man who had entered the room, I said to myself, "Oho, my dear friend, so you're here, too! So your great learning has not saved you, has it?"

He noticed that one of my eyes was open and said, "Can't you open your other eye, too?" So I opened my other eye and asked him, "When did your lordship die and take up your abode here for good?"

For some reason he didn't seem to understand me, so I asked him more plainly, "How long have you been dead, sir?"

But he just smiled and said, "No, my dear chap, you and I are still in the land of the living, for we have still to settle something here."

I didn't grasp everything he said, but since then I began to recover consciousness more and more often and for longer and longer periods and I always found by my bedside either Prince Mamuru, the President of the Noblemen's Chamber, or Julia Semyonovna, for it was she and no one else. It was the prince and Julia Semyonovna who, as the poets say, "had snatched me out of the jaws of death," and by and by Julia Semyonovna revealed to me gently that I was in the house of the President of the Noblemen's Chamber and that I had been there for over six weeks. I had been brought there unconscious and delirious by the prince himself, who had come across me in the wood where I was running about in a fit of madness, in lightning and in rain, chasing after the lithographed leaflets which were carried away by raging torrents. The prince was returning from some business trip and he was accompanied by the police officer of one of our neighbouring sub-districts. They saw that I was stark, raving mad and they seized quite a number of those revolutionary leaflets, which, of course, involved me in a charge of distributing them. The prince put me in his carriage and took me home with him as a dangerously sick person.

I listened to her unable to conceal my astonishment at the things she told me and without, of course, realising at the time that that was only one drop in the bucket of my troubles. For I was not in the prince's house as a guest, but under house arrest until I recovered sufficiently to be sent away to prison, and two men in the kitchen kept constant guard over me.

Some mess I had got myself into, eh?

The prince had to inform the authorities as soon as I got

better and then I was to be transferred to prison and later put on trial for my heinous crimes. For it seemed that my crimes were of an exceptionally grave nature, since I had attacked ontheroad one of our Government's most efficient secret agents who had been sent to track down and apprehend one of the most daring underminers of foundations responsible for the distribution of those accursed leaflets. And it was I myself who with my own hands had caught the secret agent instead of the real criminal and deprived him of his freedom and thereby contributed to the escape of the underminer of foundations and that on one of my own horses, too, for the villain, of course, was none other than my own coachman Terenka! . . .

Dear, oh dear! But what was I? Was I or was I not Terenka's accomplice? That, it seemed, had still to be discovered, for was I not seized while engaged on such an inexplicable task as salvaging those leaflets? It was obvious that the strictest possible investigation was called for to throw some light on what I had been doing in the thunderstorm in that wood on that unhappy night. What had to be established was whether it had been my intention to cover up the traces of that most pernicious of propagandists by scattering the evidence of his crime in the ditches, or whether I had actually been his accomplice and was trying to spread those damned leaflets all over the world by floating them down the raging torrents?

CHAPTER TWENTY-SEVEN

WHEN I HAD LEARNT EVERYTHING, I said to the President of the Noblemen's Chamber, "I can see, sir, that I'm languishing under a most cruel accusation, but God is my witness, sir, that that was not at all how it happened."

So I asked his permission to tell him how it did happen and I told him and Julia Semyonovna, who had entered my room just then, everything I have told you. When I finished my story, I felt so weak that my eyes closed by themselves and my face was covered with a deathly pallor. Noticing it, the prince said to Julia Semyonovna, "My dear, you see here a most unhappy man, a man who was chasing after other people's scalps and lost his own scalp in the process. What a ridiculous and pitiful condition to be in and how vile are those who brought him to such a pass!"

Then they suddenly began to talk in French and although I know quite a number of French words, I cannot speak the language because I can't manage that nasal pronunciation of theirs. Anyway, I gathered from their conversation that I myself was responsible for what had occurred, for I myself had induced Terenka to enter my service by careless talk about the existence of those "elements" in our district, whereas, in the prince's words, the only "elements" we had were *borshch* and our famous and highly-intoxicating drink which we brewed with honey in a sealed oven. Now that Terenka had made good his escape and the whole thing had assumed the aspect of a great public scandal, I was in imminent danger of being sent to Siberia! But I had got so sick and tired of all those adventures of mine that I was no longer afraid of anything and I said to myself, "So be it, for I've been wicked and I deserve to be treated the same way."

The prince, however, said to Julia Semyonovna that he would do his best to help me, and Julia Semyonovna said to him, "Please, sir, do so."

How kind they were to me! But what I liked most of all was that the prince seemed to have found some excuse for my abominable deeds.

"Upon my word," he said, "I can't honestly say that he's guilty of any crime for which society ought to punish him. Think of the terrible environment in which he lived : born in a village, all his inclinations were for a simple life, but he was constantly harried and badgered and under the pretext of receiving an education he was taught things which are not worth knowing. Here you have Ovid, and the spreading of praying carpets and singing at rehearsals of religious executions according to the poet Zhukovsky's proposals, and the candles and the comb "for my lord bishop's beard," and knowing all the decorations and the interrogation of suspects in accordance with the *Rules for the Revelation of Truth*. Good Lord, what man could stand it and remain sane? Any man could be expected to go off his head in circumstances such as these, and he did!.."

Julia Semyonovna asked him whether he really thought that I was mad.

"Yes, I do," replied the prince, "and therein lies his salvation, for otherwise he's done for. When they take him away, I shall submit my observations about him and I shall insist that before they put him on trial he should be submitted to an examination into his mental condition."

"You know," exclaimed Julia Semyonovna, "I think that's only fair, but I'm afraid they won't listen to you."

"On the contrary," the prince said, "I'm quite certain that I shall succeed. What profit can they get from giving wide

publicity to this silly affair or from sending this wretched idiot
to Siberia ? This man has not been taught any useful trade and
without that such *bêtises* are unavoidable."

At first Julia Semyonovna did not comment at all on the
prince's words, for she was measuring the socks she was knitting
on her knees, but after a short pause she smiled and said,
"*Bêtises*, indeed ! That reminds me of my grandmother, sir, who
had been a celebrated beauty and a society woman. At the age
of seventy she became stone deaf and spent all her time in her
room knitting socks. She never came out to visitors because
aunt Olga, her elder daughter and my mother's sister, objected
to her indecent behaviour in society, her indecencies consisting
in all sorts of *bêtises*, such as smacking her lips, making loud
noises while eating and, what was worst of all, picking her
nose ! Yes, that indeed was the last straw and that habit of hers
made all of us shun her. At birthday parties, however, when
our relations forgathered and other important visitors arrived,
granny was remembered and questions were asked about her
and for that reason she was brought out and sat at the table,
which certainly added a certain lustre to the party, for she was
a very grand-looking old lady. But it was just then that her
presence gave rise to awful 'qualms,' for having got used to
knitting socks when alone, she could not sit still without doing
something, so that while she was eating with a fork or a spoon
everything went off all right, but no sooner did her hands
become free than she'd start picking her nose . . . Then everybody in the room would get very angry with her and start
shouting at her, 'Stop it, granny ! *Ne faites pas de bêtises !*"
She'd look up at us and ask in a surprised voice, 'What's the
matter ? What *bêtises* have I committed now ?" And when they'd
point to her nose, she'd say, 'I wish you'd leave me alone. Give
me a sock to knit and there won't be any *bêtises!*' And the
minute she'd be given a sock, she'd start knitting and never

even touch her nose, but behave herself beautifully. I suppose, it's the same thing with everybody really."

"Quite right, my dear," the prince expressed his approval laughingly. "Your grandmother provides an excellent illustration to a moral which all people who cannot help poking their noses where they're not wanted should be made to learn."

Then Julia Semyonovna said just as a joke against herself, "I suppose that's why I'm always knitting socks."

"And a very good thing, too," said the prince, "for you, at any rate, do no wrong to anybody."

Having said that, he went out and all through the night I felt that I was among such splendid people, the like of whom I had never met before. I could not help thinking that I'd had enough of that happiness and that it was high time I relieved them of my presence and that I'd better go and take my punishment for the *bêtises* I had committed.

All my ideas had undergone a radical change.

CHAPTER TWENTY-EIGHT

MY HUMAN FEELINGS having awakened in me, I got up early next morning and, as I looked at myself in a glass, I could not help feeling shocked, for my face was all wrinkled and the light in my eyes had gone out and my teeth were bared. It was clear to me that I was finished and done for. No more running after pretty girls for me : I was an old man !

Soon Julia Semyonovna came in and I said to her, "Please let me knit one row of your sock."

She handed me her knitting, looking rather surprised that I should be able to knit, but I said to her, "I'm now going to do it always as a sign of respect for your grandmother, the grand old lady."

"But why should you want to do that?" she asked.

"Because," I replied, "I don't want to copy anyone else's *bêtises* any more : I no longer count for anything in this world now."

She smiled as if wishing to treat my words as a joke, but I said, "It isn't a joke ! Besides, it is high time I stopped sowing the wind." I added that I was deeply touched by her kindness to me, but that I didn't want to presume on the prince's generosity any more, and that I'd like to ask him to leave me to my fate.

She looked at me and instead of contradicting me, said, "Your present sentiments are so excellent that he ought not to interfere with your wishes," and she undertook to speak to the prince about me.

The prince gave me his hand and, embracing me with the other, said, "Our Ukrainian philosopher Skovoroda has an excellent saying, namely, that 'the chick is engendered in the egg only after the egg has become addled.' You, too, I'm afraid, are no longer any good for your former occupation, but, as a compensation, the best in your nature will now at last get a chance of showing itself."

"I hope you're right, sir," I said, but I could not say anything else, so deeply moved was I.

So they took me away from the prince's house and brought me straight here to this lunatic asylum for an examination, which indeed began as soon as I arrived, for no sooner did I put my foot across the threshold than a man in a tin crown came up to me and, tripping me up, gave me a sharp rap on the back of the head and shouted, "Don't you see who I am, you fool?"

"I'm quite sure that I am a fool," I said, "but I'm afraid I cannot make out your rank, sir."

"I'm the King of Small Beer," he said.

"Accept my humble greetings, your Majesty," I said.

He beamed at me and even stroked my head.

"That's right," he said, "that's how I like people to talk to me. Consider yourself, sir, one of my loyal subjects."

I glanced at his feet and noticed that he was wearing his slippers on bare feet which were blue with cold.

"I thank you humbly, your Majesty," I said, "but if you don't mind my mentioning it, your subjects do not seem to take proper care of you. See how blue your royal feet are."

"Yes, sir," he said, "they certainly are blue." Then he sighed and went on, "That, however, is only when it's cold, you see. When it's cold, sir, we can do nothing about it, for then we, too, are cold, for no command of ours can make things different in my kingdom."

"Quite right, your Majesty," I said.

"Alas, that's how it is, sir. Mind you, I've issued very strict instructions to the clerk of the weather, but it doesn't seem to make any difference."

"Don't give up hope, your Majesty," I said, "for I shall knit a pair of socks for your royal feet."

"Will you?"

"On my word of honour, your Majesty."

"In that case, sir," he said, "do so, for, you see, I have a special duty to perform, I have to fly to the swamps to hatch out some herons' eggs there : a fire-bird will come out of them !"

When I had knitted the socks for him, he put them on and said, "You have warmed our feet, sir, and as this has given us great pleasure, we graciously appoint you our court sock-knitter-in-chief and order you to knit socks for all our bare-footed subjects."

Well, sir, I have lived here for many years now and every-body loves me because, I suppose, I'm doing something useful.

CHAPTER TWENTY-NINE

DURING ONE OF MY VISITS to the lunatic asylum I asked Onopry Opanassovich how the examination into his mental condition had gone off. He told me everything had gone off very well and that he had been certified a lunatic because that was exactly what he was and, indeed, everybody could see it quite plainly, for, surely, it was quite impossible for a man who was sane to go in pursuit of a sheep and come back shorn himself.

He spoke very little and that with great reluctance about the actual way in which he had been certified, for he did not share the general view according to which the act of certification was a matter of the greatest moment. It was thus hard to find out from him who was present at the examination into his mental state. When I asked him about it, he just pulled a long face, the cast of his countenance looking somewhat soured, and he said :

"Why, sir, there were quite a number of important gentlemen there, but I'm hanged if I can remember them all. Every one of them, however, stared hard at me and each in turn let loose a flood of words at me and it seemed to me that he'd never stop talking. The devil take' em, made me feel nervous, they did."

"But you did have a good talk with them, didn't you ?"

"Of course I did. I talked to them all right . . . But, mind you, whether what I said was quite to the point or not I am not in a position to say, for, you see, they pestered me so much that I got rather excited and . . . well . . . began to do things . . . Perhaps that was because they had taken away my knitting. Took the sock out of my hands, they did, and put it on a bookshelf on top of the Code of Laws. Not that I didn't warn them. I told them plainly, 'Don't take it away from me, gentlemen, for I'm used to knitting socks and I'm quite capable of answering your questions while I'm knitting,' but the public prosecutor, or perhaps he wasn't the public prosecutor, but just some colonel or other, said that that was quite impossible and that I must try to concentrate, since everything depended on that. So they started to question me what had first led me to fear the underminers of foundations and look for them in hats of the Greek country. I told them everything, just as it was, the whole truth, namely, that that was how everybody expected them to appear and that I wished to serve my country and obtain a decoration. The colonel was quite ready to believe me, but the other gentlemen, I'm afraid, thought that I was lying, for I saw them exchanging glances and smiling. Then they asked me, 'Why did you arrest the Government agent?' and I replied, 'I'm afraid it was a mistake, for, if you'll pardon my mentioning it, he was travelling in a hat of the Greek country.' Then they suddenly began to fire different questions at me, such as 'Did you ever change your views and intentions?' and when I said that I was not aware of ever having had any intentions, they asked, 'What made you so frightened?' Well, I naturally explained to them that I couldn't help getting frightened after Terenka had brought me to a dark wood in a thunderstorm and after he had unharnessed one of my horses and driven a nail into the hoof of the other and told me that I would receive the Order of the Mad Dog! . . . Then I discovered the leaflets and I, of course, immediately realised that the matter they contained was the same sort of thing the poor Frenchmen had been taught just before France had become a republic. I naturally wanted to destroy them at once, but I couldn't remember what happened after that . . . If, however, they wished to know that, they'd better ask the prince who had taken me to his home where he had given me shelter and fed and protected me against the terrors of the night. So they asked me, 'What happened to you

at the prince's house to bring about such a change in you?'
But how could I possibly tell them that, if I myself never
noticed how it had happened. Perhaps that was because I was
ill and kept on thinking of death and the Last Judgment and
realised how insignificant I was. Or again it might have been
because under the influence of good people I had grown fond
of peace and quiet and had begun to hate rushing about and
bullying people and trying to listen to their songs in the hope
that I might hear them singing the 'Marseillaise.' 'Let them
sing what they like,' I said, 'but I don't want to commit any
bêtises and that's why I'm asking you, gentlemen, to let me
have my sock!' I went on demanding my sock in a louder
and louder voice, working myself up into an ever greater fury,
'Give me my knitting! Give me my knitting!' and as they
refused to let me have my knitting, was it my fault that I got
so excited that I began doing things? Lord, I don't even remember how I jumped on to the table and began to sob
and stamp my feet and curse and swear and call them the most
terrible names and every now and then I'd scream at the top
of my voice, 'Give me my knitting, you confounded swine!
Give me my knitting at once, damn you, or I shall commit
some *bêtise* on the table!' I can't remember what happened
after that, for when I came back to my senses I found myself
in my bed in a straitjacket. I again demanded my knitting
and when they gave it to me, I calmed down. And now that I
have remembered how those blackguards wanted me to sing
the 'Marseillaise,' now . . . it's coming back again . . . oh dear,
quick, give me my knitting, sir, or I shall have another fit! . . ''

CHAPTER THIRTY

I ASKED PEREGOOD many other questions, such as whether his long detention in the lunatic asylum was getting him down.

"Not a bit," he replied, "but why do you call this place a lunatic asylum? Aren't you ashamed of talking like that, sir? I find life here very good: I knit socks and I think what I like and I give my socks away to people who are in need of them and everybody loves me for that. Every man, sir, likes to get presents. Yes, they all like presents and they never forget to say 'thank you,' either. There are some, of course, who are ungrateful just like anywhere else in the world . . . Good Lord, I've nothing to complain about, except perhaps that sometimes it does get a bit noisy here. It's, you know, that . . . that abyss of madness. Oh, what a terrible abyss it is! But at night when everybody's asleep, everything gets very peaceful even here and then I pick up my wings and fly away."

"You mean in your imagination?"

"Why, no, sir, not in my imagination, but in truth, in real truth."

"But where do you fly to, if I may ask?"

"Of course you may ask, sir, you may ask anything you like," he said, heaving a deep sigh, and he added in a whisper that he flew away to "the swamp" where he too, it seemed, was hatching out herons' eggs among the mounds, for out of those eggs fire-birds were quite sure to hatch out.

"But don't you feel afraid in the swamp at night?"

"Not at all, sir. We have many friends there and all of them are trying to hatch out fire-birds, but so far not one of us has been successful, for there's too much pride in us, I'm afraid."

"And who are your friends? I expect Julia Semyonovna is among them, isn't she?"

"Yes, she's been sitting a long time there and on the first mound, too."

"And what about the prince? Is he there also?"

"No, sir, the prince is not there. You see, he believes in civilisation! He tried to convince me—just imagine it, sir!—that people ought to live by their reason. He is against knitting and he told me that ever since I stopped one kind of folly, I had fallen a victim to another. Yes, indeed. He told me of a German who had learnt the whole of the Russian grammar by heart and when a man called Ivan Ivanovich Ivanov came to see him, he thought that a great joke and he said, 'I know Ivan is possible, and I know Ivanish is possible, but Ivanoff—no, that's not possible!' I asked him what grammar had to do with me and he said, 'I'm telling you that so that you should realise that if a man is successful in doing one thing, that does not mean that he should go on doing it until he's exhausted. You'd better remember,' said he, 'what our philosopher Skovoroda has said about every one of us having to drag along with him his clod of earth'."

I said that that seemed to me to be quite true.

"True," Peregood repeated softly and, sighing again, he said once more, "True," then he picked up his knitting and began talking quickly to himself, "That's grammar, that's grammar : I walk on a carpet and I lie and I walk and I lie, and you walk and you lie, and he walks and he lies, and we walk and we lie and they walk and they lie . . . Oh Lord, have mercy upon us miserable sinners! Why are they all staring at me and their mouths open and speech bursts forth out of them and they change like the moon and fidget like Satan . . . The fire-bird cannot be hatched out, if they all want to eat herons' eggs . . . Oh dear, they've turned the head of the poor fool and his brains have got all addled! Farewell!"

He grew sulky, and the cast of his countenance became

decidedly gloomy, and he walked away quickly, knitting furiously.

Now he was a real lunatic whose words hardly anyone would admit to make any sense, but no lover of truth and goodness could help feeling sorry to see the divine spirit, burdened by the clod of earth leaving him. He wanted to make the whole world happy by his own loving-kindness, but the force of circumstances merely permits him to knit socks for his fellow inmates.

EPILOGUE

ONOPRY PEREGOOD DIED GLORIOUSLY and his memory lived on after him in the lunatic asylum. He left it for his last journey into the unknown when full of years and in the hope of being able to carry out "all possible deeds of loving-kindness."

During the last days of his sojourn on this earth, Peregood experienced the great happiness of believing in the possibility of a better life even in this valley of the shadow of death. Towards the end he became as weak as a grasshopper that had lived on far into the autumn, and he had long since been eager to tear himself off the stalk like a ripe berry, and he was constantly thinking of the discoveries with which the "renewal of the dwindling senses" must begin. While incessantly knitting socks, Peregood hit upon the idea that "man ought to invent a way of printing thoughts." He considered Guthenberg's invention of printing on paper of no importance, for such an invention was powerless against suppression. A real invention would be something that would spread its light throughout the whole world unhindered. It was stupid to print on a rag or a papyrus or even on the skins of calves and donkeys . . . . Animals would no longer be slaughtered . . . Every morning before dawn, in the hour when the murderous knife is being sharpened with which "the ox, having thrown off the yoke of the plough, is to be slaughtered," Peregood saw Ovid's spirit cleaving the clouds and forbidding men "to devour their own benefactors," but the people neither heard, nor saw. Peregood, however, wanted them to hear and to see not only that, but also many other things. He wanted them to realise the horror of the things they were doing and understand what they had to do. Then life and death would present no such terrors as they did now. It was this message that he was going to print straight on the face of the heavens. Oh, it was such a simple business really ! The only thing he had still to discover before he could do it was what made light to shine and darkness to grow so dense...

Peregood used to throw away his sock and begin to cut huge old-fashioned letters out of paper, intending to throw their reflections straight on to the sky, for those letters would reflect the message which was to be announced by the voice crying in the wilderness : "Prepare the way ! Prepare the way ! The trumpet shall sound and lo ! he who holdeth back the fountains of living waters shall open the great gulf and the hard ice will melt and gush forth and refresh all nature and the trees of the woods, and the terrible glory of the Lord will thunder forth !"

And so, after a hot day, about which Ovid's shadow had as usual warned Peregood, the sky began to be overcast and, as the clouds gathering from all directions met in one spot and clashed, a dreadful storm arose, dust went whirling into the air, lightning began to flash and thunder to roar without cessation.

This fearful natural phenomenon which is frequent towards the summer solstice in the South, was particularly awe-inspiring on that dark night during which the sky was continuously rent by flashes of lightning of quite remarkable brightness, and wherever the lightning lit up the sky, strange figures could be seen, and the darkness on the ground seemed at that moment to grow more impenetrable.

In the lunatic asylum, as indeed everywhere else where the storm kept people awake, panic reigned. Some of the inmates raised a loud moaning, others trembled all over and cried, while one madman recited in a loud voice :

The abhorred grave yawns wide, cold and dark,
Winds sweep howling through it, coffins crash and fly
    open,
White bones rattle and dance.

But Peregood had "conquered death," he was tired, he had felt tired a long time, and he had been longing to depart to the tents of the blessed. There one could sleep much better than under the weight of the pyramids which the Pharaos had piled up for themselves with the hands of slaves, tortured by hunger and the lash. He would rest in those tents where no oppressor gained admittance and he'd again find himself among those who, though they had been oppressed, did not try to become the masters of anyone . . . He felt that his time had come!

Peregood seized two letters from among his giant letters, the letter G, signifying *Glagol*, to wit, the Word, and the letter D, signifying *Dobro*, to wit, Goodness, and jumped with them on to the window-sill, intending to put them up against the glass so that they should be reflected all over the world.

The "terrible glory" of the Lord shone upon his letters and some kind of reflection was actually thrown on to the wall, but what it was nobody knew. Peregood himself fell off the window-sill and did not get up again, for he had departed to "the tents of the blessed."

Many of the lunatics who went to Peregood's funeral wore the socks he had knitted for them, and some of these even wept and the few among them who were more tender-hearted prostrated themselves during the burial service and kicked out with their stockinged feet.

THE END